Pregnancy Cookbook Trimester by Trimester

The Expecting Mother's Companion to Prenatal Nutrition

Everything You Need to Know for a Happy Pregnancy and a Healthy Baby with 200+ Nourishing Recipes

Laura W. Peterson

Disclaimer

First Printing Edition, 2024

Printed in the United States of America
Available from Amazon.com and other retail outlets

Table of Contents

Introduction 6

A Plate for Two: Understanding Prenatal Nutrition 7

   Eating for two? 7

Whole Foods vs. Processed Foods 8

Balancing Macronutrients 8

   Carbohydrates 8

   Proteins 10

   Healthy fats 10

   Non-starchy Vegetables 11

Get your Micronutrients 11

Vitamins 11

   Folate (Vitamin B9) 11

   Vitamin D 11

   Vitamin C 12

   Vitamin A 12

   Vitamin B6 (Pyridoxine) 12

   Vitamin B12 (Cobalamin) 12

   Vitamin E 12

   Vitamin K 12

Minerals 12

   Iron 12

   Calcium 12

   Zinc 12

   Iodine 12

   Magnesium 13

   Copper 13

   Phosphorus 13

   Supplements by trimester 13

The Plate Method 14

Fluid intake 14

   Beverages to avoid 14

Salt 15

Baby-Building Superfoods 16

Eggs 16

Liver 16

Bone Broth 17

Leafy Greens 17

Salmon (and other fatty fishes and seafood) 17

Full-fat and fermented dairy products 17

Whole grains 17

Berries 18

Avocado 18

Legumes 18

Sweet Potato 18

First Trimester Cookbook 19

How to Fight Morning Sickness and Deal with Food Aversions 19

   Ways to Alleviate Nausea During Pregnancy 19

   Soothing Ginger-Chamomile Tea 20

   Raspberry-Peppermint Cooler 20

   How to Manage Food Aversions 20

Breakfasts to fuel your day 21

   Ginger Banana Smoothie 21

   Immunity Boost Smoothie 21

   Avocado Toast with a Twist 22

   Oatmeal with Almonds and Pear 23

   Scrambled Eggs with Spinach 24

   Quinoa and Berry Bowl 24

   Chia Seed Pudding with Kiwi 25

   Whole Wheat Pancakes with Blueberry Compote 25

   Rice Cakes with Hummus and Tomato Slices 26

   Sweet Potato and Black Bean Breakfast Burrito 27

   Overnight Oats with Dried Fruits and Nuts 27

   Baked Avocado Egg Boats 28

   Toasted Muesli with Greek Yogurt 29

   Coconut Milk Porridge with Raspberries 29

   Veggie Omelette with Feta Cheese 30

Energizing lunches and dinners 31

   Lentil and Spinach Stew 31

   Kale, Roasted Beet, and Grilled Chicken Salad 31

   Salmon with Roasted Sweet Potatoes and Green Beans 32

   Grass-fed Beef and Vegetable Kabobs 33

   Roasted Butternut Squash Stuffed with Black Beans and Quinoa 33

   Poached Eggs over Sauteed Spinach and Mushrooms . 34

   Tomato, and Spinach Spaghetti Squash Bowl 35

   Grilled Lamb Chops with Garlic Broccoli and Carrots 36

   Tofu and Snap Pea Stir-Fry with Almonds 36

   Liver and Onions with Steamed Asparagus 37

   Mackerel Salad with Mixed Greens, Cucumber, and Radishes 38

   Chicken and Vegetable Soup with Bone Broth 38

   Stuffed Bell Peppers with Ground Turkey and Cauliflower Rice 39

Grilled Sardines with Olive Tapenade and Arugula Salad 40

Pork Tenderloin with Roasted Root Vegetables............40

Baked Trout with Lemon, Dill, and Roasted Beets.......41

Sautéed Chicken Livers with Garlic, Kale, and Tomatoes 42

Kale, Blueberry, and Walnut Salad with Lemon Vinaigrette..................42

Spinach, Avocado, and Poached Egg Salad with Dijon Dressing..................43

Quinoa, Roasted Beet, and Goat Cheese Salad 44

Mixed Greens with Grilled Chicken, Orange Slices, and Almond Slivers..................44

Broccoli, Chickpea, and Sunflower Seed Salad with Tahini Dressing..................45

Lentil and Spinach Soup with Turmeric..................46

Beef and Vegetable Soup with Bone Broth 46

Nutrient-dense Snacks..................47

Greek Yogurt Parfait with Berries and Granola 47

Hummus-Stuffed Mini Bell Peppers 48

Nut & Seed Trail Mix..................48

Apple & Goat Cheese Bites with Honey Drizzle..........49

Cottage Cheese, Kiwi & Mint Bowl 50

Whole Grain Toast with Smashed Avocado & Cherry Tomatoes 50

Edamame & Black Sesame Salt Dip 51

Chocolate Dipped Strawberries with Crushed Walnuts 51

Roasted Sweet Potato Cubes with Cinnamon & Yogurt Dip 52

Spinach & Feta Mini Muffins..................52

Second Trimester Cookbook..................**54**
How to Handle Cravings 55

Nutrient-rich Breakfasts..................56

Avocado and Poached Egg Whole Grain Toast............56

Mixed Berry and Chia Seed Overnight Oats..................56

Spinach, Feta, and Mushroom Breakfast Casserole.....57

Quinoa Breakfast Bowl with Fresh Fruit and Nuts.......57

Almond Butter and Banana Stuffed Whole Wheat Pancakes..................58

Sweet Potato and Black Bean Breakfast Burrito...........59

Mango and Greek Yogurt Smoothie with Ground Flaxseed..................59

Zucchini and Carrot Breakfast Muffins 60

Smoked Salmon and Cream Cheese on Whole Rye Bread 61

Pumpkin and Walnut Oatmeal Porridge..................61

Chicken and Apple Breakfast Sausages..................62

Satisfying Lunches and Dinners 63

Lamb Koftas with Cucumber Yogurt Sauce..................63

Turkey and Cranberry Stuffed Acorn Squash..................63

Pork Loin with Apple Cider Glaze and Roasted Parsnips 64

Sesame Chicken Stir-Fry with Baby Corn and Snow Peas 65

Herbed Beef Skewers with Chimichurri and Roasted Sweet Potatoes..................66

Shrimp and Pineapple Curry over Coconut Rice..........67

Grilled Swordfish with Avocado Mango Salsa 67

Red Snapper in Parchment with Leeks and Cherry Tomatoes 68

Smoked Mackerel Salad with Pickled Beets and Horseradish Cream 69

Chard and Ricotta-Stuffed Cannelloni with Marinara 69

Falafel Bowl with Hummus and Tzatziki 70

Spaghetti Squash Primavera with Seasonal Vegetables 71

Jackfruit Tacos with Avocado Crema 71

Roasted Vegetable and Quinoa-Stuffed Bell Peppers ...72

Surf and Turf Skewers with Asparagus and Cherry Tomatoes 73

Seitan and Mushroom Bourguignon 74

Chickpea and Chorizo Paella with Saffron and Peas ...74

Grilled Calamari and Roasted Red Pepper Flatbread with Olive Tapenade 75

Butternut Squash Mac'n'Cheese 76

Mediterranean Stuffed Sweet Potatoes 76

Slow-cooker Beef Bone Broth..................77

Mushroom Burger and Oven-baked Green Been Fries 78

Craving-killing Snacks..................78

Quinoa and Black Bean Stuffed Mini Peppers..............78

Tahini and Date Smoothie 79

Coconut Yogurt Parfait with Kiwi and Flaxseeds.........80

Mango and Turkey Jerky..................80

Olive and Sun-dried Tomato Tapenade on Rye Crispbread 81

Cucumber Slices with Hummus and Pomegranate Seeds 82

Miso Soup with Tofu and Seaweed..................82

Watermelon and Feta Skewers..................83

Balsamic Glazed Brussels Sprouts with Almonds.........83

Spicy Choco-Latte..................84

Third Trimester Cookbook..................**85**
Unique Challenges of the Third Trimester..................85

Essential Nutrients for the Third Trimester 85

Helpful Notes: 85

Do's: 85

Don'ts: 85

Heartburn During the Third Trimester 86

Constipation During Pregnancy 86

Wholesome Breakfasts 87

Spiced Apple and Walnut Quinoa Bowl 87

Moroccan Lentil Soup with Whole Wheat Pita 87

Roasted Root Vegetable Hash with Farm Fresh Eggs 88

Turmeric and Ginger Smoothie with Hemp Hearts 89

Wild Rice and Mushroom Pilaf with Steamed Greens .89

Pomegranate and Pistachio Overnight Oats 90

Warm Farro Salad with Roasted Beet and Goat Cheese
....90

Chia Seed Pudding Infused with Matcha and Topped
with Mango 91

Apple and Cinnamon Overnight Oats with Collagen ..92

Baked Oatmeal with Blueberries 92

Salsa Verde Baked Eggs 93

Hearty Lunches and Dinners 94

Roasted Cauliflower Salad 94

Ingredients: 94

Instructions: 94

Roast Chicken with Garlic and Herb Root Vegetables ..94

Veggie-Stuffed Portobello Mushrooms with Lentils 95

Moroccan Chickpea Stew with Whole Grain Couscous
....96

Grilled Sea Bass with Avocado and Mango Salsa 96

Tofu and Broccoli Stir-Fry with Brown Rice 97

Pumpkin and Black Bean Enchiladas with Cashew Cream
....98

Stuffed Bell Peppers with Bison and Wild Rice 98

Butternut Squash Risotto with Sage and Pecorino 99

Lamb Tagine with Apricots and Almonds 100

Spicy Shrimp Tacos with Cilantro Lime Slaw 101

Sautéed Spinach and Feta-Stuffed Chicken Breast 101

Thai Beef Salad with Mixed Greens and Lime Dressing
....102

Curried Lentils with Spinach and Tomatoes 103

Minestrone 104

Cod and Summer Vegetable Foil Packets 104

Grilled Eggplant Parmesan with Zucchini Noodles ..105

Creamy Polenta with Roasted Cherry Tomatoes and Basil
....106

Pulled Pork with Cabbage and Apple Slaw 107

Beet and Walnut Pesto Pasta with Grilled Chicken 107

Comforting Snacks 108

Roasted Chickpeas with Turmeric and Black Pepper .108

Almond Butter and Banana-Stuffed Dates 109

Spicy Tuna and Avocado Lettuce Wraps 109

Cantaloupe and Prosciutto Skewers 110

Guacamole-Stuffed Cherry Tomatoes 111

Yogurt and Dill Dip with Veggie Sticks 111

Baked Sweet Potato Fries with Greek Yogurt Dip 112

Garlic and Rosemary Marinated Olives 113

Celery Sticks with Almond Ricotta and Chives 113

Fig and Cashew Energy Bites 114

Homemade Granola Bars 114

Fitness By Trimester 116

Fitness in the First Trimester 117

Safe Exercises 117

What to Avoid 117

Fitness in the Second Trimester 118

Safe Exercises 118

What to Avoid 118

Fitness in the Third Trimester 119

Safe Exercises 119

What to Avoid 120

Pregnancy-Related Conditions 121

Conclusion 122

Appendix A: Building the Perfect Prenatal-Friendly Pantry
....123

GRAINS 123

LEGUMES 124

CANNED GOODS 125

HEALTHY FATS, OILS, AND NUT BUTTERS 126

NUTS AND SEEDS 127

DRIED FRUITS 128

SPICES AND HERBS 129

Appendix B: Prenatal-Friendly Refrigerator Regulars 130

Vegetables 130

Fruits 132

Proteins 133

Dairy Products 134

Index 135

Introduction

Before we begin, let me congratulate you on this remarkable journey you've embarked upon. Pregnancy is a beautiful, awe-inspiring experience filled with joy, wonder, and yes, a bit of trepidation. But fear not, for you've taken a wonderful first step by choosing this book, designed to guide you towards the best possible nutrition for a worry-free pregnancy and a healthy baby.

As we turn these pages together, we'll walk hand in hand through the magical journey of nurturing a new life within you. The power of nutrition during this time cannot be overstated, and together, we'll explore how the foods you choose can support not just your own well-being, but also the flourishing development of your little one.

You are embarking on one of the most incredible, challenging, and rewarding chapters of your life. This book aims to inspire and empower you with knowledge, wisdom, and positivity, helping you to embrace this miraculous journey with both open arms and an open heart.

Know that by choosing to focus on nutrition, you are already demonstrating the qualities of an amazing mother. You're making conscious choices for the well-being of both you and your baby. As we delve into this book, let's celebrate the journey of motherhood and the nourishing choices that will enrich this special time.

Let's start by discussing why this book is so important. The first section is not just a nutritional guide; it's a comprehensive resource designed to demystify prenatal nutrition. We'll cover essential nutrients, vitamins, and minerals needed during each trimester, and how they contribute to the healthy development of your baby. This information is vital for understanding the 'why' behind each recipe you'll encounter in the subsequent sections.

Following the nutritional guide, you'll find the heart of our book: a collection of carefully curated recipes. These recipes are more than just delicious—they are crafted to provide optimal nutrition for each stage of your pregnancy. We've included a variety of meals for breakfast, lunch, and dinner, ensuring that you have plenty of options to suit your palate and nutritional needs. Additionally, we've incorporated a selection of snacks and teas, perfect for those times when you need a little something extra.

Remember, every bite you take is a building block for your baby's future. This book is here to guide you, providing you with the tools and knowledge to make the best choices for you and your baby.

So, let's embark on this culinary adventure together, nurturing your body and your baby with every delicious, healthful meal. Welcome to 'Pregnancy Cookbook Trimester by Trimester'—your trusted companion in this beautiful journey of motherhood.

A PERSONAL NOTE

If the absence of color pictures and the overall **minimal photographic content** in my cookbook caught your eye, <u>here's why that is:</u>

I've made a thoughtful choice to opt out of color printing **to reduce our ecological footprint,** which is also why this book is printed on recycled paper.

Moreover, I've put a lot of effort into making the instructions **super easy to follow and accessible to everyone,** regardless of your cooking experience. I aimed to write them in a way that feels like I'm right there in the kitchen with you, guiding you through each step.

I know that pictures can be helpful, but I believe these **straightforward directions** will help you nail those recipes much better than a photo could.

I appreciate your understanding and support as I make choices that benefit our planet, **ensuring a healthier world for our children.**

Thank you for allowing me to be part of your journey.

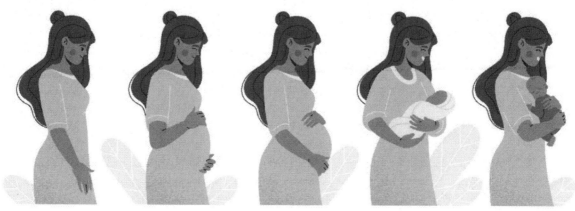

A Plate for Two: Understanding Prenatal Nutrition

Embarking on the journey of pregnancy is a remarkable and transformative experience, and as you step into this new chapter, it's important to recognize the profound impact that balanced prenatal nutrition has on both your health and the healthy development of your baby. Think of it as a journey not just for you, but for the little life growing inside you, where every meal becomes an act of love and care, a contribution to a strong and vibrant beginning. The nutrients you consume during this crucial time—be it folic acid, iron, calcium, or omega-3 fatty acids—are not just supplements; they are the very foundation of your baby's future, supporting everything from brain development and bone strength to blood production.

These early stages of life are where your dietary choices can have a lasting impact, influencing your child's health well beyond the womb. It's about creating an environment rich in nutrition that encourages optimal growth and development, an environment where every bite counts. Moreover, balanced nutrition is not just about the baby's well-being; it's equally about your health. Proper nutrition can significantly reduce the risk of pregnancy complications like gestational diabetes and preeclampsia, ensuring a healthier and more comfortable pregnancy journey for you.

While understanding what's best to eat during pregnancy can sometimes feel overwhelming, the focus should be on a diet rich in a variety of fruits, vegetables, lean proteins, whole grains, and healthy fats, all packed with essential nutrients for every stage of your baby's development. Remember, every pregnancy is unique, and what works for one may not work for another. It's crucial to listen to your body and seek personalized advice from healthcare providers or dietitians as needed. In the upcoming chapters, every macro and micronutrient will be carefully explained, and you will be provided with a comprehensive list of the best food sources.

Additionally, the second section of the book will offer trimester-specific recipes, tailored to meet the changing nutritional needs throughout your pregnancy. Your role in this journey is empowering, as you nurture not only your body but the new life within you. By embracing balanced prenatal nutrition, you're actively participating in your baby's health and your own, setting the stage for a lifetime of wellness and happiness. This journey of mindful eating is a testament to your commitment and love for your unborn child, and as you make each healthy choice, know that you're doing an incredible job nourishing the future.

Eating for two?

You may be familiar with the concept of "eating for two" during pregnancy, which seems to make sense, but is actually inaccurate. Instead, set the intention to focus on quality over quantity: Think "eat better, not more" or focus on eating "twice as healthy".

You actually don't need to increase your food intake by much. If you are carrying a single baby, it's advisable to increase your daily calorie intake by approximately 340 calories starting in the second trimester, and increasing this slightly in the third trimester. To put this in perspective, this is roughly equivalent to consuming a glass of skim milk and half a sandwich. In the case of a twin pregnancy, it is recommended to aim for an additional 600 calories daily. If you are expecting triplets, your calorie intake should be further increased to approximately 900 extra calories per day.[3]

Focusing on quality means increasing your intake of several nutrients to ensure the optimal health of you and your baby. These include vitamins C and D, B vitamins, iron, choline, folic acid, calcium, and omega-3 fatty acids. The recipes in this book will heavily focus on these nutrients to help you meet your and your baby's needs.

By eating a variety of whole foods, you also give your baby the gift of exposing him or her to these foods and flavors as well. Research has shown that what a mom eats travels through the amniotic fluid and is swallowed by the fetus. By exposing your baby to a variety of tastes, he/she will be more likely to enjoy those flavors later in life - how wild, right? Therefore, by eating a variety of healthy foods and flavors, you are setting your child up for enjoying a healthy diet in the future; and trust me, this will make your life less stressful too!

When it comes to your weight, typical weight gain during pregnancy falls within the range of 25 to 35 pounds, although this can vary based on your body type and height. On average, you can expect to gain approximately ¾ to 1 pound per week starting from the second trimester.

It's important to note that morning sickness can sometimes lead to temporary weight loss, so it's essential to focus on regaining lost weight once this phase passes by boosting your appetite.

WHOLE FOODS VS. PROCESSED FOODS

What are whole foods and why are they essential during pregnancy?

Whole foods are minimally processed or are completely unprocessed. They exist in their natural form as they are found in nature, without any additives or artificial substances.

Some examples of whole foods are fruits and vegetables; whole grains such as basmati rice, quinoa, and oats; legumes like lentils, chickpeas, and black beans; nuts and seeds like almonds, walnuts, chia seeds, and flaxseeds; and lean proteins such as eggs, chicken breast, and beef.

On the other hand, processed foods undergo alterations from their original state through various processes like refining or milling. Additionally, ingredients are often added to enhance flavor or texture and for preservation purposes. Examples of these include packaged snacks like chips, pretzels and granola bars, sugary cereals, white bread and sugary beverages.

Whole foods are widely recognized as ideal choices for pregnant women because of their rich nutritional content, their wide range of flavor profiles, and the benefits they offer to both the mother and the developing baby. These natural and unprocessed foods are packed with essential vitamins, minerals, fiber and antioxidants that promote optimal growth and development of the fetus. For example, fruits and vegetables provide a wide range of important vitamins like vitamin C and folate, as well as various minerals that are crucial for neural tube development and overall health. In addition to that, lean proteins and healthy fats help to build the skin, brain and tissues of your baby.

Moreover, opting for whole foods helps reduce exposure to harmful additives, preservatives, excessive sugar levels and unhealthy fats often found in processed foods.

Research highlights the importance of a well-balanced diet rich in nutrients during pregnancy to lower the risk of complications such as gestational diabetes, preterm birth or low birth weight. Consuming unprocessed whole foods can also contribute to managing weight gain throughout pregnancy while promoting a healthier journey for both you and your child.

BALANCING MACRONUTRIENTS

Macronutrients are the nutrients we need to consume in larger amounts, such as fat, protein, and carbohydrates. Experts say that the breakdown for pregnant women should be 20% protein, 40% fat, and 40% carbohydrates when looking at your overall diet.

But it's not just about the amounts, food combination also matters. Blood glucose levels are important to be aware of during your pregnancy and combining carbohydrates with protein and/or fat during a meal leads to lower blood sugar levels than eating carbohydrates alone. A good example of this would be eating quinoa with salmon or oatmeal with some nuts or an egg.

Carbohydrates

Carbohydrates are one of the essential macronutrients and play a vital role as one of the main energy sources for our bodies. These molecules serve various important functions in our bodies, such as providing fuel for brain activity, supporting physical activities, and contributing to cell structure. Simple carbs get absorbed quickly and can cause sudden increases in blood sugar levels, while complex carbs release energy more steadily over time.

Research has shown that consuming a diet that is moderately low in carbohydrates helps prevent gestational diabetes and is beneficial for the baby as well. Focusing on complex carbohydrates like vegetables, low glycemic whole grains, and beans provides the carbohydrates needed for optimal health as well as an abundance of fiber, vitamins, and minerals. However, it is best to minimize or avoid simple carbohydrates like baked goods, candy, pasta, and sugary drinks. These carbs not only raise your blood sugar faster and higher and increase the risk of gestational diabetes, lack the nutrients that are beneficial for you and your baby.

The two main ways you can keep your blood sugar low are through exercise and good nutrition. In the next several pages, I will provide you with a list of the most nutrient-dense, low-glycemic foods to integrate into your pregnancy diet to keep your blood sugar low.

Recommended sources of carbohydrates
(Fiber content indicated is per 1 cup)

- **Quinoa**, 5g fiber: protein, calcium, iron, magnesium, phosphorus, potassium, zinc, folate, choline, beta carotene, Vitamin A, Vitamin E
- **Gluten-free oatmeal** (fortified), 10g fiber: protein, calcium, iron, magnesium, phosphorus, potassium, zinc, folate, choline, Vitamin A, Vitamin K
- **Chia seeds**, 52g fiber: protein, calcium, iron, magnesium, phosphorus, potassium, zinc, Vitamin C, niacin, folate, Vitamin A, fatty acids

- **Pumpkin**, 2.7g fiber: protein, calcium, iron, magnesium, phosphorus, potassium, Vitamin C, folate, choline, Vitamin A, carotene, Vitamin A, Vitamin E, Vitamin K
- **Fingerling potatoes**, 2g fiber: protein, calcium, potassium, phosporus, magnesium Vitamin C, fatty acids, Vitamin B6, iron, zinc, thiamine, niacin, riboflavin
- **Sweet potatoes**, 8.2g fiber: protein, calcium, iron, magnesium, phosphorus, potassium, Vitamin C, niacin, folate, choline, Vitamin A, Vitamin E, Vitamin K
- **Butternut squash**, 6.6g fiber: protein, calcium, iron, magnesium, phosphorus, potassium, selenium, niacin, folate, Vitamin A, carotene, Vitamin A, Vitamin E, Vitamin K
- **Acorn squash**, 9g fiber: protein, calcium, iron, magnesium, phosphorus, potassium, selenium, Vitamin C, niacin, folate, Vitamin A
- **Artichoke**, 9.6g fiber: protein, calcium, magnesium, phosphorus, potassium, Vitamin C, folate, choline, carotene, Vitamin K
- **Broccoli**, 5.1g fiber: protein, calcium, magnesium, phosphorus, potassium, selenium, Vitamin C, folate, choline, Vitamin A, carotene, Vitamin A, Vitamin E, Vitamin K
- **Kale**, 4.7g fiber: protein, calcium, magnesium, phosphorus, potassium, Vitamin C, Vitamin A, carotene, Vitamin E
- **Brussels Sprouts**, 2g fiber: protein, calcium, magnesium, phosphorus, potassium, Vitamin C, folate, choline, Vitamin A, carotene, Vitamin K
- **Strawberries**, 4g fiber: magnesium, phosphorus, potassium, Vitamin C, folate, choline, carotene, Vitamin A, Vitamin K
- **Blueberries**, 3.6g fiber: protein, calcium, magnesium, phosphorus, potassium, Vitamin C, folate, choline, Vitamin A, Vitamin K
- **Raspberries**, 8.1g fiber: protein, calcium, magnesium, phosphorus, potassium, Vitamin C, folate, choline, Vitamin A, Vitamin K
- **Blackberries**, 7.6g fiber: protein, calcium, magnesium, phosphorus, potassium, folate, choline, carotene, Vitamin A, Vitamin E, Vitamin K
- **Apricot**, 3.1g fiber: protein, calcium, magnesium, phosphorus, potassium, Vitamin C, folate, choline, Vitamin A, carotene, Vitamin E, Vitamin K
- **Grapefruit**, 2.5g fiber: protein, calcium, magnesium, phosphorus, potassium, Vitamin C, folate, choline, Vitamin A, carotene, Vitamin A
- **Tomato**, 2g fiber: calcium, magnesium, phosphorus, potassium, Vitamin C, Vitamin A, carotene, folate, Vitamin K
- **Avocado**, 10g fiber: calcium, magnesium, phosphorus, potassium, Vitamin C, folate, choline, Vitamin A, Vitamin E, Vitamin K, fatty acids
- **Lentils**, 15.6g fiber: protein, calcium, iron, magnesium, phosphorus, potassium, zinc, Vitamin C, folate, choline, Vitamin A, Vitamin K
- **Chickpeas**, 10.6g fiber: protein, calcium, iron, magnesium, phosphorus, potassium, folate, zinc, Vitamin B-6, Vitamin A, carotene, Vitamin K

- **Green beans**, 4g fiber, protein, calcium, magnesium, phosphorus, potassium, Vitamin C, folate, Vitamin A, carotene, Vitamin K
- **Pinto beans**, 15.2g fiber, protein, calcium, iron, magnesium, phosphorus, potassium, zinc, folate

Carbohydrates to avoid
- White bread
- Whole wheat bread
- White pasta
- Cereal
- White crackers
- Tortillas
- Granola bars
- Muffins
- Croissants
- Pita bread
- White flour
- Whole wheat flour
- Bagels
- Mult-grain/whole wheat crackers
- Sugary drinks
- Candy
- Cookies
- Cake
- Donuts
- Ice Cream
- Artificial sweeteners

RECOMMENDED CARBOHYDRATE INTAKE
Experts recommend that you consume around 175-210g of carbohydrates per day, or about 40% of your daily diet; but it's important that these carbs are complex, nutrient-dense carbs such as the ones listed above in the recommended sources.

Proteins

Proteins, which are essential for life, are complex and large molecules comprised of amino acids. They serve vital roles in organizing, operating and controlling the body's tissues and organs. During pregnancy, protein contributes to brain growth as well as the formation of other fetal tissue, and contributes to a higher birth weight. It also helps to increase your blood supply, allowing more blood to be sent to your baby.

Protein is an essential building block for your baby! Below I will provide some recommended sources of protein. It's important when choosing animal protein to eat organic and grass-fed as much as possible to limit exposure to toxins and added hormones.

RECOMMENDED SOURCES OF PROTEIN

- Chicken
- Beef
- Duck
- Turkey
- Lamb
- Venison
- Bison
- Eggs
- Wild salmon
- Halibut
- Sole
- Rockfish
- Mahi-Mahi
- Opah
- Sardines
- Oysters
- Clams
- Shrimp
- Mussels
- Crab
- Lobster
- Scallops
- Squid
- Chunk-light tuna
- Almonds
- Cashews
- Pistachios
- Pecans
- Macadamia nuts
- Walnuts
- Hazelnuts
- Sesame seeds
- Pumpkin seeds
- Chia seeds
- Quinoa
- Lentils
- Beans

PROTEINS TO AVOID

While protein is necessary, there are some forms of protein that not considered to be safe for the fetus during pregnancy:

- Meat, fish and eggs that are raw or not thoroughly cooked
- Fish that are high in mercury content such as tilefish, shark, mackerel and swordfish
- Soft cheeses such as brie, camembert, Roquefort, feta, gorgonzola, and Mexican style cheeses such as queso blanco and queso fresco.
- Hot dogs and deli meat

RECOMMENDED PROTEIN INTAKE

Experts recommend that protein make up about 20% of your diet, or about 75-100g of protein per day during pregnancy.

Healthy fats

Healthy fats, like monounsaturated and polyunsaturated fats and omega-3 fatty acids, play a crucial role in promoting overall well-being and are especially beneficial during pregnancy. These fats are necessary for various bodily functions such as cell structure, hormone production and the absorption of fat-soluble vitamins like A, D, E, and K. Including healthy fats in your diet can help you maintain a healthy weight and manage cholesterol levels, reducing the risk of heart disease and other chronic conditions. When you're pregnant, these fats become even more important as they contribute to the development of your baby's nervous system, brain, and eyes. They also assist in forming the placenta and absorbing essential nutrients needed for your growing fetus.

Moreover, healthy fats possess anti-inflammatory properties that can help reduce inflammation in your body. This may potentially decrease the likelihood of complications during pregnancy such as preeclampsia and gestational diabetes. Omega 3 fatty acids are particularly vital during pregnancy as they support the growth of your baby's brain and eyes. It's crucial to include sources of healthy fats like fatty fish, nuts, seeds, avocados, and olive oil in your diet to ensure both you and your baby receive these necessary nutrients for optimal growth and development.

RECOMMENDED SOURCES OF HEALTHY FATs

These whole food or minimally processed fats are recommended during pregnancy:

- Avocados
- Raw almond and cashew butter
- Raw walnuts, almonds, and cashews
- Eggs
- Wild salmon
- Coconut, avocado and extra-virgin olive oils
- Chia seeds and ground flax seeds
- Grass-fed beef
- Fish oil supplement

FATS TO AVOID

When you're pregnant, it's important to be mindful of the types of fats you consume, especially processed fats. Processed fats are often found in fried foods, packaged snacks and baked goods. They can contain trans fats and high levels of saturated fats. Trans fats are known to raise bad cholesterol (LDL) and lower good cholesterol (HDL), which could increase the risk of heart related problems. Excessive saturated fats can also have negative effects on cardiovascular health.

These fats are best to avoid during pregnancy:
- Processed foods such as potato chips
- Fried foods such as French fries, fried chicken, etc.
- Vegetable oil
- Margarine
- Flaxseed oil supplement

RECOMMENDED HEALTHY FATS INTAKE
Healthy fats should make up about 20%-40% of your daily diet from the sources listed above.

Non-starchy Vegetables

While they are not a macronutrient, they deserve a category of their own. Here is a list of some fantastic non-starchy vegetables to include in your diet:
- Leafy Greens:
  - Spinach
  - Kale
  - Swiss chard
  - Romaine lettuce
  - Arugula
  - Collard greens
- Cruciferous Vegetables:
  - Broccoli
  - Cauliflower
  - Brussels sprouts
  - Cabbage
  - Bok choy
  - Radishes
- Peppers:
  - Bell peppers (all colors)
  - Jalapeños
  - Anaheim peppers
  - Banana peppers
- Cucumbers:
  - Cucumbers (English, Persian, etc.)
- Asparagus
- Tomatoes (in moderation, as they contain some carbs)
- Zucchini and Summer Squash
- Mushrooms
- Green Beans
- Onions (in moderation)
- Carrots (in moderation)
- Radishes
- Eggplant
- Artichokes
- Celery

- Snow Peas
- Okra
- Spaghetti Squash
- Turnips
- Kohlrabi

These vegetables are low in carbohydrates (besides the 3 indicated "in moderation"), making them excellent choices for pregnancy and overall managing blood sugar levels. They're also rich in vitamins, minerals, and fiber, providing essential nutrients for a balanced and healthy diet.

RECOMMENDED NON-STARCHY VEGETABLES INTAKE
Experts recommend that about 50%-75% of your daily vegetable intake be non-starchy vegetables, or about ½ of your plate at each meal.

GET YOUR MICRONUTRIENTS

Ensuring a well-rounded diet of vitamins and minerals throughout pregnancy is vital for the well-being of both you and your developing baby. This will not only safeguard against birth defects but also aids in fostering fetal growth, maintaining maternal health and preventing complications like anemia and preeclampsia. Additionally, it boosts the immune system, promotes strong bones and facilitates healthy weight gain. These essential nutrients play a significant role in supporting the baby's brain development and overall welfare.

VITAMINS

Folate (Vitamin B9)

Folate is one of the most important nutrients during pregnancy since research shows that neural tube defects are reduced by 70% when an adequate amount is consumed.

Some natural sources of folate are lentils, asparagus, cauliflower, brussels sprouts, spinach and beans.

A good prenatal vitamin will contain enough folate to support a healthy pregnancy in addition to these foods.

Vitamin D

Getting enough vitamin D is essential for the absorption of calcium, which plays a crucial role in the development of your baby's bones and teeth when you consume foods rich in calcium. Scientific studies have indicated that insufficient vitamin D during pregnancy can lead to negative outcomes such as premature birth, gestational diabetes and preeclampsia. Natural sources of vitamin D include responsible sun exposure, fatty fish such as sockeye salmon, canned tuna and sardines, eggs and beef liver.

It is recommended that a daily supplementation ranging from 1000-6400 IUs of vitamin D would be a more effective approach to prevent deficiency without causing harm

Vitamin C

Vitamin C is important for maintaining a strong immune system and preventing illness and also helps with the absorption of iron when paired with iron-rich foods. Some wonderful natural sources of vitamin c are citrus fruits, brussels sprouts, broccoli, dark leafy greens, tomatoes, organic berries, avocado, bell peppers and strawberries.

Vitamin C is contained in prenatal vitamins if you are not able to get an adequate amount from natural food sources.

Vitamin A

Vitamin A and beta carotene help with your baby's bone and teeth growth and eye health. It is found naturally in cantaloupe, eggs, liver, spinach, carrots, green and yellow vegetables, pumpkin, broccoli and potatoes.
The general recommendation is to get your Vitamin A intake through your prenatal vitamin and natural food sources and to not take a separate Vitamin A supplement, as this has been shown to be correlated with congenital birth abnormalities.

Vitamin B6 (Pyridoxine)

Vitamin B6 has been found to increase progesterone, which is a hormone that helps to sustain your pregnancy after conception. Additionally, taking a B6 supplement can be really helpful in reducing nausea if you suffer from morning sickness! It is naturally found in spinach, avocado, olives, wild salmon, turkey, cauliflower, sweet potatoes, garlic, sunflower seeds, pistachios, flaxseeds, walnuts, dried prunes, hazelnuts, raisins, dried apricots, beef and chicken.

Unless you are using it to help with morning sickness, a B6 supplement is usually not needed.

Vitamin B12 (Cobalamin)

Vitamin B12 plays a vital role in supporting the health of your nervous system and when taken with folic acid in supplements, it may help prevent spina bifida and other birth defects. Natural food sources include wild salmon, shrimp, grass-fed beef liver or tenderloin, yogurt, red meat, Swiss cheese, milk, cottage cheese, and cod.

Because B12 is primarily contained in animal products, it is recommended to speak with your doctor about supplementation if you eat a vegetarian or vegan diet.

Vitamin E

Vitamin E is essential in forming and using muscles and red blood cells. It is naturally occurring in papaya, spinach, coconut oil, olive oil, almonds, sunflower seeds, pumpkin seeds, spinach, kale, avocado and broccoli.
Vitamin E supplements are not recommended during pregnancy but can be consumed in adequate amounts through foods and a standard prenatal vitamin.

Vitamin K

Vitamin K helps with blood clotting and bone development in your baby and is naturally found in spinach, broccoli, asparagus, soybeans, eggs, strawberries, and liver.

Vitamin K supplements are not typically needed or recommended during pregnancy.

MINERALS

Iron

Iron during pregnancy is essential to prevent anemia and support the baby's brain development. It reduces the risk of preterm birth and low birth weight. Iron also boosts energy and strengthens the immune system in pregnant women. Iron can be naturally found in foods like clams, mussels, beef, sardines, walnuts, almonds, peas, broccoli, pumpkin seeds, turkey, halibut, chicken, wild salmon, beans, collard greens, kale and sesame seeds.

Iron supplementation is generally recommended during pregnancy, especially for those who follow a vegetarian or vegan diet, and is typically included in a prenatal vitamin or can be taken as a separate supplement.

Calcium

Calcium is important in the development of your baby's teeth and bones and also prevents pre-eclampsia. If your baby is not getting enough calcium, your body will start taking calcium from your body and bones, so therefore it's beneficial for both of you to ensure you are getting enough and can prevent you from developing osteoporosis later in life. Calcium is naturally found in whole foods like sunflower seeds, sweet potatoes, butternut squash, oranges, almonds, green beans, clams, figs and broccoli, and non-whole food sources are fortified non-dairy milks.

Most experts recommend taking a calcium supplement, and timing is also important. Studies have shown that calcium can interfere with your body's ability to absorb iron; therefore, taking these two supplements a different time of the day is beneficial.

Zinc

Zinc helps prevent preterm birth and for cell growth and brain development. Some natural sources of zinc are lentils, quinoa, oysters, pumpkin and sesame seeds, shrimp, beef and lamb.

Zinc is not typically needed as an additional supplement, and is usually included in prenatal vitamins.

Iodine

Iodine helps with immunity, metabolism and weight management for you and for the growth and development of your baby's brain. It can be found naturally in foods like shrimp, strawberries, potatoes, cod, and navy beans.

While iodine supplements are not typically recommended, it is advisable to use salt that contains iodine, which we will discuss in the next few pages.

Magnesium

Magnesium can increase birth weight and prevent pre-eclampsia. Natural sources of magnesium include organic berries, banana, butternut squash, avocados, hummus, lentils, beans, mushrooms, spinach, chard, pumpkin seeds and wild white fish.

A magnesium supplement is generally recommended during pregnancy in addition to what is in prenatal vitamins.

Copper

Copper is essential for brain development and is naturally found in eggs, peas, cooked carrots, apricots, tomatoes, beans, lentils, mushrooms, bell peppers, broccoli, asparagus, brussels sprouts, kale, collard greens and spinach.

Copper supplements are not typically recommended during pregnancy, and are usually contained in prenatal vitamins.

Phosphorus

Phosphorus helps build strong bones for you and your baby. Natural sources include red meat and poultry, fish, eggs, nuts and beans.

Research shows that deficiency in phosphorus is rare, and supplementation outside of a prenatal vitamin is not typically recommended.

Supplements by trimester

Supplements are important during the first trimester of pregnancy, and throughout pregnancy in general, to ensure that both the mother and the developing fetus receive adequate nutrients essential for proper growth and development. The first trimester, in particular, is a critical period for the formation of the baby's organs and tissues. Here I will break down the nutrients to focus on by trimester.

First Trimester: Vitamins A, D, E, C, B1, B2, B3, B6, folic acid, calcium, choline, iodine, iron, fiber, protein, omega-3 fatty acids and zinc.

Second Trimester: Calcium, Vitamin D, magnesium and iron

Third Trimester: Iron, protein, Vitamins B6, D3 and K2, calcium, magnesium, choline, and healthy fats
While it is important to maintain a healthy diet, there are several reasons why doctors often recommend taking supplements during pregnancy. One is that pregnancy requires higher levels of certain nutrients like folic acid, iron,

calcium, vitamin D and iodine to support the baby's growth and maintain the mother's health. Meeting these increased needs solely through food can be challenging.

Second, even with a well-balanced diet, pregnant women may still experience deficiencies in essential vitamins and minerals. Common deficiencies during pregnancy include iron, folic acid, calcium, vitamin D and omega 3 fatty acids.

Another reason is that nausea, vomiting and aversions to certain foods are common during pregnancy. These factors can limit food choices and affect nutrient intake. Supplements can help bridge the nutritional gaps when specific foods are difficult to consume.

We also want to ensure optimal fetal development. For instance, folic acid plays a critical role in preventing neural tube defects in the developing baby during early pregnancy stages. By supplementing with specific vitamins and minerals, we can ensure optimal development of the fetal brain, spinal cord and organs.

It's also important to recognize that people have diverse dietary habits that may not always meet the increased nutritional demands of pregnancy adequately for everyone. Some people may have certain dietary limitations or personal preferences that restrict the amount of nutrients they can consume.

Finally, bioavailability is an important factor to consider when it comes to nutrients. Even if a particular nutrient is included in one's diet, its bioavailability, which refers to how effectively the body can absorb and utilize it, can vary. Supplements can be a helpful way to provide specific nutrients in forms that are readily absorbed by the body.

When looking at supplement brands, it's not one size fits all. Starting with a prenatal vitamin, you want to make sure it has the full spectrum of nutrients, that they are bioavailable or able to be easily absorbed by your body, that they contain high-quality ingredients, that they are third-party tested for purity and that they are clean, meaning they don't contain harmful additives.

Here is a list of prenatal vitamins that meet these criteria:

- Ritual Prenatal Vitamin Capsules
- FullWell Prenatal Vitamin
- MegaFood Baby & Me 2 Prenatal Multivitamin (especially beneficial for vegetarians)
- Thorne Basic Prenatal
- Nature Made Prenatal Folic Acid + DHA Softgels
- SmartyPants Prenatal Formula Gummies
- Natalist Prenatal Daily Packets

THE PLATE METHOD

The USDA Plate Method is a helpful visual tool and dietary approach created by the United States Department of Agriculture (USDA) to assist in planning and enjoying well-balanced and nutritious meals. It offers a straightforward and efficient way to guide portion sizes and food choices for a wholesome diet.

To follow the USDA Plate Method, start by dividing a standard dinner plate into four equal sections;

1. **Vegetables**: Fill half of the plate with an assortment of vibrant vegetables, with an emphasis on non-starchy options such as leafy greens, carrots, broccoli and peppers.

2. **Fruits**: Fill half of your plate with low-glycemic fruits such as cherries, grapefruit, avocados, apricots, pears, apples, oranges, plums, strawberries, peaches and grapes.

3. **Grains**; Allocate about one fourth of the plate for whole grains or starchy foods like quinoa and other low-glycemic grains such as rye, barley, amaranth and buckwheat.

4. **Proteins**; Reserve another one fourth of the plate for lean protein sources such as poultry, fish, beans, nuts, legumes or lean cuts of meat.

In addition to these sections on your plate, you can also add a small serving size of dairy or dairy alternatives, being mindful to choose full-fat options.

The USDA Plate Method aims to promote a well-rounded and diverse diet by emphasizing portion management and the inclusion of various food groups to fulfill nutritional requirements. It offers a flexible and realistic approach to meal planning while encouraging healthy eating habits.

In addition to being mindful of what you eat, when you eat is also worth considering. The American Pregnancy Association recommends eating three meals and three small snacks a day, which consist mostly of whole nutritious foods.

FLUID INTAKE

Staying hydrated during pregnancy is essential because you are producing more blood, and it helps you to feel good too! A general recommendation is at least 80 ounces a day. Water is ideal, but if you find that water is becoming a little boring, there are some fantastic herbal teas you can try. These are all easy to find or make and are safe throughout pregnancy.

- Red Raspberry Leaf tea is naturally caffeine-free and is readily available in most stores. It helps to promote uterine health in the first trimester.
- Ginger Tea is especially helpful to manage nausea if you are dealing with morning sickness. You can buy tea bags or place a few slices of fresh ginger in hot water. Similarly, adding a mint leaf to hot water to form a tea can also help relieve nausea.
- Rooibos tea helps strengthen your immune system and is an antioxidant.
- Chamomile tea helps alleviate constipation or other GI issues and it also promotes good sleep, which benefits you and your baby.
- Lemon Balm tea promotes relaxation and sleep and helps with anxiety.

When it comes to drinking teas, it's best to minimize added sugar and artificial sweeteners and use natural sources like a small amount of honey, or low glycemic/natural sources like coconut sugar or agave if you prefer your tea sweetened.

Beverages to avoid

- Sugary beverages such as soda, energy drinks, sweetened iced teas, fruit juices, flavored waters and bottled smoothies are high in sugar, contain empty calories and can contain artificial sweeteners.
- Alcoholic beverages are high in calories and sometimes sugar, and in general alcohol has been found to have negative effects on your baby's growing and developing brain.
- Caffeinated beverages such as coffee, black and green tea, energy drinks and pre-workout supplements are not recommended because they can affect the quality of your sleep and could cause digestive issues. Additionally, research has shown that it can contribute to low birth weight and impaired brain development in your baby.

SALT

Salt is an important component of our diet as it plays a crucial role in various bodily functions, including maintaining fluid balance, facilitating muscle contractions, and supporting nerve function. When you're pregnant, the demand for salt may slightly increase due to the needs of the growing fetus and changes happening in your body.

However, it's crucial to maintain a balanced salt intake during this period. Consuming too much salt can lead to issues such as high blood pressure and water retention. On the other hand, insufficient salt intake can result in low blood pressure and other complications. Therefore, it's important to aim for a moderate salt intake from iodized sea salt rather than table salt.

While table salt and sea salt are primarily composed of sodium chloride, sea salt often contains small amounts of other minerals like potassium, magnesium and calcium. Some prefer the complex taste and coarser texture of sea salt.

One advantage of certain types of table salts is that they are iodized; meaning they have iodine added to them.

If you choose to use sea salt instead of regular salt, it's important to be aware that you might not be getting enough iodine unless you intentionally include other foods rich in iodine in your diet.

The role of iodine in maintaining thyroid health is crucial. These hormones are essential for regulating metabolism, supporting neurological development and promoting overall growth.

During pregnancy, the significance of iodine becomes even more pronounced. Thyroid hormones play a critical role in the development of the fetus, particularly in relation to brain and nervous system growth. Insufficient iodine levels during pregnancy can lead to conditions like intellectual disabilities and developmental delays in children. Even mild deficiencies can have long term effects on cognitive function. Therefore, it is extremely important for expectant mothers to maintain adequate levels of iodine.

Baby~Building Superfoods

Now that you know how to balance all of those important pregnancy nutrients, let's explore some specific foods that aid in fetal development.

EGGS

Eggs are a nutritional powerhouse that offer various health benefits, including support for overall health and fetal development during pregnancy. They are a rich source of high-quality protein, essential amino acids, and various vital nutrients such as protein, choline, folate, and essential fatty acids, which are indispensable for neural tube formation and the brain development of your baby. Deficiency in these nutrients may lead to complications such as neural tube defects, low birth weight, and developmental delays. Given their nutritional density, eggs can be an excellent addition to a balanced diet and pasture-raised eggs are recommended because they contain more Vitamin E and omega-3 fatty acids than those raised in cages. It's also important to note that raw or undercooked eggs should be avoided during pregnancy to reduce the risk of foodborne illness.

There are no restrictions on how often you can consume eggs, so if you are craving an egg, go for it!

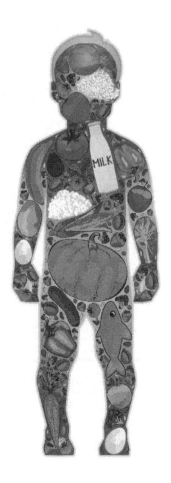

LIVER

Liver, often referred to as nature's multivitamin, is an exceptional food, particularly during pregnancy. It's the only major dietary source of choline apart from eggs, and is abundant in almost every vitamin and mineral recognized by modern nutrition science. Notably, liver is the top source of heme iron, which is highly absorbable and doesn't cause constipation like iron supplements often do. This form of iron is crucial for preventing maternal anemia, preeclampsia, hypothyroidism, and preterm birth, and is essential for the proper brain development and growth of your baby.

The liver's importance is further highlighted by its rich content of folate and vitamin B12. These are key for healthy red blood cells and fetal brain development. The natural folate in liver is far superior to synthetic folic acid in supplements, which up to 60% of people can't utilize effectively due to a genetic variation in the MTHFR enzyme. For those with the MTHFR mutation, which can be determined through genetic testing, liver provides a readily usable form of folate. Liver also contains up to 200 times more vitamin B12 than muscle meats, addressing risks associated with inadequate vitamin B12 intake like neural tube defects and miscarriage.

Liver's richness in fat-soluble vitamins A, D, E, and K is also significant. Despite concerns over vitamin A toxicity, especially during pregnancy, natural vitamin A from liver is safe, particularly when combined with adequate vitamin D and K2, which are also present in liver. This safety profile underscores the advantage of sourcing nutrients from food rather than supplements.

Concerns over vitamin A toxicity from liver are often overblown, especially considering the prevalence of vitamin A deficiency in pregnant women. Liver, as a primary food source of vitamin A, is crucial for fetal development, including the growth of lungs, kidneys, heart, eyes, and other organs. Studies show that women who include liver in their diet are more likely to meet their vitamin A needs, while a significant portion of those who avoid liver fall short of the recommended dietary allowance (RDA).

Liver's role in prenatal nutrition is further complicated by advice to avoid it based on outdated studies linking synthetic vitamin A to birth defects. However, food-sourced vitamin A, particularly in liver, doesn't pose the same risks. Liver's safety and efficacy highlight the disconnect between research and nutrition policy.

The advice to rely on plant sources of vitamin A, as an alternative to liver, is flawed. Plant sources contain carotenoids (provitamin A), which have a highly variable and often inefficient conversion rate to true vitamin A (retinol).

This variability can be influenced by genetics, making liver an essential dietary source of preformed vitamin A.

Including liver in your diet, even just a few ounces weekly, along with carotenes from vegetables and other vitamin A sources, is crucial for meeting you and your growing baby's nutritional needs. The benefits of consuming liver, particularly during pregnancy, far outweigh the outdated concerns about its vitamin A content.

BONE BROTH

Bone broth contains a variety of nutrients that can be beneficial for overall health, especially during pregnancy. It provides essential minerals like calcium, magnesium and phosphorus, as well as important amino acids such as proline and glycine. These nutrients play a crucial role in promoting the development of strong bones, teeth and connective tissue in the growing fetus. Glycine, in particular, is involved in the production of hemoglobin and collagen, which are vital for both the mother and the baby. Moreover, bone broth's collagen content can help maintain skin elasticity and joint health during pregnancy when a woman's body undergoes significant changes. Ensuring an adequate intake of these essential nutrients is important to prevent issues like weak bones or dental problems and to support the overall well-being of the baby.

As a dietary supplement, bone broth can be consumed multiple times per week.

LEAFY GREENS

Green leafy vegetables such as spinach, kale, Swiss chard, arugula and collard greens are packed with important nutrients that offer numerous health benefits, especially during pregnancy. They are abundant in essential vitamins and minerals like folic acid, iron, calcium and vitamin K, which all play vital roles in maintaining good health and supporting the development of the fetus. Iron contributes to both the mother's and baby's blood supply, while calcium aids in building a strong skeletal system for the fetus. Vitamin K plays a significant role in blood clotting. Deficiencies in these nutrients can lead to various health issues like anemia, weakened bone health and even neural tube defects if severe. Apart from leafy greens, other non-starchy vegetables like bell peppers, cauliflower and zucchini also provide essential nutrients and fiber that promote overall well-being.

These vegetables can be consumed daily and are easily integrated into many recipes.

SALMON (AND OTHER FATTY FISHES AND SEAFOOD)

Salmon and other types of fatty fish, such as mackerel, sardines and tuna, and other seafood such as shrimp and scallops contain important nutrients like omega 3 fatty acids—specifically EPA (eicosatetraenoic acid) and DHA (docosahexaenoic acid). These nutrients are crucial for maintaining good overall health and are especially beneficial during pregnancy for the development of the baby. They play a vital role in the growth of the baby's brain, eyes and nervous system. Moreover, they help reduce inflammation, promote heart health and potentially lower the risk of premature birth. Insufficient levels of omega 3s can lead to less-than-optimal brain development and cognitive function in children while also increasing the chances of maternal depression.

Current guidelines recommend that pregnant women or those who are breastfeeding should aim to consume around 8-12 ounces of various seafood per week that is low in mercury. This includes up to 6 ounces of fatty fish like salmon.

FULL-FAT AND FERMENTED DAIRY PRODUCTS

Nutrient-dense dairy products like yogurt, kefir, and whole milk in your diet during pregnancy can provide you with essential nutrients like calcium, vitamin D, and protein. These nutrients are important for the overall health of both you and your developing baby. Fermented dairy products like yogurt and kefir also contain probiotics that support good digestive health and a strong immune system. Calcium is crucial for the development of your baby's bones and teeth, while vitamin D helps with calcium absorption and supports immune function. Protein is necessary for cell growth and contributes to your baby's increasing body mass. If you don't get enough of these nutrients, it could affect bone development, weaken your immune system, or result in a lower birth weight for your baby. Full-fat dairy products can also provide healthy fats like omega-3 fatty acids that are beneficial for brain development.

While individual needs may vary, incorporating these dairy products into your diet 3-4 times a week can help ensure you're getting these important nutrients in a balanced way.

WHOLE GRAINS

Including high fiber and low glycemic whole grains like, quinoa, oatmeal, barley and buckwheat in your diet is incredibly beneficial for overall health, especially during pregnancy. Both the you and your baby benefit from these nutritious grains. Fiber helps with digestion and prevents constipation, which is a common issue during pregnancy. It also plays a crucial role in maintaining stable blood sugar levels, which is important for avoiding gestational diabetes. Low glycemic whole grains release sugar into the bloodstream slowly, providing consistent energy levels and reducing the risk of sudden spikes in blood sugar. This not only benefits the mother but also contributes to optimal brain development and overall growth of the baby.

It's generally recommended for pregnant women to incorporate whole grains into their daily meals, aiming for around 6-11 servings per day based on individual caloric and nutritional needs.

BERRIES

Berries, such as blueberries, strawberries, and raspberries, are packed with essential nutrients that are incredibly beneficial for overall health. During pregnancy, they become even more important as they contribute significantly to the development of the fetus. These fruits are abundant in vital nutrients like vitamin C, fiber and antioxidants like flavonoids and polyphenols. These elements possess remarkable anti-inflammatory and antioxidant properties that support the immune system and aid in maintaining healthy digestion. Additionally, they have the potential to counteract any increased oxidative stress that may occur during pregnancy.

When it comes to the development of the fetus, berries also provide a valuable source of folic acid needed to prevent birth defects as mentioned above.

Fruit is recommended in 2-4 servings per day, so incorporating berries into your daily fruit dose is a great idea.

AVOCADO

Avocados are incredibly nutritious and can provide significant support for overall health, particularly during pregnancy. They contain essential nutrients like folic acid, potassium, fiber, and healthy monounsaturated fats. Folic acid plays a vital role in the proper development of the neural tube in unborn babies, reducing the risk of birth defects such as spina bifida. Moreover, the healthy fats found in avocados contribute to brain development and hormone production. The fiber and potassium content can also help manage common pregnancy symptoms like constipation and high blood pressure. It's important to ensure an adequate intake of these crucial nutrients as deficiencies may lead to higher risks for both mother and baby, including poor fetal development and increased chances of complications during pregnancy.

Avocados can also be eaten several times a week as part of your 2-4 servings of daily fruit.

LEGUMES

Including legumes like lentils, chickpeas, black beans, navy beans, pinto beans, kidney beans, and lima beans in your diet is highly beneficial due to their abundance of essential nutrients. These nutrients, such as protein, fiber, folate, and iron, play a crucial role in supporting overall health and are particularly important during pregnancy. Protein aids in the growth of fetal tissue while fiber helps regulate blood sugar levels and alleviate constipation, which is commonly experienced during pregnancy. Folate is especially vital during the first trimester as it helps prevent neural tube defects in the developing fetus. Additionally, iron supports increased blood volume and reduces the risk of anemia – a condition that can lead to preterm delivery and low birth weight. Ensuring adequate intake of these essential nutrients is crucial to avoid complications such as poor fetal development, low energy levels, and heightened susceptibility to illness.

Legumes are a protein and therefore can be included in your daily 60-100 grams of daily protein.

SWEET POTATO

Sweet potatoes are a wonderful food choice during pregnancy as they offer numerous health benefits for both the mother and baby. They are packed with nutrients, such as beta carotene, which is converted into vitamin A and plays a vital role in the development of the baby's organs like the heart, lungs, and kidneys. Moreover, sweet potatoes provide a good amount of fiber that aids digestion and prevents common pregnancy issues like constipation. These tubers also contain essential nutrients like folate that are crucial for early fetal development, as well as potassium which helps regulate blood pressure.

Since sweet potatoes are loaded with Vitamin A which can become toxic if overconsumed, incorporating them into your diet once or twice per week can be a beneficial way to ensure you and your baby receive these essential nutrients and don't overdo it.

First Trimester Cookbook

The first trimester of pregnancy, covering those tenders first twelve weeks, is filled with hope, anticipation, and quite often, a whirlwind of emotions. It's not just the start of your baby's life journey, but also a profound transition for you. During this period, your little one is quietly laying down the foundation for all the milestones to come, forming vital organs and structures. The food and nutrients you consume play a heartfelt role in supporting this magical transformation. Something as simple as folic acid, a kind of B-vitamin, becomes a silent guardian, ensuring your baby's brain and spine develop appropriately. By embracing a nourishing diet, you're not just giving your baby the best possible start but also sending a message of love with every bite.

1 MONTH   **2** MONTH   **3** MONTH

For you, the first trimester might bring its share of challenges – maybe it's the morning sickness, the unexpected fatigue, or those mood swings that take you by surprise. Believe it or not, the food you eat has the gentle power to comfort and help you through these moments. A balanced diet can give you that much-needed energy boost, soothe your nausea, and uplift your spirits. On the other hand, missing out on certain nutrients might make those days feel a bit tougher. For instance, not having enough iron could leave you feeling more tired than usual. By prioritizing nutrition early on, you're not just taking care of your baby, but also nurturing yourself, ensuring that both of you have the strength and vitality for the journey ahead.

There are specific nutrients that are critical during these first twelve weeks:

- **Vitamin A** - growth of bones and teeth
- **Vitamin D** - supports growth of bones and teeth; helps the body with calcium and phosphorus absorption
- **Vitamin E** - muscle and red blood cell formation
- **Vitamin C** - boosts immunity, prevents tissue damage and helps with iron absorption
- **Vitamin B1** - helps with energy and the nervous system
- **Vitamin B2** - helps with absorption of other nutrients, promotes healthy eyes and skin
- **Vitamin B3** - supports healthy skin and nervous system; helps with digestion

- **Vitamin B6** - supports red blood cell formation and helps with morning sickness
- **Folic acid** - prevents birth defects and support placenta health
- **Calcium** - supports healthy development of teeth and bones
- **Choline** - prevents birth defects and supports nervous system development
- **Iodine** - regulates thyroid and metabolism; supports nervous system development
- **Iron** - prevents premature birth and low birth weight; prevents anemia
- **Fiber** - helps with digestion and helps prevent high blood pressure
- **Protein** - supports overall healthy fetal growth and development
- **Omega-3 fatty acids** - supports healthy nervous system development
- **Zinc** - supports insulin and enzyme production

HOW TO FIGHT MORNING SICKNESS AND DEAL WITH FOOD AVERSIONS

Nausea during pregnancy, commonly referred to as morning sickness even though it can happen at any time of the day, is a prevalent symptom experienced by many expectant mothers, especially in the initial trimester. Although its precise cause is still a mystery, several researchers speculate that it is linked to lower blood sugar and/or the increase in pregnancy hormones like human chorionic gonadotropin (hCG) and estrogen. These hormonal fluctuations are vital for a healthy pregnancy but can result in feelings of queasiness and vomiting. Another theory suggests that morning sickness may have evolved as a protective mechanism, discouraging pregnant women from consuming potentially harmful substances during a period when the developing fetus is most susceptible. Despite being unpleasant, morning sickness generally indicates that the pregnancy is progressing normally.

Ways to Alleviate Nausea During Pregnancy

Completely avoiding nausea during pregnancy might be challenging, but there are various strategies that can help alleviate its severity. Firstly, it's important to consume small and frequent meals throughout the day to maintain stable blood sugar levels. You can keep something bland, like soda crackers, beside your bed and nibble on a few before getting up in the morning. Additionally, steering clear of spicy, greasy and acidic foods may make a difference since they tend to trigger feelings of nausea. Ensuring regular fluid intake in small quantities can also help keep you hydrated without overwhelming your stomach.

Ginger is a great natural way to alleviate nausea and there are different ways you can consume it, such as ginger tea, ginger juice or even ginger candy. You can also try using acupressure wristbands, which are commonly used for motion sickness and can be quite effective. And don't forget to take some time to rest because feeling tired can make nausea worse.

If you are experiencing nausea, here are a few safe and delicious teas you can try.

Soothing Ginger-Chamomile Tea

Ingredients:

- 1 fresh ginger slice (about 1 inch, thinly sliced)
- 1 chamomile tea bag
- 1 teaspoon honey or to taste (optional)
- 1 slice of lemon (optional)
- 2 cups boiling water

Instructions:

1. In a teapot or heatproof pitcher, combine the fresh ginger slices and chamomile tea bag
2. Pour the boiling water over the mixture.
3. Allow the tea to steep for about 5 minutes.
4. Strain the tea into a cup, discarding the ginger slice
5. Stir in honey if desired, and add a slice of lemon for an added zesty flavor.
6. Enjoy your soothing blend!

Raspberry-Peppermint Cooler

Ingredients:

- 2 peppermint tea bags or 2 tablespoons fresh peppermint leaves
- 2 raspberry tea bags
- 2-3 teaspoons honey or to taste
- 1 lemon (juiced)
- 4 cups boiling water
- Ice cubes

Instructions:

1. In a large teapot or heatproof pitcher, combine the peppermint tea bags or fresh peppermint leaves, and raspberry tea bags.
2. Pour the boiling water over the tea blend.
3. Let the tea steep for about 5-7 minutes.
4. Strain the tea into a new pitcher, removing and discarding the tea leaves if needed
5. Stir in honey to taste and the juice of one lemon.
6. Allow the tea to cool down to room temperature and then refrigerate until chilled.
7. Serve the tea over ice cubes in a glass.

How to Manage Food Aversions

If you are experiencing aversions to particular foods, you are not alone. These can be attributed to a combination of hormonal changes, heightened sense of smell and shifting taste preferences. It's not unusual for expectant mothers to suddenly find certain foods that they once enjoyed to be repulsive or even develop cravings for completely new types of food. These dislikes are believed to be nature's way of safeguarding the developing fetus from potentially harmful substances. For example, many women report aversions towards coffee, alcohol and strongly scented or spicy foods. However, the exact causes and the specific range of foods that can trigger these dislikes vary from person to person. While some food dislikes are mild inconveniences, others can be more intense and make it challenging when it comes to meal planning and eating.

Effectively managing aversions begins with acknowledging and respecting your changing preferences. It's important to listen to your body and avoid eating foods that trigger strong reactions, since trying to force yourself into eating disliked foods can lead to feelings of nausea or vomiting. However, if these dislikes prevent you from getting in your essential nutrients, you can explore alternative sources. For instance, if meat becomes repulsive, you could consider incorporating plant-based proteins such as beans and lentils into your diet instead.

Exploring a variety of meals and experimenting with different cooking techniques can also be beneficial. Certain vegetables that may not seem appealing in their raw form could become more enjoyable when prepared as a soup or stew. If you're experiencing nausea, opting for smaller, frequent meals and avoiding spicy or greasy foods could also help.

BREAKFASTS TO FUEL YOUR DAY

Having a nutritious breakfast is extremely important during pregnancy for several reasons. First and foremost, it helps to kickstart your metabolism and provides a steady supply of energy, which is essential for both you and your baby. If you are experiencing morning sickness, having a small meal in the morning can help. Additionally, breakfast foods like eggs or oatmeal with fruit often contain important nutrients like protein, calcium, iron and fiber. By regularly eating breakfast, you can ensure you are meeting your increased nutrient needs while also giving your baby the best possible start in life.

Ginger Banana Smoothie

VEGETARIAN

A refreshing and invigorating smoothie that combines the tropical sweetness of bananas with the zesty kick of fresh ginger. This drink is not only delicious but also offers a great energy boost, thanks to the natural sugars in bananas and protein in Greek yogurt, and ginger can help with morning sickness.

Preparation Time: 5 minutes
Cooking Time: 0 minutes
Total Time: 5 minutes
Serves: 1

Ingredients:

- 1 ripe banana, peeled and sliced
- 1/2-inch piece of fresh ginger, peeled and grated (adjust to taste)
- 1/2 cup of unsweetened almond milk (or any milk of your choice)
- 1/4 cup of unsweetened, whole milk Greek yogurt (or any yogurt of your choice) for creaminess (optional)
- A pinch of ground cinnamon (optional)
- Ice cubes (optional)

Instructions:

1. Before you begin, make sure the bananas are ripe, as this will give the smoothie a natural sweetness.
2. Peel the ginger and grate it finely to ensure it blends well.
3. In a blender, combine the sliced bananas, grated ginger, almond milk, and yogurt.
4. If you prefer your smoothies cold or a bit icy, add a handful of ice cubes. You can also sprinkle in a pinch of cinnamon for an extra layer of flavor.
5. Blend on high until the mixture is smooth and creamy. Depending on your blender, this can take anywhere from 30 seconds to a couple of minutes.
6. Pour the smoothie into glasses, garnish with a banana slice or a sprinkle of cinnamon on top if desired, and enjoy!

Chef's Notes:

- For a thicker consistency, you can freeze the bananas beforehand.
- If you're not a fan of almond milk, feel free to substitute with coconut milk, regular dairy milk, oat milk, or any other milk of your preference.
- Ginger is quite potent, so if you're new to its flavor, you might want to start with a smaller piece and adjust to taste.
- If you don't finish it, you can store it in an airtight container in the refrigerator for up to 24 hours
- For a variation, you can add ½ cup of cauliflower and/or ½ cup mango for flavor variety. Cauliflower contains Vitamin B6 which can help with nausea and folate which helps to prevent birth defects. Mango is packed with Vitamin C so it helps to keep you healthy and promotes iron absorption.

Nutritional Information (per serving):

- Calories: 250kcal
- Total Fat: 8g
- Monounsaturated Fat: g 3.54
- Polyunsaturated Fat: 1g
- Total Carbohydrates: 34.1g
- Dietary Fiber: 3.4g
- Protein: 13.3g
- Sodium: 140.4mg
- Vitamin B6: .5mg
- Vitamin B12: 1mcg
- Vitamin C: 10.4mg
- Vitamin D:1.3mcg
- Vitamin E: 8.4mg
- Folate: 31.5mcg
- Calcium: 374.9mg
- Iron: .7mg
- Potassium 699.2mg
- Phosphorus: 210.7mg
- Magnesium: 54.7mg
- Zinc: .9mg

Immunity Boost Smoothie

VEGETARIAN

A refreshing and nutrient-packed smoothie designed to fortify your immune system with vitamins and antioxidants in a delicious way. It's easy to customize and make it different every time.

Preparation Time: 5 minutes
Cooking Time: 0 minutes
Total Time: 5 minutes
Serves: 1

Ingredients:

- 1 fresh orange, peeled and seeds removed
- 1/4 cup of frozen blueberries
- 1/4 cup of frozen strawberries
- 1/4 cup of unsweetened, whole milk Greek yogurt (plain or vanilla)
- 1/2 tablespoon of chia seeds
- 1/2 cup almond milk

Instructions:
1. Peel the orange and remove any seeds.
2. In a blender, start by adding the fresh orange and Greek yogurt. Add in the blueberries, strawberries, chia seeds, and almond milk.
3. Start the blender on a low setting, and gradually increase the speed. Continue blending until you achieve a smooth and creamy consistency. If the smoothie seems too thick, you can add a bit of water.
4. Pour the smoothie into a glass and savor immediately.

Chef's Notes:
- If you have morning sickness, you can add 1/2-inch piece of fresh ginger, peeled and grated
- For extra nutrients like folate, Vitamins C & K, iron and fiber, add small handful of spinach or kale, stems removed
- Can be kept in a sealed container in the refrigerator for up to 24 hours.
- If you're not a fan of almond milk, feel free to substitute with coconut milk, regular dairy milk, oat milk, or any other milk of your preference.

Nutritional Information (per serving):
- Calories: 208kcal
- Total Fat: 6.3g
- Monounsaturated Fat: 2.17g
- Polyunsaturated Fat: .67g
- Total Carbohydrates: 31g
- Dietary Fiber: 7.4g
- Protein: 8.8g
- Sodium: 118.6mg
- Vitamin B12: .5mcg
- Vitamin C: 93.2mg
- Vitamin D: 1.3mcg
- Vitamin E: 8.7mg
- Folate: 53.2mcg
- Iron: 1.4mg
- Calcium: 400.2mg
- Magnesium: 34.1mg
- Zinc: .6mg

Avocado Toast with a Twist

VEGETARIAN

Enjoy a healthy breakfast with this easy avocado toast on sprouted grain bread. Creamy avocado meets zesty lemon, spicy arugula, and crunchy sunflower seed will start your day with healthy fats and fiber.

Preparation Time: 5 minutes
Cooking Time: 0 minutes
Total Time: 5 minutes
Serves: 1

Ingredients:
- 1 slice of sprouted grain bread
- ½ ripe avocado
- ½ cup fresh arugula
- 1 tablespoon sunflower seeds
- Fresh lemon juice from half a lemon (adjust to taste)
- Salt, to taste
- Black pepper, to taste
- Optional: a drizzle of extra-virgin olive oil

Instructions:
1. Toast the sprouted grain bread to your desired crispness in a toaster
2. While the bread is toasting, halve the avocado and remove the seed. Scoop the flesh into a bowl. Add a pinch of salt and pepper and a squirt of lemon juice to the bowl. Use a fork to mash the avocado until it's a creamy, yet slightly chunky texture. Adjust salt and lemon juice to taste.
3. Once your bread is toasted, spread the mashed avocado generously over the slice.
4. Place a handful of fresh arugulas over the avocado layer.
5. Sprinkle the sunflower seeds over the arugula and drizzle a bit more lemon juice on top if desired.
6. If you wish, you can finish the toast with a slight drizzle of extra-virgin olive oil for added flavor and healthy fats.

Chef's Notes:
- You can store the other half of the avocado in the refrigerator with the core and a sprinkle of lemon juice to use the next day.
- You can use spinach or kale instead of arugula if preferred; you can also use chia seeds or pumpkin seeds in place of sunflower seeds.

Nutritional Information (per serving):
- Calories: 349kcal
- Total Fat: 20.5g
- Monounsaturated Fat: 11g
- Polyunsaturated Fat: 3.5g
- Total Carbohydrates: 38g
- Dietary Fiber: 10.6g
- Protein: 8.8g
- Sodium: 321.6mg
- Vitamin C: 22.1mg
- Vitamin A: 19.1mcg
- Vitamin K: 32mcg
- Folate: 111.8
- Iron: 2.9mg
- Calcium: 55.1mg
- Magnesium 58mg

Oatmeal with Almonds and Pear

MIX-AND-MATCH RECIPE

This oatmeal recipe is packed with wholesome oats, crunchy almonds, and sweet pear. It provides fiber and protein, and pears add natural sweetness. It's easy to make and customize and is a great way to start your day.

Preparation Time: 5 minutes
Cooking Time: 10 minutes
Total Time: 15 minutes
Serves: 1

Ingredients:

- 1/4 cup old-fashioned rolled oats
- 1/2 cup whole milk
- 1/4 ripe pear, cored and diced
- 1 tablespoon almonds, roughly chopped
- 1/2 tsp honey
- A pinch of ground cinnamon (optional)
- A pinch of ground nutmeg (optional)

Instructions:

1. Dice a quarter of the pear into bite-sized pieces and roughly chop the almonds.
2. In a small pot, bring the 1/2 cup of milk to a boil. Once boiling, add the rolled oats. Reduce the heat to a simmer.
3. Stir in the diced pear, chopped almonds, honey, ground cinnamon, and ground nutmeg. Mix well.
4. Let the mixture simmer for about 5 minutes, stirring occasionally, until the oats have absorbed most of the liquid. If you prefer creamier oatmeal, add a little more milk and cook for an additional minute.
5. Transfer the oatmeal to a bowl. Add toppings if desired and enjoy!

Chef's Note:

- Whole milk or any unsweetened milk alternative can be used
- Recipe variations:
  - Blueberry and Almond Oatmeal:
    - Instead of pears, add 1/4 cup of fresh or frozen blueberries.
    - Replace honey with maple syrup for a different sweetness.
    - Top with a handful of sliced almonds and a drizzle of almond butter.
  - Banana and Walnut Oatmeal:
    - Substitute the pear with 1/2 ripe banana, sliced.
    - Replace almonds with chopped walnuts.
    - Sweeten with a teaspoon of brown sugar or maple syrup.
  - Coconut and Mango Oatmeal:
    - Replace the pear with 1/4 cup of diced fresh mango.
    - Use coconut milk instead of whole milk for a tropical twist.
    - Top with toasted shredded coconut and a sprinkle of chopped macadamia nuts.
  - Apple Cinnamon Oatmeal:
    - Swap the pear for 1/4 cup of diced apple (use a sweeter variety like Honeycrisp or Gala).
    - Increase the ground cinnamon to 1/4 teaspoon.
    - Garnish with apple slices and a drizzle of caramel sauce.
  - Pumpkin Spice Oatmeal:
    - Mix in 2 tablespoons of canned pumpkin puree and 1/4 teaspoon of pumpkin pie spice.
    - Use chopped pecans instead of almonds.
    - Drizzle with a bit of maple syrup and top with a dollop of Greek yogurt.
  - Berries and Cream Oatmeal:
    - Add 1/4 cup of mixed berries (strawberries, raspberries, and blueberries) instead of pear.
    - Swirl in a spoonful of yogurt for a creamy texture.
    - Sprinkle with granola for extra crunch.
  - Chocolate Peanut Butter Oatmeal:
    - Stir in 1 tablespoon of cocoa powder and 1 tablespoon of peanut butter.
    - Replace almonds with crushed peanuts.
    - Top with chocolate chips and an extra drizzle of peanut butter.
  - Tropical Oatmeal:
    - Use 1/4 cup of diced pineapple instead of pear.
    - Mix in shredded coconut into the oatmeal while it cooks.
    - Garnish with sliced bananas and a sprinkle of chopped macadamia nuts.
  - Mixed Nut Oatmeal:
    - Use a combination of chopped nuts like almonds, walnuts, and pecans.
    - Add a teaspoon of your favorite nut butter.
    - Sweeten with a drizzle of honey or agave syrup.

Nutritional Information (per serving):

- Calories: 259 kcal
- Total Fat: 8.8g
- Monounsaturated Fat: 2.9g
- Polyunsaturated Fat: 1g (indicate omega-3 fatty acids if applicable)
- Total Carbohydrates: 38g
- Dietary Fiber: 5.5g
- Protein: 8.9g
- Sodium: 53.4mg
- Vitamin A: 56.8mcg
- Vitamin C: 3.1mg
- Vitamin D: 1.6mcg
- Vitamin K: 3.5mcg
- Folate: 13.8mcg
- Iron: 1.8mg
- Calcium: 170.8mg
- Magnesium 33.5mg

Scrambled Eggs with Spinach

GLUTEN-FREE

Indulge in a Mediterranean-inspired breakfast with this protein and micronutrient rich dish. Quick to prepare and cook, this delightful scramble offers a burst of flavors, ensuring a vibrant start to your day.

Preparation Time: 7 minutes
Cooking Time: 10 minutes
Total Time: 17 minutes
Serves: 1

Ingredients:

- 2 large eggs
- 1/2 cup fresh spinach leaves, washed and roughly chopped
- 1 tablespoon grated Parmesan cheese
- 1/2 tablespoon olive oil
- 1 tablespoon diced tomatoes
- 1 tablespoon diced red onion
- 1 garlic clove, minced
- 1 tablespoon chopped Kalamata olives
- Salt and freshly ground black pepper to taste

Instructions:

1. Chop spinach and olives, dice tomatoes and onion, and mince garlic.
2. In a bowl, whisk together the egg with a pinch of salt and black pepper. Set aside.
3. In a small non-stick skillet over medium heat, add the olive oil. Once hot, add the red onions and sauté for 2 minutes or until they start to soften. Add the minced garlic and continue sautéing for another 30 seconds.
4. Incorporate the chopped spinach to the skillet. Stir occasionally and cook until the spinach is wilted.
5. Pour the whisked egg over the spinach mixture. Let it set for a few seconds and then gently stir with a spatula, ensuring the egg and spinach mix together. Cook, stirring occasionally, until the eggs are mostly set but still slightly runny.
6. Mix in the diced tomatoes, grated Parmesan cheese, and Kalamata olives. Continue to cook, stirring gently, until the egg is fully set and the cheese begins to melt.
7. Adjust the seasoning with more salt and pepper if needed.
8. Transfer the scrambled eggs to a plate and serve immediately.

Chef's Notes:

- Add a teaspoon of fresh basil or parsley for garnish
- If you can tolerate spice, you can add a pinch of red pepper flakes
- You can replace diced tomatoes with sun-dried tomatoes for a richer flavor

Nutritional Information (per serving):

- Calories: 310kcal
- Total Fat: 24.8g
- Monounsaturated Fat: 11.7g
- Polyunsaturated Fat: 2.7g
- Total Carbohydrates: 412.9g
- Dietary Fiber: .9g
- Protein: 16.3g
- Sodium: 258mg
- Vitamin A: 252.9mcg
- Vitamin C: 11.1mg
- Vitamin D: 1.1mcg
- Vitamin K: 86.6mcg
- Folate: 61.6mcg
- Iron: 3.6mg
- Calcium: 126.2mg
- Potassium: 291.1mg
- Phosphorus: 291.2mg
- Magnesium: 31.5mg

Quinoa and Berry Bowl

GLUTEN-FREE

Refreshing, nutritious, and full of flavor, this quinoa and berry bowl makes an ideal breakfast or snack. The combination of fluffy quinoa with sweet and tangy berries provides a delicious balance of taste and texture.

Preparation Time: 10 minutes
Cooking Time: 15 minutes
Total Time: 25 minutes
Serves: 1

Ingredients:

- 1/4 cup quinoa (uncooked)
- 1/2 cup water
- 3 strawberries, hulled and sliced
- 1/3 cup blueberries
- 1/3 cup raspberries
- 1/4 cup blackberries
- 1 tbsp chopped almonds
- 1/4 tsp of chia seeds
- 1 tsp honey

Instructions:

1. Quinoa Preparation:
   a. Rinse the quinoa under cold water using a fine mesh strainer.
   b. In a small pot, bring the 1/2 cup of water to a boil. Add the rinsed quinoa.
   c. Reduce the heat to low, cover, and let it simmer for about 15 minutes or until the quinoa is tender and the water is absorbed.
   d. Remove from heat, fluff with a fork, and let it cool slightly.
2. Assembling the Bowl:
   a. In your serving bowl, place the cooked quinoa.
   b. Top with strawberries, blueberries, raspberries, and blackberries.
   c. Drizzle with honey.
   d. If desired, add a dollop of Greek yogurt on top.
   e. Sprinkle with the chopped nuts and chia seeds.
   f. Garnish with a fresh mint leaf.

3. Serving:
   a. Serve immediately or refrigerate for an hour before serving.

Chef's Notes
- You can use walnuts, cashews and/or pecans instead of or with the almonds
- You can add sliced banana for some fruity variety
- To add some additional protein and calcium, use ¼ cup water and ¼ cup whole milk to cook quinoa and/or add 2 tablespoons of greek yogurt on top

Nutritional Information (per serving):
- Calories: 222kcal
- Total Fat: 7.8g
- Monounsaturated Fat: 1.82g
- Polyunsaturated Fat: 4.69g
- Total Carbohydrates: 34.8g
- Dietary Fiber: 13.1g
- Protein: 6.8g
- Sodium: 7.2mg
- Vitamin C: 44.3mg
- Vitamin E: 2.5mg
- Vitamin K: 20.5mcg
- Folate: 57.1mcg
- Iron: 2.7mg
- Calcium: 136.7mg
- Potassium: 376.7mg
- Phosphorus: 244.4mg
- Magnesium: 110.9mg
- Zinc: 1.8mg

Chia Seed Pudding with Kiwi

GLUTEN-FREE

Preparation Time: 5 minutes
Cooking Time: 0 minutes
Total Time: 5 minutes + 4+ hours refrigeration time
Serves: 1

Ingredients
- 1 tbsp chia seeds
- 1/4 cup whole milk
- 1/2 tbsp honey
- 1/4 tsp vanilla extract
- 1 ripe kiwi fruit

Instructions:
1. In a small mixing bowl, combine the chia seeds and milk. Stir well to make sure the chia seeds are evenly distributed.
2. Add the honey and vanilla extract. Mix well.
3. Cover the bowl with plastic wrap or a lid and place it in the refrigerator. Allow it to set for at least 4 hours, or ideally overnight. This will let the chia seeds absorb the liquid and swell, creating a pudding-like texture.
4. Once the pudding is ready, slice off both ends of the kiwi.
5. Use a teaspoon to separate the kiwi's flesh from its skin, and then slice or dice the kiwi.

6. Stir the set chia pudding to ensure it has a smooth consistency.
7. Spoon the chia pudding into a serving glass or bowl.
8. Top with kiwi slices or chunks and add any other desired toppings.

Chef's Notes:
- If you wish, add ingredients like cocoa powder, cinnamon, or nut butter to give your chia pudding a different flavor.
- Though this recipe is for one serving, chia pudding can be stored for about 4-5 days in the fridge if you decide to make a larger batch in the future.
- Additional topics options are berries, nuts or coconut flakes
- Plant-based milks can be used in place of dairy milk

Nutritional Information (per serving):
- Calories: 183kcal
- Total Fat: 6.7g
- Monounsaturated Fat: XX g
- Polyunsaturated Fat: XX g (indicate omega-3 fatty acids if applicable)
- Total Carbohydrates: 27.8g
- Dietary Fiber: 7g
- Protein: 5.1g
- Sodium: 31.1mg
- Vitamin C: 64.2mg
- Vitamin E: 1.1mcg
- Vitamin K: 28mcg
- Folate: 27.5mcg
- Iron: 1.4mg
- Calcium: 182.7mg
- Potassium: 360.6mg
- Phosphorus: 197.3mg
- Magnesium: 65.7mg

Whole Wheat Pancakes with Blueberry Compote

VEGETARIAN

Delightfully fluffy and nutrient-packed, these whole wheat pancakes paired with a tangy blueberry compote are not only scrumptious but also beneficial for pregnant mothers. Whole wheat flour offers extra fiber and essential nutrients like folic acid, iron, and magnesium, which can support fetal development and maternal health. Blueberries, on the other hand, are a powerhouse of antioxidants and vitamin C, aiding in boosting immunity and preventing oxidative stress during pregnancy.

Preparation Time: 10 minutes
Cooking Time: 20 minutes
Total Time: 30 minutes
Serves: 2

Ingredients:
For the Pancakes:
- 2/3 cup whole wheat flour

- 1/2 teaspoon baking powder
- A pinch of salt
- 1 teaspoon cinnamon
- 1/2 cup whole milk
- 1 tablespoon melted butter
- 2 tablespoons honey
- 1/2 teaspoon pure vanilla extract

For the Blueberry Compote:
- 1 cup fresh or frozen blueberries
- 2 tablespoons honey
- 1 teaspoon lemon zest
- 2 tablespoons lemon juice

Instructions:
1. In a small saucepan, combine blueberries, honey, lemon zest, and lemon juice.
2. Cook over medium heat, stirring occasionally, until the blueberries begin to break down and release their juices, about 10 minutes.
3. Once the mixture has thickened slightly, remove from heat and set aside.
4. In a mixing bowl, whisk together the whole wheat flour, baking powder, salt, and cinnamon.
5. In another bowl, mix the milk, olive oil/melted butter, honey, and vanilla extract.
6. Pour the wet ingredients into the dry ingredients and stir until just combined. Let the batter sit for a few minutes.
7. Heat a non-stick skillet or griddle over medium heat. Lightly grease with a bit of oil or butter.
8. Pour 1/4 cup portions of the batter onto the skillet. Cook until bubbles form on the surface, then flip and cook until the other side is golden brown.
9. Repeat with the remaining batter.
10. Place the pancakes on a plate, spread with butter, spoon the blueberry compote on top, and enjoy!

Chef's Notes
- Will keep in the refrigerator for a week or the freezer for a month
- Add berries, bananas or chia or flax seeds into the pancake mix for variety
- Top with slivered almonds for some additional protein
- Substitute any plant-based milks for the whole milk if desired

Nutritional Information (per serving):
- Calories: 418kcal
- Total Fat: 9.4g
- Monounsaturated Fat: 2.2g
- Polyunsaturated Fat: .45g
- Total Carbohydrates: 80.4g
- Dietary Fiber: 6.5g
- Protein: 8g
- Sodium: 182.7mg
- Vitamin A: 79mcg
- Vitamin C: 31mg
- Vitamin D: .8mcg
- Vitamin E: .75mg

- Vitamin K: 15.3mcg
- Folate: 20.5mcg
- Calcium: 94.3mg
- Iron: 2mg
- Magnesium: 16mg
- Zinc: .5mg

Rice Cakes with Hummus and Tomato Slices

SO FAST

This light and refreshing rice cake breakfast topped with creamy hummus and fresh tomato slices is not only a delight for the taste buds but also a nutritious choice for expecting mothers. It's an ideal start to your day that packs the benefits of protein, fiber, antioxidants and essential vitamins C and E- key nutrients required during pregnancy and help with fetal development and strengthening the immune system.

Preparation Time: 5 minutes
Cooking Time: 0 minutes
Total Time: 5 minutes
Serves: 1

Ingredients:
- 1 rice cake
- 2 tbsp hummus
- 2 fresh tomato slices

Instructions:
1. Lay the rice cake on a plate.
2. Spread the hummus evenly over the rice cake using a knife or the back of a spoon.
3. Place the fresh tomato slices on top of the hummus.
4. If desired, season with salt, black pepper, and dried herbs.
5. Optionally, for added taste and nutrition, drizzle with a touch of olive oil or sprinkle with sesame seeds.
6. Serve immediately and enjoy!

Chef's Notes:
- Add a pinch of salt, black pepper, everything seasons or dried herbs (like basil or oregano) for added flavor
- Explore different hummus flavors, such as garlic, roasted red pepper, etc.
- Add a drizzle of olive oil or sprinkle of sesame seeds for added taste and nutrition
- Add slices of avocado or cucumber for extra nutrition.

Nutritional Information (per serving):
- Calories: 131kcal
- Total Fat: 6g
- Monounsaturated Fat: XX g
- Polyunsaturated Fat: XX g (indicate omega-3 fatty acids if applicable)
- Total Carbohydrates: 16.7g
- Dietary Fiber: 2.6g
- Protein: 4g
- Sodium: 261.9mg
- Vitamin A: 34.4mcg

- Vitamin C: 11.1mg
- Vitamin K: 13.3mcg
- Folate: 26.6mcg
- Iron: 1mg
- Magnesium: 31.4mg

Sweet Potato and Black Bean Breakfast Burrito

VEGETARIAN

A nutritious and delicious breakfast burrito that's perfect for expectant mothers. Sweet potatoes provide essential vitamins and minerals, including vitamins A and C, which are vital for the growth and development of your baby. Black beans add protein, iron and fiber, ensuring you feel full and satisfied. Together, they create a delightful combination of flavors and textures that's perfect for a hearty morning meal.

Preparation Time: 15 minutes
Cooking Time: 25minutes
Total Time: 40 minutes
Serves: 1

Ingredients:

- 1 small sweet potato, peeled and diced
- 1/2 cup canned black beans
- 1 large whole wheat tortilla
- 1/4 cup chopped red bell pepper
- 1/4 cup chopped onion
- 1 clove garlic, minced
- 1/2 tsp cumin powder
- Sprinkle of salt and pepper, to taste
- 1 tbsp olive oil
- 1/4 cup shredded cheddar cheese

Instructions:

1. Chop pepper and onion, dice and mince sweet potato and garlic. Strain beans.
2. In a medium-sized skillet, heat olive oil over medium heat. Add the onions and bell pepper and sauté until they begin to soften, around 3-4 minutes. Add garlic and continue to sauté for another minute.
3. Add the diced sweet potatoes to the skillet. Cook, stirring occasionally until they are tender and slightly golden brown, about 15 minutes. You can add a little water if they start to stick or to expedite the cooking process.
4. Stir in the black beans, cumin, salt, and pepper. Cook for another 5 minutes until beans are heated through and flavors meld.
5. Warm the tortilla in a dry skillet or microwave for about 20 seconds. Lay it flat on a plate. Spoon the sweet potato and black bean mixture onto the center of the tortilla. Sprinkle with cheese.
6. Fold the sides of the tortilla in and roll up from the bottom. Cut in half and serve hot.

Chef's Notes:

- Add fresh cilantro (optional, for garnish)
- Top with salsa, guacamole, avocado or sour cream for additional flavor and nutrients
- Filling will last for 3-4 days in the refrigerator if you make extra
- Can be eaten in a bowl instead of on a tortilla for a lower carb option

Nutritional Information (per serving):

- Calories: 615kcal
- Total Fat: 29g
- Monounsaturated Fat: 10.5g
- Polyunsaturated Fat: 3.17g
- Total Carbohydrates: 71.5g
- Dietary Fiber: 15.6g
- Protein: 20.6g
- Sodium: 409.6mg
- Vitamin A: 958.3mg
- Vitamin B5: 1.4mg
- Vitamin C: 50.2mg
- Vitamin B6: .5mg
- Vitamin E: 3.9mg
- Vitamin K: 17.9mcg
- Folate: 150.7mcg
- Iron: 4.2mg
- Calcium: 368.9mg
- Magnesium: 100.6mg
- Zinc: 1.5mg

Overnight Oats with Dried Fruits and Nuts

VEGETARIAN

This nutrient-dense and delicious overnight oats recipe is a perfect breakfast choice for expecting mothers. Packed with essential nutrients like fiber, protein, omega-3 fatty acids, and vitamins, it provides sustained energy, supports digestion, promotes your baby's brain health and contributes to the overall well-being of both you and your baby. The combination of fruits and nuts not only enhances the flavor but also offers a variety of essential nutrients that are beneficial during pregnancy.

Preparation Time: 10 minutes
Cooking Time: 0 minutes
Total Time: 10 minutes + overnight refrigeration
Serves: 1

Ingredients:

- 1/2 cup rolled oats
- 1 tbsp chia seeds
- 1 cup whole milk
- 1/2 banana, sliced
- 1/4 cup mixed berries (e.g., blueberries, strawberries, or raspberries)
- 1 tbsp chopped nuts (e.g., walnuts, almonds, or pecans)
- A pinch of salt
- 1/4 tsp vanilla extract

Instructions:

1. In a bowl or mason jar, combine the rolled oats, chia seeds, and a pinch of salt.
2. Pour in the milk and vanilla extract. Mix well to ensure that the oats and chia seeds are fully submerged.
3. Add in the sliced banana, berries, and chopped nuts. Gently stir to combine.
4. Cover the bowl or jar with a lid or plastic wrap.
5. Refrigerate overnight or for at least 6 hours.
6. In the morning, give the oats a good stir. If the mixture is too thick, you can add a little more milk to reach your preferred consistency. Enjoy

Chef's Notes

- Use any plant-based milk instead of dairy milk if desired
- Add some Greek yogurt for extra protein and calcium
- Add additional fruit and nuts as a topping when ready to serve

Nutritional Information (per serving):

- Calories: 467kcal
- Total Fat: 18.9g
- Monounsaturated Fat: XX g
- Polyunsaturated Fat: XX g (indicate omega-3 fatty acids if applicable)
- Total Carbohydrates: 62.4g
- Dietary Fiber: 11.1g
- Protein: 17.2g
- Sodium: 155mg
- Vitamin A: 114mcg
- Vitamin B5: 1.1mg
- Vitamin B6: .3mg
- Vitamin B12: 1.1mcg
- Vitamin C: 12.6mg
- Vitamin D: 3.2mcg
- Folate: 24mcg
- Iron: 3.1mg
- Calcium: 382.5mg
- Magnesium: 60.2mg
- Zinc: 1.3mg

Baked Avocado Egg Boats

GLUTEN-FREE

Baked Avocado Egg Boats are a delightful combination of creamy avocado and baked egg, making a nutritious and delicious breakfast. Rich in folic acid, healthy fats, and protein, this dish is an excellent choice during pregnancy. The presence of folic acid is vital for the neural tube development of the baby, while the healthy fats in the avocado brain and eye development.

Preparation Time: 5 minutes
Cooking Time: 15-20 minutes
Total Time: 20-25 minutes
Serves: 1

Ingredients:

- 1 ripe avocado
- 1 large egg
- Salt, to taste
- Pepper, to taste

Instructions:

1. Preheat the oven to 425°F (220°C). Cut the avocado in half and remove the pit. Scoop out a bit of the avocado flesh from each half to create a small well, ensuring the egg fits comfortably. Place the avocado halves in a baking dish, making sure they sit flat. If they wobble, you can slice a thin layer from the bottom to make them stable.
2. Crack the egg into a bowl and blend with salt and pepper. Spoon ½ of mixture into each avocado half.
3. Place the baking dish in the preheated oven and bake for about 15-20 minutes. The cooking time might vary depending on the size of the avocado and egg. The desired outcome is a set white and a slightly runny yolk. If you prefer a firmer yolk, extend the baking time by a few minutes.
4. Once out of the oven, sprinkle with optional toppings of your choice. Serve immediately.

Chef's Notes

- Optional toppings: grated cheese, arugula, chives, red pepper flakes, or fresh herbs.
- Serve with a light salad or bacon

Nutritional Information (per serving):

- Calories: 393kcal
- Total Fat: 34.2g
- Monounsaturated Fat: 21.5g
- Polyunsaturated Fat: 4.6g
- Total Carbohydrates: 17.5g
- Dietary Fiber: 13.5g
- Protein: 10.3g
- Sodium: 302.6mg
- Vitamin A: 94.1mcg
- Vitamin B5: 3.6mg
- Vitamin B6: .6mg
- Vitamin B12: .4mcg
- Vitamin C: 20.1mg
- Vitamin D: 1mcg
- Vitamin E: 4.7mg
- Vitamin K: 42.4mcg
- Folate: 180.3mcg
- Iron: 2mg
- Calcium: 52.1mg
- Magnesium: 64.3mg
- Zinc: 1.9mg

Toasted Muesli with Greek Yogurt

VEGETARIAN

A delicious and wholesome breakfast option, this toasted muesli paired with Greek yogurt offers a satisfying crunch and a creamy counterpart. Perfect for pregnant individuals, it packs the essentials: fiber, calcium, and protein, along with essential vitamins and minerals such as healthy fats and protein for fetal development and vitamins and antioxidants to boost your immune system.

Preparation Time: 5 minutes
Cooking Time: 5 minutes
Total Time: 10 minutes
Serves: 1

Ingredients:
- 1/3 cup store-bought muesli
- 1/4 tbsp honey
- 1/2 cup whole milk unsweetened Greek yogurt
- 3 strawberries
- 1/2 banana
- A sprinkle of chia seeds

Instructions:
1. In a dry skillet over medium heat, toast the muesli, constantly stirring, for about 3-5 minutes or until it's lightly golden and aromatic. Be careful as nuts and seeds can burn quickly.
2. Remove from heat and let it cool for a moment. If you prefer your muesli a bit sweeter, you can drizzle it with honey and mix well.
3. In a serving bowl, lay down the Greek yogurt. Top it with the toasted muesli. Add fresh fruits on top and sprinkle with chia seeds if desired.
4. Enjoy immediately!

Chef's Notes:
- As an alternative to store-bought muesli, you can make your own homemade blend from your favorite oats, nuts, seeds, and dried fruit
- Use a variety of berries and fruits
- Add flax seeds or sub for chia seeds

Nutritional Information (per serving):
- Calories: 296kcal
- Total Fat: 6g
- Monounsaturated Fat: 1.2g
- Polyunsaturated Fat: .7g
- Total Carbohydrates: 51g
- Dietary Fiber: 5.4g
- Protein: 11.8g
- Sodium: 35.6mg
- Vitamin B6: .3mg
- Vitamin C: 26.5mg
- Folate: 26.4mcg
- Iron 1.3mg
- Calcium: 157.4mg
- Potassium: 563mg
- Magnesium: 136.7mg
- Zinc: .9mg

Coconut Milk Porridge with Raspberries

VEGAN

Indulge in a comforting bowl of creamy coconut porridge garnished with juicy raspberries. This nutrient-rich dish offers a delightful blend of textures and flavors, making it a perfect breakfast treat for expectant mothers. During pregnancy, it's essential to provide both mother and baby with key nutrients, and this porridge does just that. The coconut milk offers healthy fats for baby's brain development, raspberries provide essential vitamins, and the oats serve as a great source of fiber. This dish is easily digestible so is a good option if you are experiencing morning sickness.

Preparation Time: 5 minutes
Cooking Time: 15 minutes
Total Time: 20 minutes
Serves: 1

Ingredients:
- 1/2 cup rolled oats
- 1 cup full-fat coconut milk
- A pinch of salt
- 1/4 cup fresh raspberries

Instructions:
1. In a saucepan, combine the rolled oats, coconut milk, and a pinch of salt.
2. Place the saucepan over medium heat and bring the mixture to a simmer. Stir occasionally to prevent the oats from sticking to the bottom.
3. Allow the porridge to cook for about 10-15 minutes or until the oats have absorbed most of the coconut milk and are soft and creamy in texture.
4. Remove from heat.
5. Transfer the porridge to a bowl and top with fresh raspberries or any other desired toppings.
6. Serve warm and enjoy!

Chef's Notes:
- Top with coconut flakes, additional fruits, nuts or seeds for extra flavors and texture

Nutritional Information (per serving):
- Calories: 601kcal
- Total Fat: 50.9g
- Monounsaturated Fat: 2.58XX g
- Polyunsaturated Fat: 1.3g
- Total Carbohydrates: 37g
- Dietary Fiber: 6g
- Protein: 9.9g
- Sodium: 155mg
- Vitamin C: 10.3mg
- Folate: 38.1mcg
- Iron: 9.4mg

- Calcium: 68.4mg
- Magnesium: 110.7mg
- Zinc: 1.4mg

Veggie Omelette with Feta Cheese

GLUTEN-FREE

A nutrient-rich, colorful vegetable omelet paired with the creamy goodness of feta cheese. This dish offers a delectable combination of flavors and textures while providing a myriad of essential nutrients beneficial during pregnancy. Eggs provide choline for your baby's brain development, feta cheese provides calcium for bone development and vegetables provide various micronutrients to support your health and your baby's!

Preparation Time: 10 minutes
Cooking Time: 10 minutes
Total Time: 20 minutes
Serves: 1

Ingredients:

- 2 large eggs
- 1/4 cup diced bell peppers
- 1/4 cup chopped spinach
- 1/4 cup diced tomatoes
- 1/8 cup diced red onion
- 1/4 cup crumbled pasteurized feta cheese
- 1 tablespoon olive oil
- Salt and pepper to taste

Instructions:

1. Wash and dice all the vegetables. Crumble the feta cheese if not already crumbled.
2. In a bowl, crack open the eggs and whisk them until well beaten. Season with a pinch of salt and pepper.
3. Heat the olive oil in a non-stick frying pan over medium heat. Add the red onions and sauté for a minute. Then, add the bell peppers and sauté until they're slightly softened. Follow up with the tomatoes and spinach, and cook for another 2 minutes until the spinach is wilted.
4. Spread the sautéed vegetables evenly in the pan. Pour the beaten eggs over the vegetables, ensuring an even distribution.
5. Sprinkle the crumbled feta cheese evenly over the top of the egg mixture.
6. Allow the omelet to cook without stirring until the edges start to set. Gently lift the edges with a spatula, allowing the uncooked egg to flow underneath. Continue to cook for another 3-4 minutes, or until the bottom is golden and the top is mostly set.
7. Carefully fold the omelet in half using a spatula. Cook for an additional 1-2 minutes if you prefer a well-done omelet.
8. Slide onto a plate and garnish with fresh herbs if desired and serve immediately.

Chef's Notes:

- Garnish with basil, cilantro, parsley or chives if desired.

Nutritional Information (per serving):
- Calories: 452kcal
- Total Fat: 38.5g
- Monounsaturated Fat: 17.62g
- Polyunsaturated Fat: 6.17g
- Total Carbohydrates: 8.7g
- Dietary Fiber: 1.4g
- Protein: 18.5g
- Sodium: 485.13mg
- Vitamin A: 330.7mcg
- Vitamin B6: .5mg
- Vitamin C: 51.8mcg
- Vitamin D: 2.3mcg
- Vitamin E: 4.6mg
- Vitamin K: 57.3mcg
- Folate: 80.2mcg
- Calcium: 283mg
- Iron: 2.4mg
- Magnesium: 35.7mg
- Zinc: 2.5mg

ENERGIZING LUNCHES AND DINNERS

Lentil and Spinach Stew

VEGAN

This hearty lentil and spinach stew is a nutritional powerhouse perfect for expectant mothers. Lentils are an excellent source of essential nutrients like protein, iron, and folate. Spinach, on the other hand, is rich in vitamin A, vitamin C, calcium, and folic acid. Together, they create a delicious and nurturing dish that supports fetal growth and maternal health and provides energy.

Preparation Time: 15 minutes
Cooking Time: 40 minutes
Total Time: 55 minutes
Serves: 4

Ingredients:
- 1 cup dried green or brown lentils, rinsed and drained
- 3 cups fresh spinach, washed and roughly chopped
- 2 tablespoons olive oil
- 1 large onion, finely chopped
- 3 garlic cloves, minced
- 1 carrot, diced
- 1 celery stalk, diced
- 4 cups vegetable broth
- 1 can (14 oz) diced tomatoes, with their juices
- 1 teaspoon ground cumin
- 1/2 teaspoon ground turmeric
- Salt and pepper, to taste
- A squeeze of lemon juice to taste

Instructions:
1. Chop and dice the onion, garlic, carrot, and celery
2. Heat the olive oil in a large pot over medium heat. Add the chopped onion, garlic, carrot, and celery. Sauté until the onions are translucent and the vegetables have started to soften, about 5 minutes.
3. Add the lentils to the pot and stir well to coat with the vegetable mixture.
4. Pour in the vegetable broth and the canned tomatoes with their juices. Stir in the cumin and turmeric.
5. Bring the mixture to a boil, then reduce heat, cover, and let simmer for about 30 minutes, or until the lentils are tender.
6. Five minutes before the lentils are fully cooked, add the chopped spinach to the pot, stirring it in until it wilts and integrates into the stew.
7. Season with salt and pepper according to your taste. For a touch of citrus, you can also add a squeeze of lemon juice.
8. Once cooked, remove from heat, and let it stand for a couple of minutes, then serve.

Chef's Notes:
- Make extra to store in the refrigerator for 3-4 days or the freezer for up to a month.
- Add extra vegetables and/or beans such as cauliflower, kale or chickpeas
- Garnish with fresh parsley or cilantro
- As an alternative, try serving over cauliflower rice

Nutritional Information (per serving):
- Calories: 200kcal
- Total Fat: 8.2g
- Monounsaturated Fat: 4.97g
- Polyunsaturated Fat: .88g
- Total Carbohydrates: 24.9g
- Dietary Fiber: 9.4g
- Protein: 8.7g
- Sodium: 580mg
- Vitamin A: 259.3mcg
- Vitamin B6: .3mg
- Vitamin C: 37.5mg
- Vitamin E: 1.7mg
- Vitamin K: 120.9mcg
- Folate: 149.7mcg
- Iron: 3.7mg
- Calcium: 83.9mg
- Magnesium: 45mg

Kale, Roasted Beet, and Grilled Chicken Salad

GLUTEN-FREE

For expectant mothers seeking a nutrient-rich, delicious meal, this salad is an ideal choice. It combines the heartiness of roasted beets, the lean protein of chicken, and the superfood qualities of kale. Packed with essential nutrients like folic acid for healthy fetal development, iron for blood formation, and vitamin C for immunity, it's perfect for supporting a healthy pregnancy and baby.

Preparation Time: 15 minutes
Cooking Time: 40 minutes
Total Time: 55 minutes
Serves: 2

Ingredients:
- 2 medium-sized beets, peeled and diced
- 2 chicken breasts
- 4 cups of kale, washed, stems removed and torn into bite-sized pieces
- 2 tablespoons olive oil (for roasting)
- 1 tablespoon olive oil (for the dressing)
- 1 tablespoon balsamic vinegar
- 1 teaspoon Dijon mustard
- Salt and pepper, to taste
- 2 tablespoons crumbled feta cheese
- 2 tablespoons roasted walnuts

Instructions:

1. Roast the Beets:

   a. Preheat your oven to 400°F (205°C).

   b. Toss the diced beets in 1 tablespoon of olive oil, sprinkle with salt and pepper, and spread them out on a baking sheet.

   c. Roast for about 35-40 minutes or until the beets are tender and lightly caramelized.

   d. Remove from the oven and let cool.

2. Prepare the Chicken:

   a. Season chicken breasts with salt and pepper.

   b. In a pan over medium heat, add a tablespoon of olive oil. Once hot, place the chicken breasts in the pan.

   c. Cook for about 5-7 minutes on each side, or until the chicken is cooked through and has a golden-brown crust.

   d. Remove from heat and let it rest for a few minutes. Slice into bite-sized pieces.

3. Prepare the Dressing:

   a. In a small bowl, whisk together 1 tablespoon of olive oil, balsamic vinegar, Dijon mustard, and honey if desired. Season with salt and pepper to taste.

4. Assemble the Salad:

   a. In a large bowl, toss the kale with the dressing until it's well-coated.

   b. Divide the kale between two plates.

   c. Top with roasted beets and sliced chicken.

   d. Sprinkle with crumbled feta and roasted nuts for added texture and flavor.

Chef's Notes:

- Use any nuts you prefer, such as almonds, pistachios, pecans or cashews.
- Add sunflower or pumpkin seeds for additional nutrients
- Add orange slices for some extra sweetness

Nutritional Information (per serving):

- Calories: 590kcal
- Total Fat: 34.6g
- Monounsaturated Fat: 18.25g
- Polyunsaturated Fat: 7.13g
- Total Carbohydrates: 9.8g
- Dietary Fiber: 2.8g
- Protein: 53.8g
- Sodium: 390mg
- Vitamin A: 106.3mcg
- Vitamin B6: 1.2mg
- Vitamin B12: .8mcg
- Vitamin C: 31.8mg
- Vitamin E: 3.7mg
- Vitamin K: 137.9mcg
- Folate: 78.2mcg
- Iron: 3.2mg
- Calcium: 194.4mg
- Magnesium: 86.8mg
- Zinc: 2.7mg

Salmon with Roasted Sweet Potatoes and Green Beans

GLUTEN-FREE

This nutritious, delectable and easy sheet pan meal combines the omega-3 rich goodness of salmon with the vitamin-packed profile of sweet potatoes and the crisp freshness of green beans. Ideal for those who are pregnant, as it delivers essential nutrients for both mother and baby including omega-3 fatty acids, protein, fiber, and a variety of essential vitamins and minerals, which help with brain, eye and skin development.

Preparation Time: 15 minutes
Cooking Time: 30 minutes
Total Time: 45 minutes
Serves: 2

Ingredients:

- 2 salmon fillets
- 2 medium-sized sweet potatoes, peeled and diced
- 200g fresh green beans, ends trimmed
- 2 tbsp olive oil
- 1 tsp garlic powder
- 1 tsp rosemary (dried or fresh)
- Salt and pepper, to taste
- Fresh squeezed lemon juice

Instructions:

1. Preheat your oven to 425°F (220°C).
2. Dice potatoes and toss them in a bowl with 1 tablespoon of olive oil, half of the garlic powder, half of the rosemary, and season with salt and pepper. Spread them out in a single layer on a baking sheet.
3. Place the sweet potatoes in the preheated oven and roast for 15 minutes.
4. While the sweet potatoes are roasting, season the salmon fillets with the remaining garlic powder, rosemary, salt, and pepper. Drizzle with a touch of olive oil.
5. After the sweet potatoes have roasted for 15 minutes, make space on the same baking sheet and place the salmon fillets skin side down.
6. In the same bowl used for the sweet potatoes, toss the green beans with the remaining 1 tablespoon of olive oil and season with a bit of salt and pepper. Spread them out on the baking sheet around the salmon.
7. Return the baking sheet to the oven and roast for another 12-15 minutes or until the salmon is cooked through and flakes easily with a fork, and the sweet potatoes are tender.
8. Plate the salmon, sweet potatoes, and green beans. Optionally, you can drizzle with a touch of olive oil or squeeze of lemon before serving. Serve immediately and enjoy!

Chef's Note:

- Roast onions, shallots and or cherry tomatoes with green beans for additional flavor
- Mix green beans with pesto for additional flavor

Nutritional Information (per serving):
- Calories: 538kcal
- Total Fat: 26,5g
- Monounsaturated Fat: 14.4g
- Polyunsaturated Fat: 7.1g
- Omega 3s: 3.9g
- Total Carbohydrates: 25,2g
- Dietary Fiber: 4g
- Protein: 45,8g
- Sodium: 292.6mg
- Vitamin A: 1118.2mcg
- Vitamin B6: 2mg
- Vitamin B12: 5.2mcg
- Vitamin C: 24.7mg
- Vitamin E: 2.8mg
- Vitamin K: 10.8mcg
- Folate: 58.4mcg
- Iron: 2.7mg
- Calcium: 71.7mg
- Potassium: 1636.2mg
- Phosphorus: 503.9mg
- Magnesium: 95.6mg
- Zinc: 1.8mg

Grass-fed Beef and Vegetable Kabobs

GLUTEN-FREE

These savory and colorful kabobs, packed with grass-fed beef and an array of vegetables, are not only delightful to the palate but also provide nutrients essential for pregnancy. Grass-fed beef is higher in omega-3 fatty acids compared to grain-fed beef, promoting fetal brain development. Together with vitamin-rich vegetables, these kabobs make for a wholesome meal suitable for expecting mothers.

Time: 45 minutes (includes marination time)
Cooking Time: 15 minutes
Total Time: 60 minutes
Serves: 4

Ingredients:
- 1 pound of grass-fed beef, cut into 1-inch cubes
- 1 red bell pepper, cut into 1-inch pieces
- 1 yellow bell pepper, cut into 1-inch pieces
- 1 zucchini, sliced into 1/2-inch rounds
- 1 red onion, cut into chunks
- 8 cherry tomatoes
- 3 tablespoons of olive oil
- 2 garlic cloves, minced
- 1 tablespoon of rosemary (or herb of choice)
- Salt and pepper to taste

Instructions:
1. In a large mixing bowl, combine olive oil, minced garlic, rosemary, salt, and pepper.
2. Add the beef cubes and toss until they're well coated. Allow to marinate for at least 30 minutes, preferably longer (up to 2 hours) in the refrigerator.
3. While the beef is marinating, prep your vegetables, cutting into evenly sized pieces.
4. If using wooden skewers, soak them in water for at least 20 minutes to prevent them from burning during cooking. Alternate between beef and vegetables, threading them onto the skewers.
5. Preheat grill or grill pan over medium-high heat. Place the skewers on the grill and cook for 10-15 minutes, turning occasionally until the beef reaches your desired level of doneness and the vegetables are tender and slightly charred.
6. Once cooked, remove the kabobs from the grill and let them rest for a few minutes.

Chef's Notes:
- Serve with quinoa or a side salad
- Leftovers can be refrigerated for 2-3 days and can be added to a cold quinoa or vegetable salad

Nutritional Information (per serving):
- Calories: 302kcal
- Total Fat: 17.5g
- Monounsaturated Fat: 7.4g
- Polyunsaturated Fat: 1.2g
- Total Carbohydrates: 11.1g
- Dietary Fiber: 3.2g
- Protein: 26.5g
- Sodium: 267.6mg
- Vitamin A: 98.9mcg
- Vitamin B6: .3mg
- Vitamin C: 92.6mg
- Vitamin E: 2.5mg
- Vitamin K: 11.3mcg
- Folate: 44.9mcg
- Iron: 4.9mg
- Calcium: 61.6mg
- Magnesium: 19.5mg

Roasted Butternut Squash Stuffed with Black Beans and Quinoa

VEGETARIAN

This is a nutrient-rich, hearty, and delicious meal that combines the natural sweetness of roasted butternut squash with the earthy flavors of black beans and quinoa. This dish offers an array of essential nutrients such as fiber, protein, iron, folic acid, and vitamins which are beneficial for both you and your baby.

Preparation Time: 20 minutes
Cooking Time: 45 minutes
Total Time: 65 minutes
Serves: 2

Ingredients:
- 1 medium butternut squash, halved lengthwise and seeds removed
- 1/2 cup quinoa, rinsed and drained
- 1 cup vegetable broth or water

- 1/2 can (about 7.5 oz) black beans, drained and rinsed
- 1 tbsp olive oil
- 1/2 small onion, finely chopped
- 1 clove garlic, minced
- 1/2 tsp ground cumin
- Salt and pepper, to taste
- 1/2 lime, juiced
- 1/2 cup crumbled feta cheese

Instructions:

1. Preheat your oven to 400°F (200°C). Place the butternut squash halves on a baking sheet, drizzle with 1 tbsp of olive oil, and season with salt and pepper. Roast in the oven for about 35-40 minutes or until the flesh is tender and slightly caramelized.
2. While the squash is roasting, in a medium-sized pot, bring the vegetable broth or water to a boil. Add quinoa, reduce heat to a simmer, cover, and cook until all the liquid is absorbed, about 15 minutes. Remove from heat and let it sit for 5 minutes before fluffing with a fork.
3. In a large skillet, heat the remaining 1 tbsp of olive oil over medium heat. Add the chopped onion and sauté until translucent, about 3-4 minutes. Add the minced garlic and cumin, cooking for an additional 1-2 minutes.
4. Stir in the black beans and cook until heated through. Finally, mix in the cooked quinoa, lime juice, and season with salt and pepper to taste. Remove from heat and stir in the chopped cilantro.
5. Once the butternut squash halves are roasted, spoon the black bean and quinoa mixture into the cavities of each squash half. If desired, sprinkle with crumbled cheese.
6. Place each stuffed butternut squash half on a plate, garnish with extra cilantro if desired, and serve warm.

Chef's Notes:

- You can spice up the filling by adding some chopped tomatoes, bell peppers, or even some corn kernels.
- For an extra protein boost, stir in some diced cooked chicken or sausage into the filling.
- Garnish with fresh cilantro or other herbs if desired.

Nutritional Information (per serving):

- Calories: 600kcal
- Total Fat: 24.7g
- Monounsaturated Fat: 8.71g
- Polyunsaturated Fat: 2.03g
- Total Carbohydrates: 75g
- Dietary Fiber: 16.5g
- Protein: 25.5g
- Sodium: 543.3mg
- Vitamin A: 1596.8mcg
- Vitamin B6: .9mg
- Vitamin C: 64.3mg
- Vitamin E: 6.4mg
- Vitamin K: 12.9mcg
- Folate: 281.9mcg
- Iron: 5.8mg
- Calcium: 557.5mg
- Magnesium: 217.6mg
- Zinc: 4.4mg

Poached Eggs over Sauteed Spinach and Mushrooms

GLUTEN-FREE

This nutritious dish combines the earthy flavors of mushrooms with tender spinach, all crowned with a delicately poached egg. When paired together, these ingredients offer a delightful mix of textures and tastes. For expecting mothers, this dish provides essential nutrients like protein, iron, folate, and vitamin D, which are crucial for fetal development and maternal health.

Preparation Time: 10 minutes
Cooking Time: 15 minutes
Total Time: 25 minutes
Serves: 2

Ingredients:

- 4 large eggs
- 2 cups fresh spinach, washed and roughly chopped
- 1 cup mushrooms, sliced (white button, shiitake, cremini, or your preference)
- 2 cloves garlic, minced
- 2 tbsp olive oil
- Salt and pepper, to taste
- 2 tbsp white vinegar (for poaching eggs)

Instructions:

Sautéing the Vegetables:
1. In a large skillet over medium heat, warm the olive oil.
2. Add the sliced mushrooms and cook until they start to release their juices and become golden brown, about 5-7 minutes.
3. Add the minced garlic and stir for about 30 seconds, or until fragrant.
4. Add the chopped spinach and cook until wilted, about 2-3 minutes. Season with salt and pepper to taste. Remove from heat and set aside.

Poaching the Eggs:
5. Fill a deep pan or skillet with water, about 2/3 full. Bring the water to a gentle simmer.
6. Add the white vinegar to the simmering water. This helps the egg whites coagulate more efficiently.
7. Crack each egg into a small bowl. One at a time, gently slide each egg into the simmering water.
8. Let the eggs poach for about 3-4 minutes for a runny yolk or 5-6 minutes for a more set yolk.
9. Using a slotted spoon, carefully remove each egg from the water and let any excess water drip off.

Assembling the Dish:
10. Divide the mushroom and spinach mixture between two plates.
11. Place two poached eggs over each serving.
12. Serve immediately with toasted whole grain bread, if desired.

Chef's Notes:

- Use fresh herbs (like parsley or chives) for garnish if desired

- Optional: Sprinkle with parmesan cheese
- Optional: Serve with toasted whole grain bread

Nutritional Information (per serving):
- Calories: 283kcal
- Total Fat: 23.1g
- Monounsaturated Fat: 13.5g
- Polyunsaturated Fat: 3.4g
- Total Carbohydrates: 4.7.g
- Dietary Fiber: 1g
- Protein: 14.6g
- Sodium: 479.1mg
- Vitamin A: 300.7mcg
- Vitamin B6: .3mg
- Vitamin B12: .8mcg
- Vitamin C: 9.4mg
- Vitamin D: 2mcg
- Vitamin E: 3.6mg
- Vitamin K: 153.3mcg
- Folate: 104.2mcg
- Iron: 2.9mg
- Calcium: 99.2mg
- Potassium: 512.5mg
- Phosphorus: 268.5mg
- Magnesium: 40.4mg
- Zinc: 2mg

Tomato, and Spinach Spaghetti Squash Bowl

VEGAN

This delectable dish provides a healthy twist to traditional spaghetti by using spaghetti squash as its base. Perfect for expecting mothers, this recipe is nutrient-dense, offering essential vitamins and minerals such as folic acid from spinach and lycopene from tomatoes that promote fetal development.

Preparation Time: 10 minutes
Cooking Time: 45 minutes
Total Time: 55 minutes
Serves: 2

Ingredients:
- 1 medium spaghetti squash
- 1 cup fresh spinach, chopped
- 1 cup cherry tomatoes, halved
- 2 garlic cloves, minced
- 2 tbsp olive oil
- Salt, to taste
- Pepper, to taste

Instructions:
1. Prep the Spaghetti Squash:
   a. Preheat your oven to 400°F (200°C).
   b. Cut the spaghetti squash in half lengthwise. Use a spoon to scrape out and discard seeds and the middle stringy pulp.
   c. Drizzle the inside of each half with olive oil and season with salt and pepper.
   d. Place the squash halves cut-side down on a baking sheet and roast in the oven for about 30-40 minutes or until the flesh is tender.
2. Sauté the Vegetables:
   a. While the squash is roasting, heat 2 tbsp of olive oil in a pan over medium heat.
   b. Add minced garlic and sauté for 1 minute or until fragrant.
   c. Add the cherry tomatoes to the pan and cook for 5 minutes or until they start to soften.
   d. Add the chopped spinach and continue cooking until it wilts. Season with salt and pepper.
3. Combine and Serve:
   a. Once the spaghetti squash is done roasting, remove it from the oven and let it cool for a few minutes.
   b. Use a fork to scrape the insides of the spaghetti squash to create spaghetti-like strands and place them into a large mixing bowl.
   c. Mix the sautéed vegetables with the spaghetti squash strands.
   d. Serve in bowls with optional ingredients below

Chef's Notes
- Top with parmesan cheese if desired
- Add additional vegetables like mushrooms or kale, or additional protein like chicken or black beans to enhance flavor and nutrition
- Garnish with fresh basil, parsley or toasted pine nuts if desired

Nutritional Information (per serving):
- Calories: 253kcal
- Total Fat: 15.3g
- Monounsaturated Fat: 9.9g
- Polyunsaturated Fat: 2.17g
- Total Carbohydrates: 28.5g
- Dietary Fiber: 6.9g
- Protein: 4.6g
- Sodium: 293.6mg
- Vitamin A: 88.5mcg
- Vitamin B6: .4mg
- Vitamin C: 22.9mg
- Vitamin K: 83.3mcg
- Folate: 65.6mcg
- Iron: 2.9mg
- Calcium: 130.5mg
- Magnesium: 49mg
- Zinc: 0.7mg

Grilled Lamb Chops with Garlic Broccoli and Carrots

GLUTEN-FREE

A balanced, nutritious meal perfect for expectant mothers, this recipe combines the protein-rich goodness of lamb chops with the vitamin-packed combination of broccoli and carrots. These ingredients offer various benefits during pregnancy. Pork is a good source of protein, while broccoli is rich in folate essential for neural tube development. Carrots are packed with beta-carotene, which the body converts to vitamin A, essential for baby's vision and growth.

Preparation Time: 15 minutes
Cooking Time: 25 minutes
Total Time: 40 minutes
Serves: 2

Ingredients:

- 2 boneless lamb chops, about 3/4-inch thick
- 1 tablespoon olive oil
- Salt and freshly ground black pepper, to taste
- 2 cups broccoli florets
- 2 medium-sized carrots, peeled and sliced into rounds
- 3 garlic cloves, minced
- 1 tablespoon butter
- 1/2 lemon, juiced

Instructions:

1. Pat the lamb chops dry with paper towels. This will help them brown better on the grill.
2. Rub the lamb chops with olive oil on both sides. Season generously with salt, freshly ground black pepper, and optional herbs. Let them sit at room temperature for about 15 minutes before grilling.
3. Preheat the grill to medium-high heat. Place the seasoned lamb chops on the grill. Cook for about 6-8 minutes on each side, or until they reach an internal temperature of 145°F (63°C). Once done, transfer to a plate and let them rest for a few minutes.
4. In a large pot, boil water with a pinch of salt. Once boiling, add the broccoli florets and carrot slices. Blanch for 2-3 minutes until they're bright in color but still firm. Drain the vegetables and set them aside.
5. In a large skillet, melt butter over medium heat. Add minced garlic and sauté for about 1 minute until fragrant.
6. Add the blanched broccoli and carrots to the skillet. Sauté for 4-5 minutes or until they're tender but still vibrant in color. Season with salt, pepper, and a squeeze of lemon juice for some zest.
7. Place the grilled lamb chops on plates and serve alongside the garlic broccoli and carrots. You can also drizzle some of the melted butter and garlic from the pan over the pork chops for added flavor.

Chef's Notes:

- Optional: Add fresh herbs such as rosemary or thyme for seasoning the lamb

- Can use pork chops instead if you prefer

Nutritional Information (per serving):

- Calories: 587kcal
- Total Fat: 31.5g
- Monounsaturated Fat: 14.7g
- Polyunsaturated Fat: 2.3g
- Total Carbohydrates: 14.7g
- Dietary Fiber: 4.6g
- Protein: 60.6g
- Sodium: 371.8mg
- Vitamin A: 586.3mcg
- Vitamin B6: .7mg
- Vitamin B12: 5.2mcg
- Vitamin C: 93.9mg
- Vitamin E: 2.6mg
- Vitamin K: 105.1mcg
- Folate: 113.1mcg
- Iron: 5.5mg
- Calcium: 92.8mg
- Potassium: 1191.9mg
- Phosphorus: 500.3mg
- Magnesium: 79.1mg
- Zinc: 10.3mg

Tofu and Snap Pea Stir-Fry with Almonds

VEGAN

This vibrant and nutritious tofu stir fry combines the crunch of almonds and snap peas with the tenderness of tofu. Loaded with proteins, vitamins, and minerals, this dish is especially beneficial during pregnancy due to its iron, calcium, and folate content. Moreover, the colorful array of vegetables provides a variety of antioxidants and nutrients that are essential for both the mother and baby.

Preparation Time: 15 minutes
Cooking Time: 20 minutes
Total Time: 35 minutes
Serves: 2

Ingredients:

- 200g firm tofu, cubed
- 1 cup snap peas, trimmed
- 1 large carrot, thinly sliced
- 1 red bell pepper, sliced
- 1/4 cup almonds, roughly chopped
- 2 tbsp soy sauce (or tamari for gluten-free)
- 2 tbsp sesame oil
- 2 tsp fresh ginger, grated
- 2 garlic cloves, minced

Instructions:

1. Preparation: Begin by prepping all the vegetables. Cube the tofu, trim the snap peas, thinly slice the carrot and bell pepper. Grate the ginger and mince the garlic.
2. In a bowl, combine soy sauce, half of the sesame oil, grated ginger and minced garlic. Mix well and then add

the tofu cubes. Allow the tofu to marinate for at least 10 minutes.

3. In a large skillet or wok, heat the other tablespoon of sesame oil over medium-high heat. Once hot, add the marinated tofu cubes, reserving the marinade. Cook the tofu until it's golden on all sides, about 5-7 minutes.
4. Push the tofu to one side of the skillet. Add the snap peas, carrot slices, and bell pepper to the skillet. Stir fry for 3-4 minutes until the vegetables are tender yet crisp.
5. Add the chopped almonds and stir fry for an additional 2 minutes.
6. Pour the reserved marinade over the tofu and vegetables in the skillet. Stir well to combine and heat everything through.
7. Transfer the stir fry to serving plates.

Chef's Notes:
- Garnish with 1 green onion, thinly sliced or sesame seeds
- Substitute tofu for any protein such as chicken, beef or shrimp
- Use quinoa or noodles such as soba or rice noodles instead of rice
- Use cashews instead of almonds, or a combination of both
- Leftovers are good in the refrigerator for 2-3 days

Nutritional Information (per serving):
- Calories: 376kcal
- Total Fat: 27.4g
- Monounsaturated Fat: 10.31g
- Polyunsaturated Fat: 11.96g
- Total Carbohydrates: 16.4g
- Dietary Fiber: 6.8g
- Protein: 22.6g
- Sodium: 922.2mg
- Vitamin A: 411mcg
- Vitamin B6: .4mg
- Vitamin C: 98.2mg
- Vitamin E: 3.9mg
- Vitamin K: 17.4mcg
- Folate: 83.1mcg
- Iron: 4.3mg
- Calcium: 748.8mg
- Potassium: 699.4mg
- Phosphorus: 311.7mg
- Magnesium: 115.8mg
- Zinc: 2.4mg

Liver and Onions with Steamed Asparagus

GLUTEN-FREE

This classic dish pairs tender, flavorful liver with caramelized onions and perfectly steamed asparagus. Liver is a powerhouse of essential nutrients such as iron, folate and vitamin B12, and when combined with fresh vegetables, it becomes a balanced meal that's especially beneficial for you and your baby.

Preparation Time: 10 minutes
Cooking Time: 25 minutes
Total Time: 35 minutes
Serves: 2

Ingredients:
- 2 slices of beef or calf liver (about 0.5 lb total)
- 2 medium onions, thinly sliced
- 1 bunch of fresh asparagus (about 0.5 lb)
- 2 tablespoons of olive oil
- Salt and pepper to taste
- 1/4 cup low sodium beef broth for added moisrure and flavor

Instructions:
1. Rinse the liver slices under cold water and pat dry with paper towels. Season both sides with salt and pepper.
2. In a large skillet, heat 1 tablespoon of olive oil over medium heat.
3. Add the sliced onions and sauté, stirring occasionally, until they are golden brown and caramelized, about 10-15 minutes. Transfer to a plate and set aside.
4. In the same skillet, add another tablespoon of olive oil.
5. Place the liver slices in the skillet and cook for about 2-3 minutes on each side until browned but still slightly pink in the middle.
6. Add the caramelized onions back to the skillet. If the mixture seems dry, add the beef broth to create a little sauce and simmer for 2 minutes.
7. Adjust seasoning with salt and pepper if necessary.
8. While the onions are caramelizing, prepare the asparagus by trimming the tough ends.
9. In a pot with a steamer insert, bring about an inch of water to a boil.
10. Place the asparagus in the steamer, cover, and steam for 3-5 minutes, or until the asparagus is tender yet still has a bit of a crunch.
11. Season with a pinch of salt.
12. Plate the liver and onions, and accompany with the steamed asparagus on the side.

Chef's Notes:
- Add fresh parsley or squeezed lemon slices for garnish
- The liver should be cooked just until pink for the best texture and flavor. Overcooked liver becomes tough and grainy.

Nutritional Information (per serving):
- Calories: 343kcal
- Total Fat: 17.7g
- Monounsaturated Fat: 10.8g
- Polyunsaturated Fat: 2.4g
- Total Carbohydrates: 21.4g
- Dietary Fiber: 5.5g
- Protein: 26,2g
- Sodium: 327.6mg
- Vitamin A: 6339.1mcg
- Vitamin B6: 1.2mg
- Vitamin B12: 67.3mcg
- Vitamin C: 18.5mg
- Vitamin D: 1mcg
- Vitamin E: 4.3mg
- Vitamin K: 84.5mcg
- Folate: 322.5mcg

- Iron: 9.1mg
- Calcium: 73.5mg
- Potassium: 811.6mg
- Phosphorus: 521.4mg
- Magnesium: 53.9mg
- Zinc: 5.6mg

Mackerel Salad with Mixed Greens, Cucumber, and Radishes

GLUTEN-FREE

A light and refreshing salad, this Mackerel Salad with Mixed Greens, Cucumber, and Radishes is the perfect blend of flavors and textures. Mackerel, a fish rich in omega-3 fatty acids, is known to support fetal brain and eye development, making this salad not just tasty but also beneficial for pregnant women. The mixed greens, cucumber, and radishes bring a crisp freshness to the dish, offering a delightful contrast to the rich taste of the mackerel as well as an assortment of beneficial micronutrients.

Preparation Time: 15 minutes
Cooking Time: 0 minutes
Total Time: 15 minutes
Serves: 2
Ingredients:

- 2 medium-sized mackerel fillets (preferably smoked or pre-cooked)
- 4 cups mixed greens (like spinach, arugula, and baby kale)
- 1 cucumber, thinly sliced
- 6-8 radishes, thinly sliced
- 2 tablespoons olive oil
- 1 tablespoon lemon juice
- Salt and pepper, to taste

Instructions:

1. If using fresh mackerel, ensure it's cooked prior to assembling the salad. If using smoked mackerel, simply flake the fillets into bite-sized pieces.
2. Wash and dry the mixed greens if needed. Thinly slice the cucumber and radishes.
3. In a small bowl, whisk together the olive oil and lemon juice. Season with salt and pepper to taste.
4. In a large mixing bowl, toss the mixed greens, cucumber, and radishes with the dressing until they are well coated.
5. Divide the salad among two plates. Top each serving with equal portions of mackerel.

Chef's Note:
- Use any healthy prepared dressing of your preference
- Add fresh herbs like dill or parsley
- Substitute mackerel with any other fish like salmon or other protein such as chicken, beef, shrimp or tofu if desired

Nutritional Information (per serving):
- Calories: 660kcal
- Total Fat: 21.6g

- Monounsaturated Fat: 12.88 g
- Polyunsaturated Fat: 3.29g
- Omega-3 fatty acids: 1.42g
- Total Carbohydrates: 22.3g
- Dietary Fiber: 8.9g
- Protein: 93.2g
- Sodium: 832.6mg
- Vitamin A: 783.7mcg
- Vitamin B6: 1.6mg
- Vitamin B12: 55.4mcg
- Vitamin C: 13.4mg
- Vitamin E: 2mg
- Vitamin K: 33mcg
- Folate: 42.8mcg
- Iron: 15.6mg
- Calcium: 389.7mg
- Potassium: 3335.1mg
- Magnesium: 147.5mg

Chicken and Vegetable Soup with Bone Broth

MEAL-PREP FRIENDLY

This nurturing and wholesome soup combines the deep flavors of bone broth with nutrient-dense vegetables and tender chicken. Tailored for expecting mothers, this soup not only warms the heart but also offers essential nutrients to support both mother and baby during pregnancy, including collagen for bone and joint health, ginger to help with nausea, protein and essential vitamins and minerals for your baby's development.

Preparation Time: 25 minutes
Cooking Time: 2 hours, 30 minutes
Total Time: 2 hours, 55 minutes
Serves: 6

Ingredients:
- 6 cups of bone broth (preferably homemade or high-quality store-bought without additives)
- 3 chicken breasts, diced
- 3 medium carrots, sliced
- 3 medium zucchinis, sliced
- 2 small onions, diced
- 6 cloves garlic, minced
- 3 inches of fresh ginger, minced
- 3 tablespoons olive oil
- Salt and pepper to taste
- 1 tablespoon fresh thyme or 1 teaspoon dried thyme
- 2 bay leaves
- 6 cups of water (or as needed)

Instructions:
1. Begin by preparing all the vegetables and chicken. Dice, slice, and mince as described in the ingredients list.
2. In a large pot over medium heat, add the olive oil. Once hot, add the onions, garlic, and ginger. Sauté until the onions become translucent.

3. Add the diced chicken breast to the pot and cook until it turns white on all sides.
4. Stir in the carrot and zucchini slices. Cook for another 5-7 minutes.
5. Pour in the bone broth and water. Add the bay leaves, thyme, salt, and pepper. Stir well.
6. Lower the heat and let the soup simmer for about 2 hours, occasionally stirring.
7. After 2 hours, taste and adjust the seasoning if needed. Remove the bay leaves. Ladle the soup into bowls.

Chef's Notes:
- Make a large batch for leftovers. Can be kept in the refrigerator for 2-3 days or the freezer for up to a month.
- Fresh parsley or cilantro for garnish (optional).
- Can also be cooked in a slow cooker on low for several hours until vegetables are soft and chicken is cooked through.

Nutritional Information (per serving):
- Calories: 268kcal
- Total Fat: 6g
- Monounsaturated Fat: .96g
- Polyunsaturated Fat: .72g
- Total Carbohydrates: 13.6g
- Dietary Fiber: 2.9g
- Protein: 37.6g
- Sodium: 292.4mg
- Vitamin A: 2786.mcg
- Vitamin B6: 1.4mg
- Vitamin B12: .3mcg
- Vitamin C: 24.7mg
- Vitamin E: 1.1mg
- Vitamin K: 8.4mcg
- Folate: 46.9mcg
- Iron: 2mg
- Calcium: 88.5mg
- Magnesium: 63.9mg
- Zinc: 1.4mg

Stuffed Bell Peppers with Ground Turkey and Cauliflower Rice

GLUTEN-FREE

Stuffed bell peppers combine the hearty flavors of ground turkey with the lightness and texture of cauliflower rice, creating a balanced meal that's both delicious and nutritious. This dish offers a variety of vitamins and minerals essential for pregnancy, such as folic acid, vitamin c, fiber and, protein. Additionally, this recipe is low in carbohydrates, making it an excellent choice for those watching their carb intake.

Preparation Time: 15 minutes
Cooking Time: 40 minutes
Total Time: 55 minutes
Serves: 4
Ingredients:
- 4 large bell peppers (any color)
- 1 lb ground turkey
- 2 cups cauliflower rice (prepackaged or freshly riced from a medium cauliflower head)
- 1 small onion, finely chopped
- 2 garlic cloves, minced
- 1 cup diced tomatoes (canned or fresh)
- 1 tsp cumin
- 1 tsp paprika
- Salt and pepper to taste
- 1 cup shredded cheese (cheddar, mozzarella, or your choice)
- Olive oil for cooking

Instructions:
Preparation
1. Preheat your oven to 375°F (190°C).
2. Wash the bell peppers, cut off their tops, and remove the seeds and membranes.
3. If using a fresh cauliflower, pulse the florets in a food processor until it resembles the texture of rice.

Cook the Filling
4. In a large skillet, heat olive oil over medium heat.
5. Add the chopped onion and sauté until translucent.
6. Add garlic and sauté for another minute.
7. Add the ground turkey, breaking it up as it cooks. Cook until no longer pink.
8. Stir in the diced tomatoes, cumin, paprika, salt, and pepper. Cook for 2-3 minutes.
9. Mix in the cauliflower rice and cook for another 5-6 minutes or until the cauliflower is tender. If you're using cheese, save a bit for topping and stir the rest into the mixture.

Assemble and Bake
10. Lightly oil a baking dish.
11. Stuff each bell pepper with the turkey-cauliflower mixture and place them in the baking dish.
12. Sprinkle the remaining cheese on top if desired.
13. Cover the baking dish with aluminum foil and bake for about 20 minutes.
14. Remove the foil and bake for an additional 5 minutes, or until the cheese is melted and slightly browned.

Serve (5 minutes):
Serve warm and enjoy!

Chef's Notes:
- Serve with side salad
- Garnish with fresh herbs if desired, such as parsley or cilantro
- Make extra for leftovers to store in the refrigerator for 2-3 days or up to a month in the freezer

Nutritional Information (per serving):
- Calories: 322kcal
- Total Fat: 15.9g
- Monounsaturated Fat: 6.16g
- Polyunsaturated Fat: 3.19g
- Total Carbohydrates: 19g
- Dietary Fiber: 6.8g
- Protein: 28.6g
- Sodium: 293.4mg

- Vitamin A: 291.4mcg
- Vitamin B6: 1.1mg
- Vitamin B12: 1.1mcg
- Vitamin C: 226.2mg
- Vitamin E: 3.5mg
- Vitamin K: 11.3mcg
- Folate: 84.9mcg
- Iron: 2.6mg
- Calcium: 111.2mg
- Magnesium: 47.6mg
- Zinc: 3mg

Grilled Sardines with Olive Tapenade and Arugula Salad

GLUTEN-FREE

This simple yet flavor-packed recipe features fresh grilled sardines complemented by a robust olive tapenade and a peppery arugula salad. Sardines are an excellent source of omega-3 fatty acids, which are beneficial for brain health and fetal development during pregnancy. Additionally, the salad offers an array of vitamins and minerals that support overall well-being. Enjoy a wholesome, Mediterranean-inspired meal that is as delicious as it is nutritious.

Preparation Time: 20 minutes
Cooking Time: 10 minutes
Total Time: 30 minutes
Serves: 2

Ingredients:
- 4 fresh sardines, cleaned and gutted
- 1 cup pitted olives (black or green or a mixture)
- 1 clove garlic, minced
- 2 tbsp capers, drained
- 1 tbsp lemon juice
- 2 tbsp extra-virgin olive oil, plus extra for drizzling
- Salt and pepper, to taste
- 2 cups fresh arugula
- Lemon wedges, for serving

Instructions:
1. In a food processor, combine olives, garlic, capers, 1 tbsp olive oil, and lemon juice. Pulse until you get a coarse paste. Taste and adjust seasoning with salt and pepper if needed. Transfer to a bowl and set aside.
2. Preheat a grill or grill pan over medium-high heat.
3. Drizzle the sardines with olive oil and season with salt and pepper.
4. Once the grill is hot, place the sardines on it and grill for about 3-4 minutes on each side, or until the skin is charred and the flesh is cooked through.
5. In a large bowl, toss arugula with 1 tbsp olive oil, a squeeze of lemon juice, and season with salt and pepper. Mix until the leaves are lightly coated.
6. Plate the grilled sardines and add a generous spoonful of olive tapenade on top or on the side.
7. Accompany with the arugula salad and serve with fresh lemon wedges for an extra zing.

Chef's Notes:
- Fresh sardines can be replaced with high-quality canned sardines if needed.
- Feel free to incorporate cherry tomatoes or parmesan shavings into the arugula salad for additional flavor.

Nutritional Information (per serving):
- Calories: 165kcal
- Total Fat: 12.8g
- Monounsaturated Fat: 7.84g
- Polyunsaturated Fat: 1.9g
- Total Carbohydrates: 7.5g
- Dietary Fiber: 2.1g
- Protein: 7.5g
- Sodium: 943.9mg
- Vitamin C: 6.9mg
- Vitamin D: 1.2mcg
- Iron: 6.8mg

Pork Tenderloin with Roasted Root Vegetables

This balanced dish features succulent pork tenderloin complemented by a medley of roasted root vegetables. Root vegetables are rich in fiber, vitamins, and minerals, making them especially beneficial for expectant mothers. The protein from the pork supports fetal tissue development, including brain growth, while the vegetables provide essential nutrients for both mother and baby.

Preparation Time: 15 minutes
Cooking Time: 45 minutes
Total Time: 60 minutes
Serves: 2

Ingredients:
- 10.5 oz Pork Tenderloin
- 2 Carrots, peeled and cut into chunks
- 1 large Sweet Potato, peeled and cut into chunks
- 1 Beetroot, peeled and cut into chunks
- 2 Potatoes, cut into chunks
- 2 tbsp Olive oil
- 1 tbsp Fresh rosemary, chopped
- 1 tbsp Fresh thyme, chopped
- Salt, to taste
- Pepper, to taste
- 2 cloves Garlic, minced

Instructions:
1. Begin by preheating your oven to 400°F (205°C).
2. Rub the pork tenderloin with half of the olive oil, minced garlic, half of the rosemary and thyme, salt, and pepper. Ensure the pork is well coated.
3. In a large mixing bowl, toss the carrots, sweet potatoes, beetroot, and potatoes with the remaining olive oil, rosemary, thyme, salt, and pepper.
4. Spread the seasoned vegetables on a baking sheet in a single layer. Place them in the preheated oven and roast

for about 25-30 minutes, or until they're tender and slightly browned.

5. While the vegetables are roasting, heat a skillet or oven-safe pan over medium-high heat. Once hot, sear the pork tenderloin on all sides until browned, about 3-4 minutes per side. After searing, transfer the pork (in the skillet or pan) to the oven and roast for 15-20 minutes or until the internal temperature reaches at least 145°F (63°C).

6. Once the pork is cooked, remove it from the oven and let it rest for about 5 minutes. After resting, slice the pork into 1-inch thick medallions.

7. Plate the roasted root vegetables alongside the sliced pork tenderloin.

Nutritional Information (per serving):
- Calories: 507kcal
- Total Fat: 6.5g
- Monounsaturated Fat: 2.26g
- Polyunsaturated Fat: 1.085g
- Total Carbohydrates: 61.8g
- Dietary Fiber: 9.1g
- Protein: 49.8g
- Sodium: 225.3mg
- Vitamin A: 1068.7mcg
- Vitamin B6: 1.9mg
- Vitamin B12: .9mcg
- Vitamin C: 32.7mb
- Vitamin D: .3mcg
- Vitamin K: 15.5mcg
- Folate: 132.8mcg
- Iron: 4.3mg
- Calcium: 90.1mg
- Potassium: 2249.8mg
- Phosphorus: 652.9mg
- Magnesium: 132.8mg
- Zinc: 5.2mg

Baked Trout with Lemon, Dill, and Roasted Beets

GLUTEN-FREE

This nutritious and delicious recipe combines the delicate flavors of trout with the zesty tang of lemon and the aromatic freshness of dill. Paired with the earthy sweetness of roasted beets, this dish provides a vibrant combination of flavors and colors. Perfect for a romantic dinner or a healthy meal, this dish has essential nutrients beneficial for you and baby, including omega-3 fatty acids, protein, Vitamin C and folate.

Preparation Time: 15 minutes
Cooking Time: 30 minutes
Total Time: 45 minutes
Serves: 2

Ingredients:
- 2 trout fillets
- 1 lemon (sliced thin)
- 2 tsp fresh dill (chopped)
- 2 medium-sized beets
- 2 tbsp olive oil
- Salt and pepper to taste

Instructions:
1. Preheat oven to 400°F (200°C).
2. Peel the beets and cut them into wedges.
3. Toss beet wedges with 1 tbsp of olive oil, salt, and pepper in a bowl. Spread them on a baking sheet lined with parchment paper.
4. Roast in the oven for about 25-30 minutes or until tender and slightly caramelized. Turn them halfway through for even cooking.
5. While the beets are roasting, prepare the trout. Lay out two sheets of aluminum foil large enough to wrap each trout fillet. Place a trout fillet in the center of each foil sheet.
6. Drizzle each fillet with the remaining olive oil, and season with salt and pepper.
7. Lay thin lemon slices on top of each fillet and sprinkle with fresh dill.
8. Fold up the sides of the foil, sealing the trout into a packet.
9. Place the packets on a baking sheet and bake in the preheated oven for 12-15 minutes, or until the trout easily flakes with a fork.
10. Once cooked, carefully open the trout packets (be cautious of the steam). Plate the trout alongside the roasted beets. Garnish with extra dill if desired.

Chef's Notes:
- Top trout with a dollop of sour cream if desired
- Add asparagus or a salad on the side for some green vegetables

Nutritional Information (per serving):
- Calories: 365kcal
- Total Fat: 22g
- Monounsaturated Fat: 12.37g
- Polyunsaturated Fat: 4.1g
- Omega-3 Fatty Acids: 1.53g
- Total Carbohydrates: 7.8g
- Dietary Fiber: 1.8g
- Protein: 34g
- Sodium: 275.1mg
- Vitamin A: 26.6mcg
- Vitamin B6: .6mg
- Vitamin B12: 9mcg
- Vitamin C: 20.9mg
- Vitamin E: 2mg
- Vitamin K: 8.2mcg
- Folate: 71.9mcg
- Iron: 1.3mg
- Calcium: 140.8mg
- Potassium: 840.7mg
- Phosphorus: 409mg
- Magnesium: 58.7mg
- Zinc: .9mg

Sautéed Chicken Livers with Garlic, Kale, and Tomatoes

GLUTEN-FREE

This recipe combines the rich, earthy flavors of chicken livers with the freshness of kale and tomatoes, all infused with the aromatic touch of garlic. The dish not only packs a burst of flavor but is also nutritionally dense. Chicken livers are rich in essential nutrients such as iron, folate, and vitamin B12, which support the health of both the mother and the developing fetus by preventing anemia and birth defects and helps with brain and blood development.

Preparation Time: 10 minutes
Cooking Time: 20 minutes
Total Time: 30 minutes
Serves: 2

Ingredients:
- 200g fresh chicken livers, cleaned and trimmed
- 2 tbsp olive oil
- 3 garlic cloves, minced
- 2 cups kale, washed, de-stemmed and roughly chopped
- 1 cup cherry tomatoes, halved
- Salt and pepper to taste

Instructions:
1. Pat the chicken livers dry with a paper towel. Season them with salt and pepper on both sides.
2. In a large skillet over medium heat, heat 1 tablespoon of olive oil. Once hot, add the chicken livers. Cook for about 2-3 minutes on each side or until they're browned but slightly pink in the center. Remove the livers from the skillet and set aside on a plate.
3. In the same skillet, add the remaining tablespoon of olive oil and the minced garlic. Cook the garlic for 1 minute or until it becomes fragrant but not browned.
4. Stir in the kale and sauté for 2-3 minutes until it starts to wilt. Add the cherry tomatoes and cook for another 3-4 minutes until they're softened.
5. Return the chicken livers to the skillet and toss everything together. Cook for another 2 minutes to let the flavors meld.
6. Taste and adjust the seasoning if needed. Transfer the mixture to plates, garnish with fresh herbs if desired, and serve immediately.

Chef's Notes:
- Chicken livers should be cooked to a safe temperature but can retain a slightly pink center. Overcooking can make them tough.
- Add fresh herbs like parsley or basil for garnish if desired

Nutritional Information (per serving):
- Calories: 279kcal
- Total Fat: 18.2g
- Monounsaturated Fat: 9.87g
- Polyunsaturated Fat: 1.54g
- Total Carbohydrates: 9.1g
- Dietary Fiber: 2.7g
- Protein: 19.7g
- Sodium: 310mg
- Vitamin A: 38.6mcg
- Vitamin C: 46.5mg
- Vitamin E: 2mg
- Vitamin K: 70.5mcg
- Folate: 10.1mcg
- Iron: 11.5mg
- Calcium: 89.3mg
- Magnesium: 6.4mg

Kale, Blueberry, and Walnut Salad with Lemon Vinaigrette

SO FAST!

This vibrant salad melds the earthy flavor of kale with the sweetness of blueberries, the crunchy texture of walnuts, and the creamy tang of feta cheese. The fresh lemon vinaigrette offers a bright and zesty finish to each bite. Not only is it delicious, but this nutrient-packed salad is particularly beneficial during pregnancy due to its mix of essential vitamins, minerals, and healthy fats that can support both the mother's health and baby's development.

Preparation Time: 15 minutes
Cooking Time: 0 minutes
Total Time: 15 minutes
Serves: 2

Ingredients:
- 4 cups of kale, de-stemmed and torn into bite-sized pieces
- 1 cup fresh blueberries
- 1/2 cup walnuts, roughly chopped
- 1/2 cup crumbled feta cheese
- 1 lemon, zested and juiced
- 3 tablespoons extra-virgin olive oil
- Salt and pepper to taste

Instructions:
1. In a large bowl, massage the kale with a pinch of salt for about 2-3 minutes until it softens and becomes a bright green. This makes the kale more palatable and easier to digest.
2. In a small bowl or jar, combine the lemon juice, lemon zest, and olive oil. Whisk together or seal the jar and shake until well mixed. Season with salt and pepper to taste.
3. To the bowl of massaged kale, add the blueberries, chopped walnuts, and crumbled feta cheese.
4. Drizzle the lemon vinaigrette over the salad and toss gently to combine. Adjust the seasoning with additional salt and pepper if desired.
5. Divide the salad between two plates and enjoy immediately.

Chef's Notes:
- Add chicken, salmon, tofu or shrimp for extra protein
- Use parmesan cheese as an alternative to feta

- Use almonds, pecans, or pistachios as an alternative to walnuts
- Add toasted pine nuts or sunflower seeds for extra crunch and nutrition
- Use strawberries, apples, mandarin slices and/or pears for fruit variety

Nutritional Information (per serving):
- Calories: 531kcal
- Total Fat: 48.2g
- Monounsaturated Fat: 19.19g
- Polyunsaturated Fat: 16.5g
- Omega-3 Fatty Acids: 3.1g
- Total Carbohydrates: 20.3g
- Dietary Fiber: 5.9g
- Protein: 11.6g
- Sodium: 446.4mg
- Vitamin A: 126.8mcg
- Vitamin B6: .4mg
- Vitamin B12: .6mcg
- Vitamin C: 52.8mg
- Vitamin E: 3.9mg
- Vitamin K: 12.6mcg
- Folate: 68.1mcg
- Iron: 2.1mg
- Calcium: 307mg
- Potassium: 360.8mg
- Phosphorus: 258.7mg
- Magnesium: 70.7mg
- Zinc: 2.2mg

Spinach, Avocado, and Poached Egg Salad with Dijon Dressing

VEGETARIAN

This nutrient-packed salad is perfect for expectant mothers as it combines essential vitamins and minerals that support pregnancy health. Spinach offers folic acid which helps prevent neural tube defects, while avocados provide healthy fats and potassium. The poached egg supplies protein and choline, vital for baby's brain development. The tangy Dijon dressing brings all the ingredients together, offering both flavor and additional nutrients.

Preparation Time: 15 minutes
Cooking Time: 5 minutes
Total Time: 20 minutes
Serves: 2

Ingredients:
- 4 cups fresh baby spinach, washed and dried
- 1 ripe avocado, sliced
- 2 large eggs
- 2 cups water (for poaching eggs)
- 1 tablespoon white vinegar (for poaching eggs)
- Salt, to taste
- Freshly ground black pepper, to taste

For the Dijon Dressing:

- 2 tablespoons extra virgin olive oil
- 1 tablespoon apple cider vinegar
- 1 teaspoon Dijon mustard
- 1/2 teaspoon honey
- 1 garlic clove, minced
- Salt and pepper, to taste

Instructions:
1. In a small bowl, whisk together the olive oil, apple cider vinegar, Dijon mustard, honey, and minced garlic. Season with salt and pepper to taste. Set aside.
2. Bring 2 cups of water to a gentle simmer in a deep skillet or saucepan. Add the white vinegar and a pinch of salt.
3. Crack one egg into a small bowl. Carefully slide the egg into the simmering water. Repeat with the second egg.
4. Let the eggs poach for about 3-4 minutes for a soft yolk or 5-6 minutes for a firmer yolk.
5. Using a slotted spoon, carefully remove the poached eggs from the water and set them on a paper towel to drain excess water.
6. Divide the baby spinach between two plates or bowls.
7. Top each with half of the sliced avocado.
8. Carefully place a poached egg on top of each salad.
9. Drizzle with the prepared Dijon dressing.
10. Season with additional salt and pepper, if desired.
11. Serve and Enjoy: Serve the salad immediately as a refreshing and nutritious meal.

Chef's Notes:
- Add chicken, salmon, shrimp or tofu for extra protein and nutrients
- Add nuts and/or seeds on top for extra crunch and nutrients

Nutritional Information (per serving):
- Calories: 377kcal
- Total Fat: 33.2g
- Monounsaturated Fat: .21.53g
- Polyunsaturated Fat: 4.3g
- Total Carbohydrates: 13.6g
- Dietary Fiber: 8.1g
- Protein: 10.1g
- Sodium: 388.9mg
- Vitamin A: 368.4mcg
- Vitamin B6: .5mg
- Vitamin B12: .4mcg
- Vitamin C: 27.4mg
- Vitamin D: 1mcg
- Vitamin E: 5.8mg
- Vitamin K: 319.1mcg
- Folate: 215.4mcg
- Iron: 3.2mg
- Calcium: 103mg
- Zinc: 1.6mg

Quinoa, Roasted Beet, and Goat Cheese Salad

GLUTEN-FREE

This nutrient-packed salad blends the earthy flavor of roasted beets with the tang of creamy goat cheese, all set on a bed of protein-rich quinoa. Not only is it delectably colorful and tasty, but this salad also offers an array of vitamins and minerals beneficial for pregnancy, such as folate from beets and protein from quinoa.

Preparation Time: 20 minutes
Cooking Time: 40 minutes
Total Time: 60 minutes
Serves: 2

Ingredients:
- 1 cup quinoa (any color)
- 2 medium-sized beets
- 1/2 cup crumbled goat cheese (ensure it's pasteurized)
- 2 tbsp olive oil
- Salt, to taste
- Pepper, to taste
- 2 tbsp lemon juice

Instructions:
1. Preheat your oven to 400°F (205°C).
2. Scrub the beets clean and trim off the leafy tops.
3. Wrap each beet in foil and place them on a baking sheet. Roast in the oven for about 40 minutes, or until they can be easily pierced with a fork.
4. Once cooked, remove from the oven and let cool before peeling the skin off. Dice the beets into bite-sized pieces.
5. While the beets are roasting, rinse the quinoa under cold water using a fine mesh strainer. In a medium saucepan, bring 2 cups of water to a boil. Add a pinch of salt.
6. Add the quinoa, reduce heat to low, cover, and cook for 15 minutes.
7. Once the quinoa is cooked, remove it from the heat and let it sit for 5 minutes, then fluff with a fork.
8. In a large mixing bowl, combine the cooked quinoa, roasted beets, and crumbled goat cheese. Drizzle with olive oil and lemon juicer. Toss to combine. Divide into two bowls. Season with salt and pepper to taste and enjoy!

Chef's Notes:
- Add 1/4 cup toasted walnuts or pecans for some crunch and extra protein
- Add additional protein sources such as chicken, salmon, shrimp or tofu
- Add some mixed greens, roasted asparagus or broccoli for some green vegetables
- Add a splash of balsamic vinegar for extra flavor

Nutritional Information (per serving):
- Calories: 594kcal
- Total Fat: 40.9g
- Monounsaturated Fat: 16.18g
- Polyunsaturated Fat: 3.09g
- Total Carbohydrates: 30.1g
- Dietary Fiber: 4.6g
- Protein: 28.1g
- Sodium: 637.8mg
- Vitamin A: 349.6mcg
- Vitamin B6: .5mg
- Vitamin B12: 134.5mcg
- Vitamin C: 5.9mg
- Vitamin D: .5mcg
- Vitamin E: 2.8mg
- Vitamin K: 10.5mcg
- Folate: 134.5mcg
- Iron: 4.5mg
- Calcium: 201.2mg
- Potassium: 501.7mg
- Phosphorus: 488.1mg
- Magnesium: 101.9mg
- Zinc: 2.5mg

Mixed Greens with Grilled Chicken, Orange Slices, and Almond Slivers

GLUTEN-FREE

This refreshing and nutritious salad combines the tender grilled chicken with sweet orange slices and the subtle crunch of slivered almonds. A perfect balance of protein, healthy fats, and essential vitamins, this salad is particularly beneficial for pregnant women. Oranges are rich in vitamin C and folate, which are vital during pregnancy, while chicken offers lean protein for muscle development. Almonds add a touch of magnesium and vitamin E.

Preparation Time: 10 minutes
Cooking Time: 15 minutes
Total Time: 25 minutes
Serves: 2

Ingredients:
- 2 boneless, skinless chicken breasts
- 2 cups mixed greens (like spinach, arugula, and romaine)
- 1 large orange, peeled and sliced
- 1/4 cup slivered almonds, toasted
- 2 tbsp olive oil (for grilling)
- Salt and pepper, to taste

For the dressing:
- 2 tbsp olive oil
- 1 tbsp fresh orange juice
- 1 tsp honey
- 1 tsp Dijon mustard
- Salt and pepper, to taste

Instructions:
1. Preheat grill or grill pan to medium-high heat.
2. Rub the chicken breasts with olive oil and season both sides with salt and pepper.
3. Grill the chicken for 6-7 minutes on each side, or until fully cooked (internal temperature of 165°F or 74°C). Remove from the grill and let it rest for a few minutes.

4. Slice the chicken into strips or bite-sized pieces.
5. In a small bowl, whisk together the olive oil, fresh orange juice, honey, and Dijon mustard. Season with salt and pepper to taste. Set aside.
6. In a large bowl, toss the mixed greens with half of the dressing.
7. Divide the greens between two serving plates.
8. Top each plate with grilled chicken slices, orange slices, and toasted slivered almonds.
9. Drizzle the remaining dressing over the top or serve on the side.

Chef's Notes:
- Use salmon, shrimp or tofu as alternative protein sources
- Add some blueberries or strawberries for additional fruit
- Add some feta cheese if desired

Nutritional Information (per serving):
- Calories: 731kcal
- Total Fat: 40.8g
- Monounsaturated Fat: 21.86g
- Polyunsaturated Fat: 4.19g
- Total Carbohydrates: 29.3g
- Dietary Fiber: 8.2g
- Protein: 63.3g
- Sodium: 287.6mg
- Vitamin A: 21.1mcg
- Vitamin B6: 1.1mg
- Vitamin B12: .6mcg
- Vitamin C: 52.5mcg
- Vitamin E: 4.5mg
- Vitamin K: 16.8mcg
- Folate: 36.7mcg
- Iron: 6.6mg
- Calcium: 223.8mg
- Magnesium: 60mg
- Zinc: 1.8mg

Broccoli, Chickpea, and Sunflower Seed Salad with Tahini Dressing

SO FAST!
This nutrient-packed salad combines the freshness of broccoli with the protein of chickpeas and the crunch of sunflower seeds, all enveloped in a creamy tahini dressing. For expectant mothers, this salad provides essential vitamins, minerals, and proteins needed for healthy pregnancy, such as folic acid, calcium, fiber, magnesium and protein, making it a delicious and beneficial choice.

Preparation Time: 15 minutes
Cooking Time: 0 minutes
Total Time: 15 minutes
Serves: 2

Ingredients:
- 1 cup of broccoli florets, cut into bite-sized pieces
- 1 cup of cooked chickpeas (if canned, drain and rinse)
- 2 tbsp sunflower seeds, roasted
- 1 spring onion, finely chopped

Tahini Dressing:
- 2 tbsp tahini
- 1 garlic clove, minced
- 1 tbsp lemon juice
- 1 tsp honey
- 2 tbsp water (or more as needed to thin)
- Salt and pepper to taste

Instructions:
1. In a mixing bowl, combine the broccoli florets, chickpeas, sunflower seeds, and spring onion.
2. In a separate small bowl, whisk together tahini, minced garlic, lemon juice, and honey. Add water a tablespoon at a time until you reach your desired consistency. Season with salt and pepper to taste.
3. Pour the tahini dressing over the salad base and toss until all ingredients are well-coated.
4. Divide the salad between two serving plates. Garnish with fresh parsley if desired. Enjoy immediately!

Chef's Notes:
- For an added touch of sweetness, consider adding a handful of dried cranberries or raisins to the salad.
- If you prefer a warm salad, you can lightly steam the broccoli before adding it to the mix.
- For additional protein, add chicken, salmon or tofu

Nutritional Information (per serving):
- Calories: 296kcal
- Total Fat: 13.9g
- Monounsaturated Fat: 4.22g
- Polyunsaturated Fat: 6.88g
- Total Carbohydrates: 34.4g
- Dietary Fiber: 9.8g
- Protein: 12.7g
- Sodium: 194.9mg
- Vitamin A: 19.1mcg
- Vitamin B6: .3mg
- Vitamin C: 45.9mg
- Vitamin E: 2.6mg
- Vitamin K: 65.3mcg
- Folate: 207.3mcg
- Iron: 4.5mg
- Calcium: 139.2mg
- Potassium: 539.3mg
- Phosphorus: 365.3mg
- Magnesium: 74.6mg
- Zinc: 2.6mg

Lentil and Spinach Soup with Turmeric

MEAL-PREP FRIENDLY

A hearty and nutritious soup that combines the richness of lentils with the freshness of spinach, enhanced by the warmth of turmeric. This soup is not only delicious but also packed with essential nutrients beneficial for pregnancy, such as iron, folate, and anti-inflammatory properties.

Preparation Time: 15 minutes
Cooking Time: 40 minutes
Total Time: 55 minutes
Serves: 6

Ingredients:

- 2 cups green or brown lentils, rinsed and drained
- 1 large onion, finely chopped
- 2 garlic cloves, minced
- 1 tablespoon olive oil
- 1 teaspoon ground turmeric
- 1 teaspoon ground cumin
- 1 bay leaf
- 6 cups vegetable broth or water
- 4 cups fresh spinach, roughly chopped
- 1 can (14 oz) diced tomatoes
- Salt and pepper to taste
- Lemon wedges and fresh coriander for garnish

Instructions:

1. In a large pot, heat the olive oil over medium heat. Add the chopped onions and sauté until translucent, about 5 minutes.
2. Add the minced garlic, ground turmeric, and cumin to the pot. Stir well and cook for another 2 minutes, ensuring the garlic doesn't burn.
3. Add the rinsed lentils, bay leaf, and vegetable broth or water to the pot. Increase the heat and bring the mixture to a boil. Once boiling, reduce the heat to low, cover, and let it simmer for 25-30 minutes, or until the lentils are tender.
4. Add diced tomatoes to the pot and stir well. Allow the soup to simmer for another 5 minutes.
5. Stir in the chopped spinach and continue cooking just until the spinach is wilted, which should take about 2-3 minutes.
6. Remove the bay leaf and season the soup with salt and pepper to taste.
7. Serve hot, garnished with a squeeze of lemon and a sprinkle of fresh coriander.

Chef's Notes:
- Can be made in a large batch for meal prepping, and stored in the refrigerator for 3-5 days or freezer for up to a month
- Serve with a side salad for extra vegetables

Nutritional Information (per serving):
- Calories: 142kcal
- Total Fat: 2.8g
- Monounsaturated Fat: 1.7g
- Polyunsaturated Fat: .41g
- Total Carbohydrates: 22.3g
- Dietary Fiber: 7.6g
- Protein: 8.4g
- Sodium: 677.2mg
- Vitamin A: 119.4mcg
- Vitamin B6: .2mg
- Vitamin C: 25.1mg
- Vitamin E: .8mg
- Vitamin K: 99.8mcg
- Folate: 160.6mcg
- Iron: 3.5mg
- Calcium: 48.8mg
- Magnesium: 44.6mg
- Zinc: 1.1mg

Beef and Vegetable Soup with Bone Broth

MEAL-PREP FRIENDLY

This nourishing soup combines the rich flavors of beef and bone broth with a medley of fresh vegetables. Perfect for expectant mothers, the bone broth provides vital nutrients such as collagen, gelatin, and amino acids that are essential for joint, skin, and gut health. The vegetables and beef offer an abundance of vitamins and minerals that support the health of both the mother and the baby, such as protein and iron.

Preparation Time: 20 minutes
Cooking Time: 2 hours
Total Time: 2 hours, 20 minutes
Serves: 6

Ingredients:
- 2 lbs beef chuck, cubed
- 6 cups bone broth
- 2 medium carrots, diced
- 2 celery stalks, diced
- 1 medium onion, diced
- 2 garlic cloves, minced
- 2 medium potatoes, diced
- 1 cup green beans, chopped
- 1 cup corn kernels
- 2 tomatoes, diced
- 2 tablespoons olive oil
- 2 teaspoons salt (adjust to taste)
- 1 teaspoon black pepper
- 2 bay leaves
- 1 teaspoon dried thyme
- Fresh parsley, chopped (for garnish)

Instructions:
1. In a large pot, heat the olive oil over medium heat. Add the beef cubes and brown on all sides. Remove and set aside.
2. In the same pot, add the onions, carrots, and celery. Sauté until the onions are translucent, about 5 minutes.
3. Add the minced garlic and sauté for another minute until fragrant.

4. Return the beef to the pot. Pour in the bone broth, ensuring the beef is submerged.
5. Add bay leaves, dried thyme, salt, and black pepper. Bring to a boil.
6. Once boiling, reduce the heat to low, cover, and let it simmer for 1 hour.
7. After 1 hour, add the potatoes, green beans, corn, and tomatoes to the pot. Let it simmer for another 30-40 minutes, or until the vegetables are tender.
8. Check for seasoning. Adjust salt and pepper if needed.
9. Once cooked, discard the bay leaves. Serve hot, garnished with fresh parsley.

Chef's Notes:
- Can be made in a large batch for meal prepping, and stored in the refrigerator for 3-5 days or freezer for up to a month
- Serve with a side salad for extra vegetables

Nutritional Information (per serving):
- Calories: 459kcal
- Total Fat: 16.4g
- Monounsaturated Fat: 8.2g
- Polyunsaturated Fat: 1.1g
- Total Carbohydrates: 20.8g
- Dietary Fiber: 3.8g
- Protein: 56.4g
- Sodium: 681.3mg
- Vitamin A: 184.8mcg
- Vitamin B6: .7mg
- Vitamin B12: 3.8mcg
- Vitamin C: 21.9mg
- Vitamin E: 1.8mg
- Vitamin K: 55.7mcg
- Folate: 66mcg
- Iron: 5.7mg
- Calcium: 72.9mg
- Magnesium: 62mg
- Zinc: 11.9mg

Are you enjoying these delicious recipes? Your feedback matters! Share your thoughts with other expecting parents by leaving a review on Amazon today. Your review can help future moms and dads discover the perfect cookbook for their journey.

NUTRIENT~DENSE SNACKS

When it comes to snacking, especially during the crucial first trimester of pregnancy, it's essential to prioritize nutrient balance. Consuming "naked carbohydrates" like a lone piece of fruit can result in rapid spikes and drops in blood sugar. This can lead to feelings of fatigue, dizziness, and irritability. To maintain sustained energy and ensure that you're nourishing both yourself and your growing baby, it's recommended to pair carbohydrates with proteins.

We have provided some nutrient-dense snack recipes below, but here are some ideas for quick and easy grab-and-go snacks

- Apple slices with almond butter
- Banana with peanut butter
- Grapes and pistachios
- Hard-boiled eggs, sprinkled with black pepper
- Dark chocolate and almonds:
- Celery sticks with cream cheese, almond butter or hummus
- Dried figs with cashews
- Kale chips
- Roasted chickpeas
- Orange slices and pumpkin seeds
- Unsweetened greek yogurt with blueberries
- A cube of cheese and cashews
- Coconut or almond yogurt with pistachios
- Cherry tomatoes and macadamia nuts
- Cucumber slices with cream cheese
- Nori/seaweed snacks with brazil nuts

Remember, balance is key. By accompanying carbohydrates with proteins, you'll be ensuring steady energy release, curbing hunger, and providing your body with essential nutrients during this special time.

Greek Yogurt Parfait with Berries and Granola

SO FAST!
This delectable Greek Yogurt Parfait layered with fresh berries and crunchy granola offers a satisfying balance of sweet, tangy, and crunchy elements. Not only is it a treat for the eyes and palate, but its nutritious components make it a fantastic choice for expecting mothers and baby such as protein, fiber and antioxidants.

Preparation Time: 10 minutes
Cooking Time: 0 minutes
Total Time: 10 minutes
Serves: 1

Ingredients:
- 1 cup Greek yogurt (plain or vanilla)
- 1/3 cup mixed berries (e.g., strawberries, blueberries, raspberries, blackberries)
- 1/4 cup granola (choose your favorite, preferably one with low sugar)

Instructions:

1. Layer 1: Begin with a layer of Greek yogurt at the bottom of a glass or bowl.
2. Layer 2: Add a layer of mixed berries on top of the yogurt.
3. Layer 3: Sprinkle a generous amount of granola over the berries.
4. Layer 4: Repeat with another layer of Greek yogurt.
5. Layer 5: Top off with more mixed berries.
6. Enjoy immediately for the best texture and freshness.

Chef's Notes:

- Customize with your favorite berries or fruits. Banana slices, mango chunks, or kiwi slices can also make delightful additions.
- If you're making this ahead of time, store the granola separately to keep it crunchy and add just before eating.
- Drizzle with a teaspoon of honey for additional sweetness
- Add a sprinkle of chia seeds or flax seeds for additional crunch and nutrients
- For a protein boost, consider adding a spoonful of nut butter or a handful of nuts.

Nutritional Information (per serving):

- Calories: 369kcal
- Total Fat: 18.8g
- Monounsaturated Fat: 8.19g
- Polyunsaturated Fat: 3.45g
- Total Carbohydrates: 25.5g
- Dietary Fiber: 2.7g
- Protein: 24.6g
- Sodium: 87.3mg
- Vitamin A: 4.8mcg
- Vitamin B6: .3mg
- Vitamin B12: 1.7mcg
- Vitamin C: .4mg
- Vitamin E: 3.4mg
- Folate: 37mcg
- Iron: 1.2mg
- Calcium: 250mg
- Potassium: 284.2mg
- Phosphorus: 437.6mg
- Magnesium: 76.2mg
- Zinc: 2.5mg

Hummus-Stuffed Mini Bell Peppers

GLUTEN-FREE

These vibrant and flavorful stuffed mini bell peppers are the perfect healthy snack or appetizer. They are packed with protein from chickpeas and an array of essential nutrients that benefit expectant mothers. Hummus offers a good source of iron, folate, and vitamin B6, which are crucial during pregnancy. Additionally, bell peppers are rich in vitamin C, which aids iron absorption and promotes healthy skin.

Preparation Time: 20 minutes
Cooking Time: 0 minutes
Total Time: 20 minutes
Serves: 4

Ingredients:

- 16 mini bell peppers
- 1 can (15 oz) chickpeas, drained and rinsed
- 2 cloves garlic, minced
- 2 tbsp tahini
- Juice of 1 lemon
- 3 tbsp extra virgin olive oil
- Salt and pepper, to taste
- 1 tsp ground cumin
- 1-2 tbsp water (or as needed)

Instructions:

1. Rinse the mini bell peppers. Slice off the tops and remove the seeds and membranes, creating a cavity to be filled with hummus.
2. In a food processor or blender, combine chickpeas, garlic, tahini, lemon juice, olive oil, salt, pepper, and cumin. Blend until smooth. If the mixture is too thick, slowly add water, a tablespoon at a time, until the desired consistency is reached.
3. Using a small spoon or piping bag, fill each mini bell pepper with the hummus mixture until they are all stuffed.
4. Arrange on a serving platter and serve immediately.

Chef's Notes:

- These can be made in advance and refrigerated for 2-3 days until serving.
- Eat with a few nuts for extra protein

Nutritional Information (per serving):

- Calories: 350kcal
- Total Fat: 17g
- Monounsaturated Fat: 9.53 g
- Polyunsaturated Fat: 4.08g
- Total Carbohydrates: 39.5g
- Dietary Fiber: 10.6g
- Protein: 12.3g
- Sodium: 171.8mg
- Vitamin C: 225mg
- Vitamin B6: .2mg
- Vitamin E: 1.9mg
- Vitamin K: 10.4mcg
- Folate: 191.8mcg
- Iron: 4.7mg
- Calcium: 95.7mg
- Magnesium: 59.7mg
- Zinc: 2mg

Nut & Seed Trail Mix

VEGAN

This nutritious trail mix is tailored for expectant mothers, packed with essential nutrients such as omega-3 fatty acids, iron, magnesium, zinc, protein, and fiber. The blend of nuts, seeds, and dried fruits provides sustained energy and supports the overall well-being of both mother and baby.

Preparation Time: 10 minutes
Cooking Time: 0 minutes
Total Time: 10 minutes
Serves: 10

Ingredients:

- 1 cup unsalted almonds
- 1 cup unsalted walnuts
- 1/2 cup unsalted cashews
- 1/2 cup unsalted pistachios
- 1/2 cup pumpkin seeds (pepitas)
- 1/4 cup sunflower seeds
- 1 cup dried cranberries or raisins (or a mix of both)
- 1/2 cup dried apricots, chopped
- 1/2 cup dried figs, chopped

Instructions:

1. In a large mixing bowl, combine the almonds, walnuts, cashews, pistachios, pumpkin seeds, and sunflower seeds. Stir them together for an even mix.
2. Gently fold in the dried cranberries, chopped apricots, and chopped figs. Ensure they're evenly distributed throughout the mix.

Chef's Notes:

- Optional Addition: If you're adding dark chocolate chips, fold them into the mix last. Their sweetness and antioxidants can be a delightful addition, but consume in moderation.
- Storing: Once mixed, store the trail mix in an airtight container. Keep at room temperature and best consumed within a month for freshness.
- Serving: A typical serving size is about 1/2 cup. This recipe should yield roughly 10 servings.
- Try all unsalted nuts and seeds or at least half unsalted to reduce sodium intake

Nutritional Information (per serving):

- Calories: 316kcal
- Total Fat: 24.6g
- Monounsaturated Fat: 10.1g
- Polyunsaturated Fat: 10.3g
- Total Carbohydrates: 19.8g
- Dietary Fiber: 5.3g
- Protein: 9.7g
- Sodium: 20.9mg
- Vitamin B6: .2mg
- Vitamin E: 5.2mg
- Vitamin K: 5.5mcg
- Folate: 36.7mcg
- Iron: 2.4mg
- Calcium: 79.6mg
- Magnesium: 171.7mg

- Zinc: 2mg

Apple & Goat Cheese Bites with Honey Drizzle

SO FAST!

Elevate your snack game with these delightful apple and goat cheese bites. The combination of crisp apple, creamy goat cheese, and sweet honey is not only a treat for your taste buds but also offers several health benefits for expecting mothers. Apples are rich in dietary fiber that aids digestion, goat cheese provides much-needed calcium, and honey is a natural sweetener that has antioxidant properties. Together, they make a harmonious and nutritious snack perfect for pregnancy cravings.

Preparation Time: 10 minutes
Cooking Time: 0 minutes
Total Time: 10 minutes
Serves: 1

Ingredients:

- 1 medium-sized apple
- 2 tablespoons goat cheese, pasteurized
- 1 tablespoon honey

Instructions:

1. Start by washing the apple thoroughly. Then, using a knife, slice the apple into rings, about 1/4-inch thick. Remove the core from each ring using a cookie cutter or a sharp knife.
2. Spread a generous layer of softened goat cheese onto each apple ring.
3. Drizzle a light layer of honey over the assembled apple and goat cheese bites.
4. Place the finished bites on a plate and enjoy immediately. Best when consumed fresh.

Chef's Notes:

- Top with chia seeds or finely chopped nuts of your choice for extra protein and nutrients
- Use almond butter instead of goat cheese as a non-dairy alternative

Nutritional Information (per serving):

- Calories: 233kcal
- Total Fat: 6.3g
- Monounsaturated Fat: 1.4g
- Polyunsaturated Fat: .24g
- Total Carbohydrates: 42.4g
- Dietary Fiber: 4.4g
- Protein: 5.8g
- Sodium: 133mg
- Vitamin B6: .2mg
- Vitamin C: 8.5mg
- Folate: 9.3mcg
- Iron: .8mg
- Calcium: 51.9mg
- Potassium: 213mg

Cottage Cheese, Kiwi & Mint Bowl

SO FAST!

This refreshing bowl combines the creaminess of cottage cheese with the tangy sweetness of kiwi and the invigorating flavor of fresh mint. Not only is it a delicious treat, but it's also packed with nutrients that are beneficial during pregnancy. Kiwi is a source of vitamin C, which supports the immune system. Cottage cheese provides calcium and protein, essential for the growth of the baby. Mint not only adds flavor but may also help soothe nausea.

Preparation Time: 10 minutes
Cooking Time: 0 minutes
Total Time: 10 minutes
Serves: 1

Ingredients:

- 1/2 cup full fat cottage cheese
- 1 ripe kiwi
- 1-2 fresh mint leaves

Instructions:

1. Peel the kiwi and cut it into small slices or chunks.
2. Finely chop the fresh mint leaves.
3. In a serving bowl, place the cottage cheese.
4. Layer the kiwi slices on top of the cottage cheese.
5. Sprinkle the chopped mint leaves over the kiwi and cottage cheese.
6. Gently mix, if desired, or enjoy as layered.
7. Serve immediately and relish the burst of flavors!

Chef's Notes:

- Sprinkle with chia seeds or finely chopped nuts for extra protein and nutrients

Nutritional Information (per serving):

- Calories: 145kcal
- Total Fat: 4.9g
- Monounsaturated Fat: .85g
- Polyunsaturated Fat: .33g
- Total Carbohydrates: 13.7g
- Dietary Fiber: 2.1g
- Protein: 12.5g
- Sodium: 332.8mg
- Vitamin A: 41.7mcg
- Vitamin C: 64mg
- Vitamin B12: .5mcg
- Vitamin E: 1.1mg
- Vitamin K: 27.8mcg
- Folate: 29.9mcg
- Iron: .3mg
- Calcium: 110.7mg
- Potassium: 324.8mg
- Phosphorus: 190.4mg
- Magnesium: 20.2mg
- Zinc: .5mg

Whole Grain Toast with Smashed Avocado & Cherry Tomatoes

MIX-AND-MATCH RECIPE

A delightful and nourishing snack, perfect for expectant mothers. This recipe combines the heartiness of whole grains, the creaminess of avocado, and the juicy tang of cherry tomatoes to create a delicious and nutrient-packed toast that's beneficial during pregnancy due to its high content of fiber, folate, potassium and healthy fats.

Preparation Time: 5 minutes
Cooking Time: 2 minutes
Total Time: 7 minutes
Serves: 1

Ingredients:

- 1 slice of whole grain bread
- 1/2 ripe avocado
- 5-7 cherry tomatoes
- Salt, to taste
- Pepper, to taste

Instructions:

1. Place the whole grain bread slice in a toaster or oven and toast until it's crispy and golden brown.
2. While the bread is toasting, slice the avocado in half. Remove the seed and use a spoon to scoop out the flesh. Place it in a bowl and mash it using a fork until it's relatively smooth. If you prefer chunkier avocado, you can mash it less.
3. Rinse the cherry tomatoes under cool water. Slice each tomato in half or quarters, depending on your preference.
4. Once the bread is toasted to your liking, spread the mashed avocado generously over the slice. Top with the sliced cherry tomatoes. Sprinkle with salt and pepper to taste. Enjoy!

Chef's Notes/Recipe Variations:

- Poached Egg: A perfectly poached egg adds a creamy and savory element to your avocado toast. The runny yolk pairs wonderfully with the creamy avocado.
- Sliced Tomato: Fresh tomato slices bring a juicy and slightly acidic contrast to the richness of the avocado. You can sprinkle some salt and pepper on top for extra flavor.
- Feta Cheese: Crumbled feta cheese adds a tangy and salty kick to your avocado toast. It's a great choice for those who enjoy a bit of Mediterranean flair.
- Red Pepper Flakes: If you like a bit of heat, sprinkle some red pepper flakes over your avocado toast. It adds a spicy kick that complements the creamy avocado.
- Smoked Salmon: For a luxurious twist, top your avocado toast with thinly sliced smoked salmon. The smokiness and saltiness of the salmon work beautifully with the avocado's creaminess.
- Everything Bagel Seasoning: Sprinkle some everything bagel seasoning on your avocado toast for a delightful mix of sesame seeds, poppy seeds, garlic, onion, and salt. It adds a crunchy texture and a burst of flavor.

- Grilled Shrimp: Grilled shrimp can turn your avocado toast into a seafood delight. The slightly charred shrimp pairs well with the creamy avocado.
- Cilantro and Lime: Drizzle freshly squeezed lime juice over your avocado toast and garnish it with chopped cilantro. This combination adds a bright and zesty flavor.
- Hummus: Spread a layer of hummus on your avocado toast for extra creaminess and a touch of Mediterranean flavor. You can also add some chopped cucumbers or olives for extra flair.
- Bacon: If you enjoy a savory and crispy element, crumbled bacon is a classic choice. Its smoky flavor complements the avocado's creaminess.

Nutritional Information (per serving):
- Calories: 283kcal
- Total Fat: 15.2g
- Monounsaturated Fat: 9.8g
- Polyunsaturated Fat: 1.8g
- Total Carbohydrates: 33.6g
- Dietary Fiber: 10.7g
- Protein: 7g
- Sodium: 321.5mg
- Vitamin B6: .3mg
- Vitamin C: 27.4mg
- Vitamin E: 2.1mg
- Vitamin K: 21.1mcg
- Folate: 81.4mcg
- Iron: 3.1mg
- Calcium: 52.3mg
- Magnesium: 29.1mg
- Zinc: .6mg

Edamame & Black Sesame Salt Dip

VEGAN

This creamy and flavorful dip combines the fresh taste of edamame beans with the nutty undertone of black sesame. It is not only a delightful accompaniment to chips and veggies but is also packed with nutrients beneficial for pregnancy. Edamame contains essential folate and protein, while black sesame seeds offer calcium and iron. Together, they make a power-packed snack perfect for expecting mothers.

Preparation Time: 10 minutes
Cooking Time: 5 minutes
Total Time: 15 minutes
Serves: 6

Ingredients:
- 2 cups shelled edamame (fresh or frozen)
- 2 tbsp toasted black sesame seeds
- 3 tbsp sesame oil
- 1-2 cloves garlic
- 1 tbsp lemon juice
- 1 tsp black sesame salt
- Water as needed
- Freshly cracked black pepper, to taste

Instructions:
1. Boil edamame in salted water for about 4-5 minutes until tender. Drain and rinse with cold water.
2. If your black sesame seeds are not already toasted, place them in a dry skillet over medium heat. Toast, stirring frequently, until they become fragrant. This usually takes 2-3 minutes. Remove from heat and set aside.
3. In a food processor or high-speed blender, combine the cooked edamame, garlic, lemon juice, and half of the toasted black sesame seeds. Blend until you achieve a smooth consistency. While blending, gradually add the sesame oil. If the mixture is too thick, add a little water until you achieve the desired consistency.
4. Season the dip with black sesame salt and freshly cracked black pepper. Adjust the seasoning according to your preference.
5. Serve: Transfer the dip to a serving bowl and garnish with the remaining toasted black sesame seeds. Serve with vegetable sticks, crackers, or as a spread on sandwiches or toast.

Chef's Notes:
- Store in an airtight container in the refrigerator for 2-3 days.

Nutritional Information (per serving):
- Calories: 143kcal
- Total Fat: 11g
- Monounsaturated Fat: 3.36g
- Polyunsaturated Fat: 3.94g
- Total Carbohydrates: 6.1g
- Dietary Fiber: 3g
- Protein: 6.7g
- Sodium: 158.7mg
- Vitamin C: 5.7mg
- Vitamin K: 14.6mcg
- Folate: 160.3mcg
- Iron: 1.6mg
- Calcium: 65.3mg
- Magnesium: 33.3mg
- Zinc: .7mg

Chocolate Dipped Strawberries with Crushed Walnuts

GLUTEN-FREE

Dive into the rich indulgence of chocolate dipped strawberries sprinkled with the earthy crunch of walnuts. This recipe brings together the natural sweetness of fresh strawberries, the velvety touch of melted chocolate, and the nutty aroma of walnuts. Not only is this treat deliciously luxurious, but it also packs a punch of essential nutrients beneficial for pregnant women and their babies. Strawberries are rich in Vitamin C and antioxidants, chocolate has mood-enhancing properties, and walnuts provide essential omega-3 fatty acids and proteins.

Preparation Time: 15 minutes
Cooking Time: 5 minutes
Total Time: 20 minutes

Serves: 1

Ingredients:

- 12 fresh strawberries, washed and dried thoroughly
- 200g (7oz) dark chocolate (choose 70% cocoa or more for added antioxidants)
- 1/2 cup walnuts, finely crushed

Instructions:

1. Make sure the strawberries are completely dry. Any water residue can affect the consistency of the melted chocolate.
2. In a heat-proof bowl, break the dark chocolate into pieces. Melt it over a pot of simmering water (double boiler method) ensuring that the water doesn't touch the base of the bowl. Stir continuously until the chocolate is smooth and fully melted.
3. Holding a strawberry by its green top, dip it into the melted chocolate, ensuring it's coated evenly.
4. Immediately after dipping, roll or sprinkle the chocolate-coated portion of the strawberry in the crushed walnuts.
5. Place the coated strawberries on a baking sheet lined with parchment paper.
6. Allow the strawberries to set at room temperature or, to expedite the process, place them in the refrigerator for about 15-20 minutes. Enjoy!

Chef's Notes:

- Can be stored in the refrigerator for 2-3 days
- Dip in Greek yogurt for additional nutrients
- Sprinkle a pinch of sea salt right after you dip them in chocolate for added contrast in flavor.

Nutritional Information (per serving):

- Calories: 233kcal
- Total Fat: 17.7g
- Monounsaturated Fat: 4.4g
- Polyunsaturated Fat: 4.4g
- Omega-3 Fatty Acids: .8g
- Total Carbohydrates: 16g
- Dietary Fiber: 4.1g
- Protein: 3.7g
- Sodium: 6.1mg
- Vitamin C: 14.2mg
- Folate: 14.1mcg
- Iron: 3.7mg
- Calcium: 32.9mg
- Potassium: 277.4mg
- Phosphorus: 122.7mg
- Magnesium: 81.3mg
- Zinc: 1.2mg

Roasted Sweet Potato Cubes with Cinnamon & Yogurt Dip

GLUTEN-FREE

This simple and delectable dish combines the earthy sweetness of roasted sweet potatoes with a hint of cinnamon, creating a perfect bite. Served with a creamy yogurt dip, this dish offers a balance of flavor and texture. Not only is this dish flavorful,

but it also offers numerous benefits for pregnant women, providing essential nutrients like vitamin A, potassium, and fiber from sweet potatoes, and protein and calcium from yogurt.

Preparation Time: 10 minutes
Cooking Time: 25 minutes
Total Time: 35 minutes
Serves: 1

Ingredients:

- 1 medium-sized sweet potato, peeled and cut into 1-inch cubes
- 1 tablespoon coconut oil
- 1/4 teaspoon ground cinnamon
- Salt, to taste
- 1/4 cup plain full fat Greek yogurt
- 1/4 teaspoon vanilla extract
- 1/2 teaspoon honey

Instructions:

1. Preheat your oven to 400°F (200°C).
2. In a mixing bowl, toss the sweet potato cubes with coconut oil, ground cinnamon, and a pinch of salt.
3. Spread the cubes on a baking sheet in a single layer.
4. Roast in the preheated oven for 20-25 minutes, or until the sweet potatoes are tender and have a golden-brown hue. Turn them halfway through the cooking time for even roasting.
5. Remove from oven and allow them to cool slightly.
6. In a small bowl, mix the Greek yogurt with vanilla extract and honey.
7. Mix well until smooth.
8. Serve the roasted sweet potato cubes alongside the yogurt dip and enjoy!

Nutritional Information (per serving):

- Calories: 314kcal
- Total Fat: 17.1g
- Monounsaturated Fat: 2.38g
- Polyunsaturated Fat: .58g
- Total Carbohydrates: 31.6g
- Dietary Fiber: 3.9g
- Protein: 8.4g
- Sodium: 96.5mg
- Vitamin A: 923.1mcg
- Vitamin B6: .3mg
- Vitamin B12: .5mcg
- Vitamin C: 3.1mg
- Folate: 17.9mcg
- Iron: .8mg
- Calcium: 110.2mg
- Magnesium: 40.4mg
- Zinc: .8mg

Spinach & Feta Mini Muffins

MEAL-PREP FRIENDLY

These delectable mini muffins combine the nutrition of spinach, the creaminess of feta, and the wholesome goodness of eggs to create a perfect snack for home or on-the-go. They are easy to make and portable, making them ideal for busy mornings. The nutritional benefits of these muffins, especially for pregnant women, are notable: they offer protein, calcium, iron, and folate, which are essential nutrients for mom and baby.

Preparation Time: 10 minutes
Cooking Time: 20 minutes
Total Time: 30 minutes
Serves: 6

Ingredients:

- 6 large eggs
- 1 cup fresh spinach, finely chopped
- 1/2 cup crumbled feta cheese
- 1/4 cup diced onions
- Salt and pepper, to taste
- 1/4 teaspoon garlic powder
- Olive oil or non-stick cooking spray (for greasing)

Instructions:

1. Set your oven to 375°F (190°C) and let it warm up.
2. Grease a 12-cup muffin tin with olive oil or non-stick cooking spray to ensure the muffins don't stick.
3. In a mixing bowl, whisk the eggs until smooth. Add the chopped spinach, crumbled feta, diced onions (if using), garlic powder, salt, and pepper. Mix everything together until well combined.
4. Using a ladle or a large spoon, pour the egg mixture into the muffin cups, filling each about 3/4 full.
5. Place the muffin tin in the preheated oven and bake for 20 minutes, or until the center of the muffins is set and a toothpick comes out clean.
6. Once done, remove from the oven and let them cool for a few minutes. Using a knife or a spatula, gently go around the edges of the muffins to make sure they aren't sticking to the tin. Pop them out and serve.

Chef's Notes:

- Store in an airtight container in the refrigerator for up to 4 days. They can be reheated in a microwave for a quick snack or breakfast.
- Feel free to add diced bell peppers, broccoli, kale, asparagus, or even a sprinkle of your favorite herbs for added flavor and nutrition.

Nutritional Information (per serving):

- Calories: 198kcal
- Total Fat: 14.9g
- Monounsaturated Fat: 4.45g
- Polyunsaturated Fat: 1.74g
- Total Carbohydrates: 4g
- Dietary Fiber: .6g
- Protein: 12.1g
- Sodium: 528.6mg
- Vitamin A: 223.3mcg
- Vitamin B6: .3mg
- Vitamin B12: 1.1mcg
- Vitamin E: 1.2mg
- Vitamin K: 77mcg
- Vitamin C: 6.8mg
- Vitamin D: 1.2mcg
- Iron: 1.5mg
- Calcium: 242.2mg
- Potassium:236.2mg
- Phosphorus: 240.4mg

- Magnesium: 28mg
- Zinc: 1.8mg

Second Trimester Cookbook

The second trimester, spanning from weeks 13 to 26, is a transformative period for both the mother and her developing baby. It is often referred to as the "golden period" of pregnancy because many of the tough symptoms of the first trimester ease up. However, it brings its own set of unique challenges.

II TRIMESTER

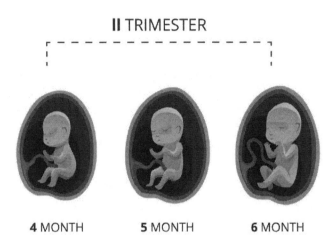

4 MONTH **5** MONTH **6** MONTH

During the fetal phase, there's a surge in your baby's growth, which continues until delivery. The placenta becomes pivotal in delivering vital nutrients and oxygen to the developing fetus. This transition might alleviate some of your earlier symptoms like fatigue and nausea, but hormone changes can present new challenges like constipation and heartburn.

Challenges of the Second Trimester:

Physical Changes: As the belly grows, many women experience backaches due to the extra weight and shifting center of gravity. The body also produces a hormone called relaxin, which can cause ligaments to soften and lead to pain.

Digestive Issues: Heartburn and constipation can become more pronounced during this phase, caused by hormonal shifts and the expanding uterus pressing on the intestines and stomach.

Nasal and Gum Problems: Increased blood flow can lead to swollen nasal passages, causing stuffiness or nosebleeds. Gums might also become more sensitive and bleed easily.

Leg Cramps and Dizziness: Some women might experience sudden leg cramps. Dizziness can also occur due to changes in blood pressure.

Essential Nutrients for the Second Trimester:

Iron: The blood volume increases to supply oxygen to the fetus. Hence, iron is crucial to prevent anemia. Leafy greens, red meat, fortified cereals, and legumes are good sources.

Calcium: This is essential for the skeletal development of your growing baby. Dairy products, fortified plant-based milk, almonds, and green leafy vegetables are great sources.

Vitamin D: Works in tandem with calcium for bone health. Sun exposure, fortified foods, and fatty fish are good sources.

Magnesium: This is part of the trio with calcium and vitamin D as it helps with absorption, and you will need all of the calcium you can get to help your baby's bones to grow and be strong.

Fiber: To combat constipation, fiber intake should be increased. Whole grains, fruits, vegetables, and legumes can help.

Helpful Tips:

Dos:
- Regular Check-ups: Continue prenatal visits and any recommended screenings.
- Stay Active: Engage in moderate exercise like walking or prenatal yoga, unless advised otherwise.
- Hydration: Drink plenty of water to help with swelling and constipation.
- Balanced Diet: Ensure you're consuming all essential nutrients and consider a prenatal vitamin if recommended.
- Dental Hygiene: With an increased risk of gum issues, maintaining good oral hygiene is crucial.
- Proper Posture: Use support pillows while sitting or sleeping to reduce backaches.

Don'ts:
- Avoid High-Mercury Fish: Such as shark, king mackerel, and swordfish.
- Limit Caffeine: Keep it to about 200mg or less per day (roughly a 12-ounce cup of coffee).
- No Alcohol or Smoking: These can severely affect fetal development.
- Avoid Heavy Lifting: It can strain your back and lead to other complications.
- Stay Away from Risky Foods: Such as raw or undercooked seafood, undercooked meats, and unpasteurized dairy products which can harbor harmful bacteria.

In conclusion, while the second trimester is often more comfortable than the first, it's important to remain informed about its unique challenges. Prioritizing essential nutrients and considering these helpful tips can help ensure a smoother journey through this critical period of pregnancy.

HOW TO HANDLE CRAVINGS

Pregnancy is an extraordinary journey that brings a whirlwind of physiological, emotional, and hormonal changes. One of the most widely discussed phenomena associated with pregnancy is food cravings. Pregnant women often report intense desires for specific foods, ranging from pickles and ice cream to more unusual combinations. Let's delve into the why and how of pregnancy cravings and shed light on the peculiar condition called Pica.

Why Do Pregnancy Cravings Happen?

The exact cause of pregnancy cravings is still under debate, but a combination of factors is believed to contribute:

- Hormonal Changes: Pregnancy is accompanied by dramatic hormonal fluctuations, primarily in progesterone and human chorionic gonadotropin (hCG). These changes can impact a woman's sense of smell and taste, potentially leading to new food preferences or aversions.
- Nutritional Needs: Some researchers theorize that cravings might be the body's way of acquiring certain nutrients that are in higher demand during pregnancy. For instance, a craving for oranges or other citrus fruits might indicate a need for vitamin C.
- Emotional Factors: Pregnancy can be an emotionally charged time. Stress, anticipation, and hormonal shifts can influence mood, which in turn may influence food preferences. Comfort foods, for instance, might be sought out more frequently.

Pica: A Unique Pregnancy Phenomenon

Beyond conventional cravings, some pregnant women experience a condition known as Pica. This is the consumption of non-food items like clay, dirt, chalk, or paper.

The exact cause of Pica is unknown, but it's believed to be a combination of psychological and physiological factors. Some theories suggest that Pica might arise from mineral deficiencies, such as iron or zinc, prompting the body to seek out alternative sources. However, the substances craved usually aren't rich in the minerals lacking in the person's diet, so this explanation is still debated. Other theories point to cultural practices, stress, or mental health disorders as potential triggers.

Managing Pregnancy Cravings

- Balanced Diet: Aim for a balanced diet rich in whole grains, fruits, vegetables, lean proteins, and healthy fats. This ensures the body gets the nutrients it needs, potentially reducing the intensity or frequency of cravings.
- Stay Hydrated: Sometimes, the body can confuse thirst with hunger or cravings. Drinking ample water can keep you hydrated and might stave off some unnecessary snacking.
- Mindful Eating: Paying attention to what and when you eat can help recognize genuine hunger from emotional eating or cravings. This doesn't mean you should ignore all cravings, but being mindful can help in distinguishing between needs and wants.
- Seek Alternatives: If you crave foods high in sugar or salt, look for healthier alternatives that satisfy the craving without compromising nutrition. For instance, if you crave something sweet, fruit might be a healthier choice than candy.
- Consult Your Healthcare Provider: If cravings become excessive or if you experience cravings for non-food items (Pica), it's essential to consult with a healthcare provider. They can offer guidance, ensure you're receiving the nutrients you and your baby need, and address any potential risks associated with Pica.

While cravings during pregnancy are a common and often amusing topic of conversation, they can be indicative of deeper physiological and emotional changes occurring within the body. Proper understanding and management of these cravings, combined with regular consultations with healthcare providers, can ensure a healthy and happy journey through pregnancy.

NUTRIENT~RICH BREAKFASTS

Avocado and Poached Egg Whole Grain Toast

VEGETARIAN

Savor a nutritious and delectable breakfast with a perfect combination of creamy avocado and delicate poached egg atop a crispy toast slice. This dish is not only a treat for your taste buds but is also packed with nutrients beneficial for pregnant women, including folic acid, healthy fats, protein, and essential vitamins.

Preparation Time: 10 minutes
Cooking Time: 5 minutes
Total Time: 15 minutes
Serves: 1

Ingredients:
- 1 slice of whole grain bread
- 1/2 ripe avocado
- 1 large egg
- 1 tablespoon of white vinegar (for poaching)
- Salt and pepper, to taste

Instructions:
1. Toast the bread in a toaster and set aside.
2. Fill a medium-sized saucepan with water, about 2/3 full, and bring it to a simmer. Add the white vinegar. This helps the egg white coagulate more easily.
3. Crack the egg into a small bowl, ensuring the yolk remains intact.
4. Create a gentle whirlpool in the simmering water by stirring it with a spoon.
5. Gently slide the egg into the center of the whirlpool. Allow it to cook for 5-6 minutes for a firmer yolk.
6. Using a slotted spoon, carefully lift the poached egg out of the water and drain it on a paper towel.
7. Cut the avocado in half and remove the seed. Scoop out the flesh and place it in a bowl.
8. Mash the avocado using a fork until you achieve a creamy texture. Season with salt and pepper to taste.
9. Spread the mashed avocado generously on the toasted bread.
10. Place the poached egg on top and season with additional salt, pepper, and your chosen garnishes.

Chef's Notes:
- Optional garnishes: chopped chives, red pepper flakes, feta cheese, everything seasoning or arugula.

Nutritional Information (per serving):
- Calories: 322kcal
- Total Fat: 20g
- Monounsaturated Fat: 11.67g
- Polyunsaturated Fat: 2.78g
- Total Carbohydrates: 27.9g
- Dietary Fiber: 8.7g
- Protein: 11.3g
- Sodium: 395.6mg
- Vitamin A: 87mcg
- Vitamin B6: .3mg
- Vitamin B12: .4mcg
- Vitamin C: 16.1mg
- Vitamin E: 2.6mg
- Vitamin K: 21.3mcg
- Folate: 98.9mcg
- Iron: 2.5mg
- Calcium: 40.1mg
- Magnesium: 35.1mg
- Zinc: 1.3mg

Mixed Berry and Chia Seed Overnight Oats

MIX-AND-MATCH RECIPE

A nutritious and delightful breakfast option, this Mixed Berry and Chia Seed Overnight Oats recipe offers an enticing blend of flavors and textures. It's a fantastic way to kickstart the day, especially during pregnancy, with an optimal blend of antioxidants and essential nutrients like fiber, calcium, vitamin C, vitamin D and omega-3 fatty acids.

Preparation Time: 10 minutes
Cooking Time: 0 minutes (besides overnight chilling)
Total Time: 10 minutes
Serves: 1

Ingredients:
- 1/2 cup rolled oats
- 1 tablespoon chia seeds
- 3/4 cup unsweetened almond milk
- 1/2 cup mixed berries (like raspberries, blueberries, strawberries)
- A pinch of salt
- 1/4 teaspoon vanilla extract

Instructions:
1. In a mason jar or a bowl, combine the rolled oats and chia seeds.
2. Pour in the almond milk, ensuring that the oats and chia seeds are well-submerged.
3. Add the mixed berries to the jar.
4. Stir in honey, if using, and a pinch of salt.
5. Add vanilla extract for a touch of flavor, if desired.
6. Mix everything thoroughly.
7. Seal the jar or cover the bowl and place it in the refrigerator.
8. Let it sit overnight.
9. In the morning, give it a good stir. If the mixture seems too thick, add a little more milk until you reach the desired consistency.

Chef's Notes:
- Tropical Twist: Swap out mixed berries for diced mango, pineapple, and a sprinkle of shredded coconut.
- Nutty Delight: Add a tablespoon of almond butter or peanut butter to the mix and top with crushed nuts.

- Chocolate Indulgence: Mix in 1 tablespoon of cocoa or cacao powder for a chocolatey treat.
- Protein Boost: Stir in a scoop of your preferred protein powder for an added protein kick.
- Dairy-Free: Use coconut milk, soy milk, or oat milk as an alternative to almond milk.

Nutritional Information (per serving):
- Calories: 274kcal
- Total Fat: 8.8g
- Monounsaturated Fat: 2.49g
- Polyunsaturated Fat: 4.83g
- Omega-3 Fatty Acids: 2.53g
- Total Carbohydrates: 44.2g
- Dietary Fiber: 11.8g
- Protein: 8.6g
- Sodium: 155 mg
- Vitamin C: 15.2mg
- Vitamin D: 2mcg
- Vitamin E: 12.5mg
- Folate: 8.9mcg
- Iron: 3.7mg
- Calcium: 481.1mg
- Magnesium: 59.4mg
- Zinc: .8mg

Spinach, Feta, and Mushroom Breakfast Casserole

MEAL-PREP FRIENDLY

This hearty and delicious breakfast casserole combines the earthy flavors of spinach, mushrooms, and feta cheese. Not only is it a treat for the taste buds, but it's also beneficial during pregnancy due to its high content of folic acid (from spinach), protein, and essential B vitamins.

Preparation Time: 15 minutes
Cooking Time: 40-45 minutes
Total Time: 60 minutes
Serves: 4

Ingredients:
- 2 cups fresh spinach, packed
- 1 cup white button mushrooms, sliced
- 1/2 cup feta cheese, crumbled (pasteurized)
- 6 large eggs
- 3/4 cup whole milk
- 1/2 medium onion, diced
- 2 cloves garlic, minced
- Salt and pepper to taste
- 1 tablespoon olive oil

Instructions:
1. Preheat your oven to 350°F (175°C).
2. In a large pan, heat the olive oil over medium heat. Add the diced onions and sauté until translucent.
3. Add garlic and sauté for another minute.
4. Add the sliced mushrooms and cook until they release their water and start to brown, about 5-7 minutes.
5. Add the spinach and cook until wilted.
6. Season with salt and pepper, then remove from heat and set aside.
7. In a large mixing bowl, whisk together the eggs, milk, salt, and pepper. Stir in the crumbled feta.
8. Gently fold the spinach and mushroom mixture into the egg mixture.
9. Pour the mixture into a greased casserole dish.
10. Bake for 40-45 minutes, or until the top is golden brown and a knife inserted into the center comes out clean.

Chef's Notes:
- Add bacon or sausage for extra protein
- Add a variety of vegetables like asparagus, bell peppers, broccoli or kale for extra nutrients.
- Store any leftovers in an airtight container in the refrigerator for up to 3 days or in the freezer for up to a month.

Nutritional Information (per serving):
- Calories: 261kcal
- Total Fat: 17.1g
- Monounsaturated Fat: 6.89g
- Polyunsaturated Fat: 2.77g
- Total Carbohydrates: 10g
- Dietary Fiber: 1.5g
- Protein: 18.1g
- Sodium: 505.4mg
- Vitamin A: 238.4mcg
- Vitamin B6: .2mg
- Vitamin B12: .9mcg
- Vitamin C: 7.3mg
- Vitamin D: 2.3mcg
- Vitamin E: 1.9mg
- Vitamin K: 78.3mcg
- Folate: 74mcg
- Iron: 2.4mg
- Calcium: 284.4mg
- Magnesium: 32.8mg
- Zinc: 1.6mg

Quinoa Breakfast Bowl with Fresh Fruit and Nuts

MIX-AND-MATCH RECIPE

A nutrient-packed breakfast bowl that combines the protein-rich qualities of quinoa with the natural sweetness of fresh fruit and the crunch of nuts. This dish not only tantalizes your taste buds but also offers numerous health benefits for you and your baby, including B vitamins, fiber, protein and healthy fats.

Preparation Time: 10 minutes
Cooking Time: 15 minutes
Total Time: 25 minutes
Serves: 1

Ingredients:

- 1/4 cup quinoa (rinsed and drained)
- 1/2 cup unsweetened almond milk
- 1/4 cup fresh blueberries
- 1/4 cup diced mango
- 1/4 cup diced strawberries
- 2 chopped almonds
- 2 chopped walnuts
- 2 chopped pecans
- 1 tablespoon honey
- A pinch of salt
- A sprinkle of cinnamon

Instructions:

1. In a small pot, bring the water or almond milk to a boil. Add the rinsed quinoa and a pinch of salt. Reduce the heat to low and cover the pot.
2. Let it simmer for about 15 minutes or until the quinoa is cooked and the liquid is absorbed. Fluff with a fork.
3. While the quinoa is cooking, prepare the fruits by washing, peeling (if necessary), and dicing them.
4. Once the quinoa is ready, transfer it to a bowl.
5. Top with blueberries, mango, strawberries, and chopped nuts.
6. Drizzle with honey for added sweetness if desired. Sprinkle with a pinch of cinnamon for extra flavor.
7. Serve warm and enjoy your nutrient-packed breakfast!

Chef's Notes:

- Tropical Twist: Use coconut milk instead of water or almond milk, and top with diced pineapple, kiwi, and shredded coconut.
- Berry Delight: Add raspberries, blackberries, and a dollop of Greek yogurt or a vegan alternative.
- Nut Butter Drizzle: Instead of honey, drizzle with almond butter or peanut butter for extra protein and creaminess.
- Seed Boost: Sprinkle chia seeds, flax seeds, or hemp seeds for added fiber, protein, and Omega-3 fatty acids.

Nutritional Information (per serving):

- Calories: 502kcal
- Total Fat: 24.6g
- Monounsaturated Fat: 9.27g
- Polyunsaturated Fat: 11.79g
- Omega-3 Fatty Acids: 1.6g
- Total Carbohydrates: 65.6g
- Dietary Fiber: 8.4g
- Protein: 11.4g
- Sodium: 253.8mg
- Vitamin B6: .4mg
- Vitamin C: 43.5mg
- Vitamin D: 1.3mcg
- Vitamin E: 10.9mg
- Vitamin K: 10.8mcg
- Folate: 127.7mcg
- Iron: 3.6mg
- Calcium: 308.9mg
- Potassium: 637.4mg
- Phosphorus: 326mg
- Magnesium: 149.5mg
- Zinc: 2.7mg

Almond Butter and Banana Stuffed Whole Wheat Pancakes

VEGETARIAN

These whole wheat pancakes, stuffed with creamy almond butter and slices of fresh banana, offer a nourishing and delectable treat perfect for expectant mothers. Packed with essential nutrients, the combination of whole grains, protein, healthy fats, and potassium-rich bananas can be a beneficial addition to a pregnancy diet, supporting both the mother's health and baby's growth.

Preparation Time: 10 minutes
Cooking Time: 15 minutes
Total Time: 25 minutes
Serves: 1

Ingredients:

- 1/2 teaspoon baking powder
- A pinch of salt
- 1/4 cup whole milk
- 1/2 teaspoon pure vanilla extract
- 1 tablespoon coconut oil
- 2 tablespoons almond butter
- 1 ripe banana, thinly sliced

Instructions:

1. In a mixing bowl, combine the whole wheat flour, baking powder, and salt. Gradually add in the milk and vanilla extract, whisking until a smooth batter forms.
2. Heat a non-stick skillet or frying pan over medium heat. Add the coconut oil or butter and let it melt. Pour half of the batter into the pan, spreading it out into a round shape.
3. As the pancake starts to set around the edges but is still uncooked in the center, spread 1 tablespoon of almond butter evenly over half of the pancake. Place half of the banana slices on top of the almond butter.
4. Using a spatula, gently fold the other half of the pancake over the almond butter and banana side, creating a half-moon shape. Press down slightly to seal. Continue cooking until the pancake is golden brown on both sides and fully cooked in the center.
5. Remove the pancake from the pan and transfer it to a plate. Repeat with the remaining batter and fillings. Drizzle with a bit more almond butter or maple syrup, if desired. Serve warm.

Chef's Notes:

- For a non-dairy option, use any plant-based milk

Nutritional Information (per serving):

- Calories: 465kcal
- Total Fat: 33.6g
- Monounsaturated Fat: 11.78g
- Polyunsaturated Fat: 4.79g

- Total Carbohydrates: 36g
- Dietary Fiber: 6.4g
- Protein: 9.9g
- Sodium: 444.8mg
- Vitamin B6: .5mg
- Vitamin B12: .3mcg
- Vitamin C: 10.3mg
- Vitamin D: .8mcg
- Vitamin E: 7.9mg
- Folate: 43.6mcg
- Iron: 1.5mg
- Calcium: 186.1mg
- Potassium: 744.4mg
- Magnesium: 127.3mg
- Zinc: 1.5mg

Sweet Potato and Black Bean Breakfast Burrito

VEGAN

A savory and nutritious breakfast burrito that combines the earthiness of sweet potatoes with the richness of black beans, wrapped in a soft tortilla. This meal is not only delicious but is also packed with essential nutrients beneficial during pregnancy. Sweet potatoes are rich in vitamin A and fiber, while black beans offer protein and iron – all of which are important for the health and growth of your baby.

Preparation Time: 15 minutes
Cooking Time: 20 minutes
Total Time: 35 minutes
Serves: 1

Ingredients:
- 1 small sweet potato, peeled and diced
- 1/2 cup canned black beans, rinsed and drained
- 1 whole wheat tortilla
- 1 tbsp olive oil
- 1/4 tsp ground cumin
- 1/4 tsp paprika
- Salt and pepper to taste

Instructions:
1. In a medium-sized skillet, heat the olive oil over medium heat. Add the diced sweet potatoes and sauté until they start to soften, about 7-8 minutes.
2. Add the ground cumin, paprika, salt, and pepper to the skillet and mix well to coat the sweet potatoes. Continue to cook until they're fully softened and slightly golden.
3. Add the rinsed black beans to the skillet, mixing them in with the sweet potatoes. Cook for another 3-4 minutes until the beans are heated through.
4. Warm the tortilla in a dry skillet or microwave for about 10-15 seconds.
5. Lay out the warmed tortilla on a plate. In the center, layer the sweet potato and black bean mixture. Add desired toppings.
6. Fold in the sides of the tortilla and then roll it up from the bottom to make a burrito.

7. Serve immediately and enjoy your nutritious breakfast!

Chef's Notes:
- Add various toppings as desired such as green onion, cilantro, shredded cheese, salsa, guacamole or sour cream.
- Double the recipe and store extras in the refrigerator for another quick breakfast.

Nutritional Information (per serving):
- Calories: 449kcal
- Total Fat: 16.6g
- Monounsaturated Fat: 9.9g
- Polyunsaturated Fat: 1.7g
- Total Carbohydrates: 64.1g
- Dietary Fiber: 14.6g
- Protein: 12.7g
- Sodium: 242.9mg
- Vitamin A: 935.9mcg
- Vitamin B6: .3mg
- Vitamin C: 3.1mg
- Vitamin E: 3.2mg
- Vitamin K: 13.8mcg
- Folate: 142.7mcg
- Iron: 3.8mg
- Calcium: 148.9mg
- Magnesium: 93.7mg
- Zinc: 1.4mg

Mango and Greek Yogurt Smoothie with Ground Flaxseed

GLUTEN-FREE

This refreshing mango and Greek yogurt smoothie is a delightful blend of tropical sweetness and creamy texture, enriched with ground flaxseed. Ideal for pregnant women, it offers a bounty of nutrients that support both the you and your growing baby, such as Vitamins A, C and B6 for brain development and immunity, as well as protein and omega-3 fatty acids.

Preparation Time: 5 minutes
Cooking Time: 0minutes
Total Time: 5 minutes
Serves: 1

Ingredients:
- 1 ripe mango, peeled and pitted
- 1 banana
- 1/2 cup unsweetened Greek yogurt
- 1 tablespoon ground flaxseed
- 1/2 cup whole milk (adjust according to desired consistency)
- A few ice cubes (optional, for a chilled smoothie)

Instructions:
1. Begin by ensuring all your ingredients are at hand. Peel the banana and mango and remove its pit.

2. In a blender, combine the mango pieces, banana, Greek yogurt, ground flaxseed, and milk. If you'd like a chilled smoothie, you can add a few ice cubes too.
3. Blend on high until you achieve a smooth, creamy consistency.
4. Pour the smoothie into a glass and enjoy immediately.

Chef's Notes:
- Add additional fruit such as strawberries and/or pineapple for additional flavor and nutrients.
- Use any plant-based milk and yogurt for a dairy-free option.

Nutritional Information (per serving):
- Calories: 564kcal
- Total Fat: 16.4g
- Monounsaturated Fat: 4.53g
- Polyunsaturated Fat: 1.23g
- Total Carbohydrates: 91.3g
- Dietary Fiber: 10.7g
- Protein: 22.1g
- Sodium: 109.5mg
- Vitamin A: 243.9mcg
- Vitamin B6: 1mg
- Vitamin B12: 1.6mcg
- Vitamin C: 132.6mg
- Vitamin D: 1.6mcg
- Vitamin E: 3.2mg
- Vitamin K: 15.1mcg
- Folate: 181.3mcg
- Iron: 1.3mg
- Calcium: 344.6mg
- Magnesium: 93.3mg
- Zinc: 1.7mg

Zucchini and Carrot Breakfast Muffins

GLUTEN-FREE

These wholesome muffins are the perfect blend of natural sweetness and moisture from zucchini and carrots. Ideal for expectant mothers, they offer essential nutrients like vitamin C, vitamin A and fiber, making them a handy and delicious snack option during pregnancy.

Preparation Time: 15 minutes
Cooking Time: 25 minutes
Total Time: 40minutes
Serves: 12

Ingredients:
- 2 cups oat flour (ensure it's gluten-free if you're catering to gluten sensitivities)
- 1 1/2 tsp baking powder
- 1/2 tsp baking soda
- 1/4 tsp salt
- 1 tsp ground cinnamon
- 1/2 cup unsweetened applesauce
- 2 large eggs
- 1/3 cup honey
- 1 tsp vanilla extract
- 1/2 cup unsalted butter, melted
- 1 cup grated zucchini (water squeezed out)
- 1 cup grated carrot

Instructions:
1. Preheat your oven to 375°F (190°C) and line a 12-cup muffin tin with paper liners or lightly grease.
2. In a large bowl, combine oat flour, baking powder, baking soda, salt, and cinnamon.
3. In a separate bowl, whisk together the applesauce, eggs, honey, vanilla extract, and melted butter.
4. Pour the wet ingredients into the dry and mix until just combined.
5. Fold in the grated zucchini, grated carrot, and any optional ingredients.
6. Evenly divide the batter among the 12 muffin cups.
7. Bake in the preheated oven for about 22-25 minutes or until a toothpick inserted into the center of a muffin comes out clean.
8. Allow the muffins to cool in the tin for 5 minutes, then transfer them to a wire rack to cool completely.

Chef's Notes:
- Muffins can be stored in an airtight container at room temperature for up to 3 days. For longer storage, freeze in a sealed container or zip-top bag. To enjoy, thaw at room temperature or warm gently in the microwave or oven.
- Optional: Add 1/2 cup raisins, nuts, or dark chocolate chips

Nutritional Information (per serving):
- Calories: 154kcal
- Total Fat: 9g
- Monounsaturated Fat: 2.49g
- Polyunsaturated Fat: .45g
- Total Carbohydrates: 16.4g
- Dietary Fiber: 1.9g
- Protein: 2.5g
- Sodium: 244.8mg
- Vitamin A: 154.2mcg
- Vitamin C: 2.4mg
- Folate: 8.4mcg
- Iron: .6mg
- Potassium: 127mg

Smoked Salmon and Cream Cheese on Whole Rye Bread

HEARTH-HEALTHY

This sumptuous homemade rye bread, layered with smooth cream cheese and delicate smoked salmon, is both a treat for the taste buds and beneficial for expectant mothers. Rye bread, a powerhouse of essential nutrients like fiber, iron, magnesium and zinc, combined with omega-3 rich smoked salmon, makes it an especially nutritious option during pregnancy.

Bread

Preparation Time: 90 minutes (includes time for dough to rise)
Cooking Time: 30 minutes
Total Time: 120 minutes
Serves: 12

Slice with Salmon and Cream Cheese

Preparation Time: 5 minutes
Cooking Time: 0 minutes
Total Time: 5 minutes
Serves: 1

Rye Bread (makes 12 servings):

Ingredients:
- 1 1/2 cups rye flour
- 1 1/2 cups all-purpose flour
- 1 tbsp sugar
- 1 tsp salt
- 2 tsp active dry yeast
- 1 1/4 cups warm water (about 110°F)
- 2 tbsp olive oil
- 1 tbsp caraway seeds (optional for flavor)
- 2 tbsp cream cheese (for 1 serving)
- 3-4 slices of smoked salmon (for 1 serving)

Instructions:
1. In a large bowl, mix the active dry yeast with warm water. Let it sit for about 5 minutes until it becomes frothy.
2. Add rye flour, all-purpose flour, sugar, salt, and olive oil to the yeast mixture. If using, fold in the caraway seeds.
3. Knead the dough on a floured surface until it becomes smooth and elastic. This might take about 10-12 minutes.
4. Place the dough in a greased bowl, covering it with a clean towel. Let it rise in a warm place for 1.5 to 2 hours, or until it doubles in size.
5. Preheat the oven to 375°F (190°C).
6. Punch down the dough and shape it into a loaf. Place it in a greased loaf pan.
7. Bake for about 30 minutes or until the top is golden brown and the bread sounds hollow when tapped.
8. Remove from oven and let it cool on a wire rack.
9. When cooled, spread the cream cheese evenly over the slice of rye bread and layer with smoked salmon slices.

Chef's Notes:
- Add thin slices of red onion, capers, and fresh dill for garnish
- Rye Bread: Once cooled, store the bread in an airtight container at room temperature for up to 4 days. For longer shelf life, slice and freeze, then toast as needed.

Nutritional Information (per serving):
- Calories: 301kcal
- Total Fat: 15.3g
- Monounsaturated Fat: 5.01g
- Polyunsaturated Fat: 1.68g
- Omega-3 Fatty Acids: .58g
- Total Carbohydrates: 17.1g
- Dietary Fiber: 1.9g
- Protein: 22.7g
- Sodium: 952mg
- Vitamin A: 115.2mcg
- Vitamin B6: .3mg
- Vitamin B12: 3.3mcg
- Vitamin D: 17mcg
- Vitamin E: 1.7mg
- Folate: 39.8mcg
- Iron: 1.8mg
- Calcium: 62.4mg
- Potassium: 265.4mg
- Phosphorus: 234mg
- Magnesium: 33.3mg
- Zinc: .8mg

Pumpkin and Walnut Oatmeal Porridge

GLUTEN-FREE

A nourishing and delicious oatmeal porridge infused with the warm flavors of pumpkin and enhanced with the crunch of walnuts. This breakfast option is not only perfect for the autumn season but also brimming with nutrients beneficial for pregnant women. The pumpkin provides a good dose of beta-carotene, which is crucial for the baby's development, while the walnuts are a great source of omega-3 fatty acids and protein. Oats, on the other hand, are high in fiber, aiding digestion and helping to keep blood sugar levels stable.

Preparation Time: 5 minutes
Cooking Time: 10 minutes
Total Time: 15 minutes
Serves: 1

Ingredients:
- 1/2 cup gluten-free rolled oats
- 1 cup whole milk
- 1/4 cup pumpkin puree (can be store-bought or homemade)
- 1 tablespoon maple syrup
- 1/4 teaspoon pumpkin pie spice (or a pinch each of cinnamon, nutmeg, and cloves)
- A pinch of salt
- 2 tablespoons chopped walnuts

Instructions:

1. In a saucepan, combine the rolled oats and milk. Bring to a gentle boil over medium heat.
2. Once boiling, reduce heat to low and simmer. Stir occasionally to ensure the oats don't stick to the bottom.
3. As the oats begin to soften and the mixture thickens (about 5 minutes in), stir in the pumpkin puree, maple syrup, pumpkin pie spice, and a pinch of salt.
4. Continue to cook for another 3-5 minutes, or until the porridge reaches your desired consistency.
5. Once done, turn off the heat and transfer the oatmeal to a bowl.
6. Garnish with chopped walnuts.
7. Serve hot and enjoy your nutritious and flavorful breakfast!

Chef's Notes:

- Optional toppings: chia seeds, flaxseeds, or a dollop of yogurt
- Use any plant-based milk as a non-dairy option

Nutritional Information (per serving):

- Calories: 603kcal
- Total Fat: 19.8g
- Monounsaturated Fat: 4.26g
- Polyunsaturated Fat: 8.11g
- Omega-3 Fatty Acids: 1.46g
- Total Carbohydrates: 98.9g
- Dietary Fiber: 6.8g
- Protein: 15.5g
- Sodium: 155mg
- Vitamin A: 589mcg
- Vitamin B6: .2mg
- Vitamin B12: 1.1mcg
- Vitamin C: 2.9mg
- Vitamin D: 3.2mcg
- Vitamin K: 11mcg
- Folate: 33.4mcg
- Iron: 4.2mg
- Calcium: 388.4mg
- Potassium: 828.2mg
- Magnesium: 89.5mg
- Zinc: 1.5mg

Chicken and Apple Breakfast Sausages

KID FRIENDLY

These savory-sweet breakfast sausages blend the lean protein of chicken with the natural sweetness of apples. Perfect for expectant mothers, the combination provides essential nutrients needed during pregnancy, such as protein for muscle and tissue development and apples for dietary fiber and essential vitamins. Plus, it's an easy and delicious way to start the day!

Preparation Time: 10 minutes
Cooking Time: 10 minutes
Total Time: 20 minutes
Serves: 10

Ingredients:

- 1 pound ground chicken breast (ensure it's of good quality and free from additives)
- 2 medium apples, grated
- 1 tsp salt (or to taste)
- 1/3 tsp black pepper
- 1/3 tsp dried sage (or fresh if available)
- 1/3 tsp dried thyme (or fresh if available)
- A pinch of nutmeg
- 4 tsp olive oil

Instructions:

1. In a mixing bowl, combine the ground chicken, grated apple, salt, pepper, sage, thyme, and nutmeg. Mix well until all ingredients are well combined.
2. Shape the mixture into 8-10 sausage patties (depending on your preferred size).
3. Heat oil in a non-stick skillet over medium heat. Once hot, add the sausage patties.
4. Cook for about 4-5 minutes on each side or until they are golden brown and fully cooked through.
5. Remove from heat and drain on a paper towel if necessary.
6. Serve immediately with your favorite breakfast sides or store in an airtight container in the refrigerator for up to 3 days.

Chef's Notes:

- You can make a batch ahead of time, cook them, and store in the refrigerator for up to 3 days or freezer up to a month.
- Add an egg, side salad or serving of fruit on the side
- When you're ready to eat, just heat them in a skillet or microwave for a quick and nutritious breakfast.

Nutritional Information (per serving):

- Calories: 232kcal
- Total Fat: 11.9g
- Monounsaturated Fat: 3.3g
- Polyunsaturated Fat: .53g
- Total Carbohydrates: 12.9g
- Dietary Fiber: 2.3g
- Protein: 19g
- Sodium: 649.5mg
- Vitamin C: 4.4mg

Satisfying Lunches and Dinners

Lamb Koftas with Cucumber Yogurt Sauce

GLUTEN-FREE

These succulent lamb koftas paired with a refreshing yogurt cucumber sauce offer a flavorful Middle Eastern touch to your meal. They are not only delicious but also packed with essential nutrients like protein and iron, making them a wonderful choice for pregnant individuals. Consuming iron-rich foods like lamb can help combat iron-deficiency anemia that some expectant mothers may experience, while the yogurt serves as a source of calcium and probiotics.

Preparation Time: 10 minutes

Preparation Time: 20 minutes
Cooking Time: 10 minutes
Total Time: 30 minutes
Serves: 2

Ingredients:

For the Lamb Koftas:
- 250g ground lamb
- 1 small onion, finely grated or minced
- 1 garlic clove, minced
- 2 tbsp fresh parsley, chopped
- 2 tbsp fresh coriander, chopped
- 1/2 tsp ground cumin
- 1/2 tsp ground coriander
- 1/4 tsp ground cinnamon
- 1/4 tsp cayenne pepper (can omit if you cannot tolerate spice)
- Salt and black pepper to taste
- 1 tbsp olive oil (for cooking)

For the Yogurt Cucumber Dipping Sauce:
- 1/2 cup plain Greek yogurt
- 1/2 cucumber, finely diced
- 1 garlic clove, minced
- 1 tbsp fresh mint, chopped
- 1 tbsp fresh dill, chopped
- Salt and pepper to taste
- 1 tsp lemon juice

Instructions:
1. In a large mixing bowl, combine ground lamb, grated onion, minced garlic, parsley, coriander, ground cumin, ground coriander, ground cinnamon, cayenne pepper, salt, and black pepper.
2. Mix until well combined. Divide the mixture into 4 equal portions and mold each into an oval shape.:
3. Heat the olive oil in a frying pan over medium-high heat.
4. Place the koftas in the pan and cook for about 4-5 minutes on each side or until they are browned and cooked through.

5. In a bowl, combine Greek yogurt, finely diced cucumber, minced garlic, fresh mint, fresh dill, and lemon juice if using. Season with salt and pepper to taste and mix well.
6. Chill in the refrigerator for a few minutes before serving.
7. Place the lamb koftas on a serving plate and accompany with the chilled yogurt cucumber sauce.

Chef's Notes:
- Serve with a side salad
- Use non-dairy yogurt if desired

Nutritional Information (per serving):
- Calories: 659kcal
- Total Fat: 40 g
- Monounsaturated Fat: 9.9g
- Polyunsaturated Fat: 1.8g
- Total Carbohydrates: 19g
- Dietary Fiber: 3.5g
- Protein:40.9 g
- Sodium: 305.3mg
- Vitamin B6: .2mg
- Vitamin B12: 1.5mcg
- Vitamin C: 14.4mg
- Vitamin E: 1.1mg
- Vitamin K: 79.2mcg
- Folate: 29.6mcg
- Iron: 3.7mg
- Calcium: 298.2mg
- Magnesium: 55.mg
- Zinc: 1.6mg

Turkey and Cranberry Stuffed Acorn Squash

GLUTEN-FREE

A delightful and wholesome dish, this stuffed acorn squash is filled with a savory mixture of turkey and cranberries, offering a perfect balance of flavors. It's a great source of lean protein, dietary fiber, vitamins, and essential nutrients. Acorn squash is rich in folic acid which is vital during pregnancy to prevent neural tube defects. Turkey is a lean source of protein and essential amino acids. The cranberries provide vitamin C and antioxidants which are beneficial for both you and your baby.

Preparation Time: 15 minutes
Cooking Time: 50 minutes
Total Time: 65 minutes
Serves: 2

Ingredients:
- 1 acorn squash, halved and seeds removed
- 1/2 lb ground turkey
- 1/2 cup cranberries, fresh or dried
- 1/4 cup onions, finely chopped
- 1 clove garlic, minced
- 1 tsp fresh rosemary, finely chopped
- 1/2 tsp salt
- 1/4 tsp black pepper
- 2 tbsp olive oil

- 1/4 cup feta cheese

Instructions:
1. Preheat the oven to 375°F (190°C).
2. Rub the cut sides of the acorn squash with 1 tablespoon of olive oil. Place them cut side down on a baking sheet lined with parchment paper or a silicone baking mat.
3. Baking the Squash: Bake the acorn squash in the preheated oven for about 25-30 minutes, or until it's tender but still holding its shape.
4. While the squash is baking, heat the remaining olive oil in a skillet over medium heat. Add onions and garlic and sauté until translucent. Add ground turkey, breaking it apart with a spatula, and cook until browned and fully cooked through.
5. Stir in cranberries, rosemary, salt, and pepper, and cook for another 3-4 minutes. If you're using dried cranberries, you might want to add a splash of water to help them rehydrate slightly.
6. Remove from heat and mix until everything is well combined.
7. Once the acorn squash halves are done baking, flip them over so the cut side faces up. Fill each half with the turkey and cranberry mixture. If you're using cheese, sprinkle it on top.
8. Return the stuffed acorn squash halves to the oven and bake for an additional 10-15 minutes, or until the tops are golden and the cheese has melted.
9. Let the stuffed squash sit for a few minutes before serving. Enjoy!

Chef's Notes:
- Pair with a side salad or steamed green vegetables such as broccoli or asparagus
- Can add sauteed kale or spinach in the bowl if desired for additional nutrients
- For a vegetarian option, use lentils or quinoa instead of turkey

Nutritional Information (per serving):
- Calories: 441kcal
- Total Fat: 25.1g
- Monounsaturated Fat: 13.42g
- Polyunsaturated Fat: 4.12g
- Total Carbohydrates: 31.9g
- Dietary Fiber: 5.6g
- Protein: 26.3g
- Sodium: 211.4mg
- Vitamin A: 78.6mcg
- Vitamin B6: 1.1mg
- Vitamin B12: 1.3mcg
- Vitamin C: 33.4mg
- Vitamin E: 2.8mg
- Vitamin K: 11.2mcg
- Folate: 53.2mcg
- Iron: 3.1mg
- Calcium: 164.8mg
- Potassium: 1105.7mg
- Phosphorus: 359.2mg
- Magnesium: 103.3mg

- Zinc: 3.4mg

Pork Loin with Apple Cider Glaze and Roasted Parsnips

GLUTEN-FREE

A sumptuous, nutrient-packed meal that combines the rich flavors of pork with a tangy apple cider glaze and the sweet earthiness of roasted parsnips. This dish is not only delightful to the palate but also offers essential nutrients beneficial for pregnant individuals, such as protein from the pork and fiber and folic acid from the parsnips.

Preparation Time: 15 minutes
Cooking Time: 50 minutes
Total Time: 65 minutes
Serves: 2

Ingredients:
- 1 lb Pork loin
- 1 cup Apple cider
- 2 tbsp Brown sugar
- 1 tbsp Dijon mustard
- 4 medium-sized parsnips, peeled and sliced into even chunks
- 2 tbsp olive oil
- Salt and pepper to taste

Instructions:
1. Preheat the oven to 375°F (190°C).
2. Season the pork loin generously with salt and pepper on all sides.
3. In a hot skillet or oven-proof pan, add 1 tablespoon of olive oil. Sear the pork loin on all sides until golden brown (around 3-4 minutes per side). Remove from heat and set aside.
4. In a small saucepan, combine the apple cider, brown sugar, Dijon mustard, and chopped rosemary.
5. Bring the mixture to a boil, then reduce heat and simmer for about 10 minutes, or until the mixture has reduced by half and has a syrupy consistency.
6. Brush the pork loin generously with half of the glaze.
7. Toss the parsnip batons in 1 tablespoon of olive oil, salt, and pepper.
8. Spread them out on a baking sheet, ensuring they are not overcrowded.
9. Place the pork loin and the baking sheet with parsnips into the preheated oven.
10. Roast the pork for about 25-30 minutes or until the internal temperature reaches at least 145°F (63°C) for medium rare or 160°F (71°C) for more well-done. Remember, cooking times might vary based on the thickness of the loin.
11. Roast the parsnips for approximately 25-30 minutes, turning them once or twice, until they are tender and golden brown.
12. Once the pork is done, remove from the oven and let it rest for at least 5 minutes. Then, slice the pork loin.

13. Place slices of pork loin on plates and drizzle with the remaining apple cider glaze. Accompany with the roasted parsnips.
14. Garnish with additional fresh rosemary if desired.

Chef's Notes:
- You can also add roasted apples or a side salad to enhance the meal and add more nutrients.
- Garnish with fresh rosemary if desired

Nutritional Information (per serving):
- Calories: 928kcal
- Total Fat: 42g
- Monounsaturated Fat: 22.47g
- Polyunsaturated Fat: 3.95g
- Total Carbohydrates: 80.6g
- Dietary Fiber: 12g
- Protein: 58.3g
- Sodium: 254.7mg
- Vitamin B6: 1.2mg
- Vitamin B12: 1.4mcg
- Vitamin C: 43.4mg
- Vitamin D: 2.6mcg
- Vitamin E: 5.7mg
- Vitamin K: 11.3mcg
- Folate: 195.5mcg
- Iron: 3.8mg
- Calcium: 181.7mg
- Magnesium: 148.3mg
- Zinc: 5.6mg

Sesame Chicken Stir-Fry with Baby Corn and Snow Peas

GLUTEN-FREE

A vibrant and nutritious stir fry that combines the succulence of chicken with the crunch of snow peas and baby corn, all tossed in a delicious sesame sauce. This dish is not only packed with flavors but also with nutrients such as vitamin c, protein, fiber, magnesium and calcium.

Preparation Time: 20 minutes
Cooking Time: 45 minutes
Total Time: 65 minutes
Serves: 4

Ingredients:
- 1 cup brown rice
- 2.5 cups chicken broth
- 1 lb (450g) boneless, skinless chicken breasts, thinly sliced
- 1 cup snow peas, trimmed
- 1/2 cup baby corn, sliced in half
- 1/2 cup broccoli, chopped
- 1/2 cup sliced carrots
- 3 tbsp sesame oil, divided
- 2 tbsp soy sauce
- 1 tbsp hoisin sauce
- 1 tbsp rice vinegar
- 2 garlic cloves, minced
- 1 tsp ginger, grated
- 1 tbsp toasted sesame seeds
- 2 green onions, thinly sliced (for garnish)
- Salt and pepper, to taste

Instructions:
1. Start by cooking the brown rice. In a saucepan, bring the water or chicken broth to a boil. Add the rice and a pinch of salt (omit if using broth). Reduce heat to low, cover, and let simmer for 35-40 minutes or until the rice is tender and water is absorbed. Remove from heat and let it stand covered for 5 minutes, then fluff with a fork.
2. While the rice is cooking, whisk together soy sauce, hoisin sauce, rice vinegar, minced garlic, and ginger in a medium bowl. Set aside.
3. In a large skillet or wok, heat 2 tablespoons of sesame oil over medium-high heat. Add the chicken slices, seasoning with a pinch of salt and pepper. Cook until the chicken is browned and cooked through, about 4-6 minutes. Remove chicken from the pan and set aside.
4. In the same pan, add the remaining 1 tablespoon of sesame oil. Stir in the snow peas, broccoli, carrots and baby corn. Cook for 2-3 minutes, or until the vegetables are slightly tender but still maintain a crunch.
5. Return the chicken to the pan. Pour the sauce over the chicken and vegetables, stirring to coat evenly. Cook for another 2-3 minutes until everything is heated through.
6. Remove from heat and sprinkle with toasted sesame seeds and sliced green onions.
7. Serve the stir fry over the cooked brown rice.

Chef's Notes:
- Store leftovers in an airtight container in the refrigerator for up to 3 days.
- For longer storage, you can freeze the stir fry in a freezer-safe container for up to 1 month. However, the texture of the vegetables might change slightly upon reheating.
- To reheat, thaw in the refrigerator overnight (if frozen) and warm in a skillet over medium heat until heated through.
- Add any additional vegetables to your liking
- Use cauliflower rice or quinoa instead of brown rice if desired.

Nutritional Information (per serving):
- Calories: 372kcal
- Total Fat: 15.1g
- Monounsaturated Fat: 5.45g
- Polyunsaturated Fat: 5.56g
- Total Carbohydrates: 27.8g
- Dietary Fiber: 4.8g
- Protein: 30.2g
- Sodium: 733.4mg
- Vitamin A: 545.8mg
- Vitamin B6: 1.2mg
- Vitamin B12: .2mcg
- Vitamin C: 55.6mg
- Vitamin E: 1.7mg

- Vitamin K: 75.3mcg
- Folate: 70.4mcg
- Iron: 2.1mg
- Calcium: 87.5mg
- Magnesium: 87.9mg
- Zinc: 1.8mg

Herbed Beef Skewers with Chimichurri and Roasted Sweet Potatoes

GLUTEN-FREE

Succulent beef skewers marinated in fresh herbs are paired with vibrant chimichurri sauce and comforting roasted sweet potatoes. This dish is not only a delight for the taste buds but also packed with nutrients beneficial for pregnancy, such as protein from the beef, vitamin C from the herbs and vegetables, and beta-carotene from sweet potatoes.

Preparation Time: 30 minutes
Cooking Time: 30 minutes
Total Time: 60 minutes
Serves: 2

Ingredients:

For the Beef Skewers:
- 3/4 pounds beef (preferably sirloin or tenderloin), cut into 1-inch cubes
- 2 garlic cloves, minced
- 1 tsp rosemary, finely chopped
- 1 tsp thyme, finely chopped
- 1 tsp oregano, finely chopped
- 2 tbsp olive oil
- Salt and pepper to taste

For the Chimichurri:
- 1 cup fresh parsley, finely chopped
- 4 garlic cloves, minced
- 2 tbsp fresh oregano, chopped
- 1/4 cup red wine vinegar
- 1/2 cup extra virgin olive oil
- Salt and pepper to taste
- A pinch of red pepper flakes (optional)

For the Roasted Sweet Potatoes:
- 2 medium sweet potatoes, peeled and diced
- 2 tbsp olive oil
- Salt and pepper to taste
- 1/2 tsp paprika

Instructions:

Marinate the Beef: In a bowl, combine beef cubes, minced garlic, rosemary, thyme, oregano, olive oil, salt, and pepper. Toss well to coat and let it marinate for at least 20 minutes (or overnight for better flavor).

Prepare the Chimichurri: In a mixing bowl, combine parsley, garlic, oregano, red wine vinegar, olive oil, salt, pepper, and red pepper flakes (if using). Mix well and set aside.

Roast the Sweet Potatoes: Preheat the oven to 400°F (200°C). Toss the sweet potatoes in olive oil, salt, pepper, and paprika. Spread them on a baking sheet in a single layer. Roast for 25-30 minutes or until tender, turning them halfway through.

Grill the Beef Skewers: Preheat the grill or grill pan over medium-high heat. Thread the marinated beef cubes onto skewers. Grill for 2-3 minutes on each side or until they reach your desired level of doneness.

Serve: Place the beef skewers on plates, drizzle with chimichurri sauce, and serve alongside roasted sweet potatoes.

Chef's Notes

- For additional nutrients, serve with a side salad, or alternate vegetables in between the beef on the skewers. Some ideas are bell peppers, mushrooms and zucchini.

Nutritional Information (per serving):
- Calories: 1065kcal
- Total Fat: 91.1g
- Monounsaturated Fat: 59.23g
- Polyunsaturated Fat: 8.77g
- Total Carbohydrates: 30.2g
- Dietary Fiber: 6g
- Protein: 37.5g
- Sodium: 129.7mg
- Vitamin A: 1238.7mcg
- Vitamin B6: .5mg
- Vitamin C: 65.7mg
- Vitamin E: 13.1mg
- Vitamin K: 558.8mcg
- Folate: 58.6mcg
- Iron: 8.3mg
- Calcium: 155.7mg
- Potassium: 1209.1mg
- Magnesium: 54.2mg
- Zinc: .9mg

Shrimp and Pineapple Curry over Coconut Rice

GLUTEN-FREE

A delightful blend of juicy shrimp and sweet pineapples, this curry takes you on a tropical culinary journey. The coconut rice complements the flavors perfectly, creating a balance of sweetness and savory goodness. This meal is not only delicious but also beneficial for pregnancy, providing a good balance of proteins, vitamins, and minerals such as omega-3 fatty acids and vitamin C.

Preparation Time: 15 minutes
Cooking Time: 30 minutes
Total Time: 45 minutes
Serves: 4

Ingredients:

- 2 cups Shrimp (peeled and deveined)
- 1 cup Pineapple (chopped into bite-sized pieces)
- 1/2 Red bell pepper (chopped)
- 1 large Onion (finely chopped)
- 3 cloves Garlic (minced)
- 1 inch Ginger (minced)
- 2 teaspoons Curry powder
- 1/2 teaspoon Turmeric powder
- 1/2 teaspoon Chili powder
- 1 can (400 ml) Coconut milk
- 2 tablespoons coconut oil
- Fresh cilantro – for garnish
- Salt to taste

For the Rice:

- 1/2 cup jasmine rice
- 1/2 cup full fat coconut milk
- 1/4 cup water
- Salt to taste

Instructions:

1. Prepare all vegetables
2. Wash the rice thoroughly and drain.
3. In a pot, combine rice, coconut milk, water, and salt.
4. Bring the mixture to a boil, then reduce the heat to low, cover, and let it simmer for about 15-20 minutes or until the rice is cooked through and all the liquid has been absorbed.
5. Fluff the rice with a fork.
6. While the rice is cooking, cook the shrimp and vegetables. Heat oil in a large skillet over medium heat. Add onions and sauté until translucent.
7. Add ginger and garlic, and sauté for another 2 minutes.
8. Add curry powder, turmeric powder, and chili powder. Cook for 1-2 minutes until fragrant.
9. Add coconut milk and let it simmer for about 5 minutes.
10. Add shrimp and pineapple pieces. Cook for another 5-7 minutes or until the shrimp turns pink.
11. Adjust salt and seasoning to taste.
12. Divide rice between bowls and top with curry.
13. Garnish with fresh cilantro before serving.

Chef's Notes:

- Store the shrimp and pineapple curry and coconut rice in separate airtight containers. Refrigerate for up to 2 days. While reheating, ensure the shrimp curry is heated thoroughly.
- The curry and rice can also be frozen for up to a month. Thaw in the refrigerator before reheating.
- Use tofu instead of shrimp for a vegetarian option.

Nutritional Information (per serving):

- Calories: 1680kcal
- Total Fat: 137g
- Monounsaturated Fat: 15.69g
- Polyunsaturated Fat: 31.92g
- Omega-3 Fatty Acids: 4.19g
- Total Carbohydrates: 92.2g
- Dietary Fiber: 11.7g
- Protein: 43.9g
- Sodium: 1345.4mg
- Vitamin A: 856.7mcg
- Vitamin B6: 2.5mg
- Vitamin B12: 2.1mcg
- Vitamin C: 889.9mg
- Vitamin E: 19.6mg
- Vitamin K: 95.6mcg
- Folate: 97.5mcg
- Iron: 13mg
- Calcium: 230.4mg
- Magnesium: 254.7mg
- Zinc: 4.7mg

Grilled Swordfish with Avocado Mango Salsa

GLUTEN-FREE

A light and refreshing dish perfect for a summer evening, this grilled swordfish is paired beautifully with a fruity, spicy salsa. The combination of omega-3 fatty acids from the swordfish and the vitamins A, C, E and potassium from the fruits make it especially beneficial for pregnancy.

Preparation Time: 20 minutes
Cooking Time: 10 minutes
Total Time: 30 minutes
Serves: 2

Ingredients:

Swordfish:

- 2 swordfish steaks
- 1 tbsp olive oil
- Salt and pepper to taste
- 1 lemon, zest and juice

Avocado Mango Salsa:

- 1 ripe mango, peeled and diced
- 1 ripe avocado, peeled, pitted, and diced
- 1 small red onion, finely chopped

- 1 jalapeño, seeded and minced (adjust to your heat preference)
- 1/4 cup fresh cilantro, chopped
- Juice of 1 lime
- Salt and pepper to taste

Instructions:

1. In a mixing bowl, combine the mango, avocado, red onion, jalapeño, cilantro, and lime juice. Season with salt and pepper to taste. Mix gently to combine and set aside to allow the flavors to meld.
2. Heat your grill to medium-high heat. While it's heating, drizzle the swordfish steaks with olive oil, lemon zest, lemon juice, salt, and pepper.
3. Once the grill is hot, place the swordfish steaks on the grill. Cook for about 4-5 minutes per side or until the fish is opaque and easily flakes with a fork.
4. Place the grilled swordfish on plates and top with a generous amount of the avocado mango salsa. Serve immediately.

Chef's Notes:

- Serve with a side salad or steamed vegetables such as broccoli or asparagus. Can also include quinoa.

Nutritional Information (per serving):

- Calories: 539kcal
- Total Fat: 30.8g
- Monounsaturated Fat: 18.79g
- Polyunsaturated Fat: 4.16g
- Omega-3 fatty acids: 1.41g
- Total Carbohydrates: 43.8g
- Dietary Fiber: 12g
- Protein: 29.3g
- Sodium: 270.5mg
- Vitamin A: 154.8mcg
- Vitamin B6: 1.2mg
- Vitamin B12: 1.7mcg
- Vitamin C: 107.8mg
- Vitamin D: 17.6mcg
- Vitamin E: 7.5mg
- Vitamin K: 40.2mcg
- Folate: 171.4mcg
- Iron: 1.8mg
- Calcium: 65.9mg
- Potassium: 1451.8mg
- Phosphorus: 421.6mg
- Magnesium: 92.4mg
- Zinc: 1.8mg

Red Snapper in Parchment with Leeks and Cherry Tomatoes

GLUTEN-FREE

This delicate and delicious dish steams red snapper inside parchment paper along with leeks and cherry tomatoes. Not only is this method simple and quick, but it also preserves the nutrients and flavors of the ingredients, making it an excellent choice during pregnancy. The dish is rich in omega-3 fatty acids, lean protein, and essential vitamins like folate and vitamin C.

Preparation Time: 15 minutes
Cooking Time: 20 minutes
Total Time: 35 minutes
Serves: 2

Ingredients:

- 2 red snapper fillets, boneless and skinless
- 1 leek, white and pale green parts only, washed thoroughly and thinly sliced
- 1 cup cherry tomatoes, halved
- 2 cloves garlic, minced
- 2 tablespoons fresh lemon juice
- 2 tablespoons olive oil
- 2 teaspoons fresh dill or parsley, chopped (optional)
- Salt and pepper, to taste

Instructions:

1. Preheat your oven to 375°F (190°C).
2. Cut two large pieces of parchment paper, each big enough to fold over and encase a snapper fillet.
3. On one half of each piece of parchment, place half of the sliced leeks. Place a snapper fillet on top of the leeks. Season the fish with salt, pepper, and half of the minced garlic. Scatter half of the cherry tomatoes over each fillet and drizzle with olive oil and lemon juice. If desired, sprinkle some fresh dill or parsley over the top.
4. Fold the other half of the parchment over the fish and crimp the edges to seal, creating a half-moon shape. Make sure the pouches are sealed well to prevent steam from escaping.
5. Place the parchment packets on a baking sheet and bake in the preheated oven for about 15-20 minutes, or until the fish is cooked through and flakes easily with a fork.
6. Carefully open the parchment (be cautious of the hot steam), and transfer the fish and vegetables to plates. Pour the flavorful juices over the top before serving.

Chef's Notes/Side Options:

- Quinoa Salad: Quinoa is a good source of protein and fiber. Toss cooked quinoa with chopped vegetables and a lemon vinaigrette for a refreshing side.
- Steamed Asparagus: A simple and nutritious side that can be quickly steamed and seasoned with salt, pepper, and a drizzle of olive oil.
- Mashed Sweet Potatoes: Sweet potatoes are rich in beta-carotene, vitamin C, and fiber, making them an excellent side for pregnant individuals.

Nutritional Information (per serving):
- Calories: 403kcal
- Total Fat: 16.6g
- Monounsaturated Fat: 10.4g
- Polyunsaturated Fat: 2.5g
- Omega-3 fatty acids: .73g
- Total Carbohydrates: 14.1g
- Dietary Fiber: 2.9g
- Protein: 47.6g
- Sodium: 336.2mg
- Vitamin A: 96.4mcg
- Vitamin B6: .9mg
- Vitamin B12: 6mcg
- Vitamin C: 24.9mg
- Vitamin E: 2.4mg
- Vitamin K: 29.1mcg
- Folate: 41.1mcg
- Iron: 2.9mg
- Calcium: 140.9mg
- Magnesium: 76.8mg
- Zinc: .8mg

Smoked Mackerel Salad with Pickled Beets and Horseradish Cream

SO FAST!

This vibrant and flavorful salad combines the smoky richness of mackerel with the tangy punch of pickled beets and the zesty kick of horseradish cream. Perfect for a light lunch or as a refreshing appetizer, it's also packed with nutrients beneficial during pregnancy such as folic acid, omega-3 fatty acids and folic acid.

Preparation Time: 15 minutes
Cooking Time: 0 minutes
Total Time: 15 minutes
Serves: 2

Ingredients:
- 2 smoked mackerel fillets, skin removed and flaked
- 4 small pickled beets, sliced
- 2 cups mixed salad greens (e.g., arugula, spinach, frisée)
- 2 tbsp chopped fresh dill
- Salt and pepper, to taste

For the Horseradish Cream:
- 1/4 cup full fat sour cream
- 1-2 tbsp prepared horseradish (adjust to taste)
- 1 tbsp lemon juice
- Salt, to taste

Instructions:
1. In a small bowl, mix together the sour cream (or crème fraiche), horseradish, lemon juice, and a pinch of salt. Adjust seasoning according to your preference. Set aside.
2. In a large mixing bowl, gently toss the flaked mackerel, pickled beet slices, salad greens, and fresh dill. Season lightly with salt and pepper.

3. Plate the salad on two individual plates. Generously drizzle with the horseradish cream.
4. Optional: Garnish with extra dill or other fresh herbs of your choice.

Chef's Notes:
- Additional salad additions can include avocado slices, walnuts, almonds, hard-boiled eggs, or feta cheese.: For

Nutritional Information (per serving):
- Calories: 525kcal
- Total Fat: 24.3g
- Monounsaturated Fat: 7.57g
- Polyunsaturated Fat: 4.91g
- Omega-3 fatty acids: 3.76g
- Total Carbohydrates: 20.2g
- Dietary Fiber: 4.8g
- Protein: 55.2g
- Sodium: 986.8mg
- Vitamin A: 80.4mcg
- Vitamin B6: .8mg
- Vitamin B12: 7.9mcg
- Vitamin C: 11mg
- Vitamin D: 21.2mcg
- Vitamin E: 2.5mg
- Folate: 29.1mcg
- Iron: 7.1mg
- Calcium: 215.5mg
- Potassium: 1785.9mg
- Magnesium: 82.5mg
- Zinc: 1.9mg

Chard and Ricotta-Stuffed Cannelloni with Marinara

VEGETARIAN

A comforting Italian classic, this dish is packed with leafy greens and creamy ricotta, making it perfect for anyone, especially expectant mothers. Chard offers essential vitamins such as A, C and K, while ricotta cheese provides calcium and protein. Enjoy a plateful of health, flavor, and warmth.

Preparation Time: 30 minutes
Cooking Time: 40 minutes
Total Time: 70 minutes
Serves: 8

Ingredients:

For the Cannelloni Filling:
- 2 tbsp olive oil
- 1 large onion, finely chopped
- 3 garlic cloves, minced
- 1 large bunch of chard, stems removed and chopped
- 2 cups ricotta cheese
- 1 cup grated Parmesan cheese
- 1 egg
- Salt and pepper, to taste

For the Marinara Sauce:
- 2 tbsp olive oil
- 1 small onion, finely chopped
- 2 garlic cloves, minced
- 1 can (28 oz.) crushed tomatoes
- 2 tsp dried basil
- 1 tsp dried oregano
- Salt and pepper, to taste
- 1/4 cup fresh basil, chopped

Other:
- 16 cannelloni tubes
- 1 cup mozzarella cheese, shredded

Instructions:
1. In a large skillet, heat olive oil over medium heat. Add onions and garlic and sauté until translucent. Add chard and cook until wilted. Allow to cool slightly. In a mixing bowl, combine the chard mixture, ricotta cheese, Parmesan, egg, salt, and pepper.
2. In a pot, heat olive oil and sauté onion and garlic until translucent. Add crushed tomatoes, dried basil, oregano, salt, and pepper. Allow the sauce to simmer for 20 minutes. If desired, add sugar for a touch of sweetness. Stir in fresh basil just before turning off the heat.
3. Preheat oven to 375°F (190°C). Fill each cannelloni tube with the chard and ricotta mixture.
4. Spread a thin layer of marinara sauce at the bottom of a large baking dish. Place the stuffed cannelloni on top. Pour the remaining marinara sauce over the cannelloni and sprinkle with mozzarella cheese.
5. Place the dish in the oven and bake for 30-40 minutes, or until the cheese is bubbly and golden brown.
6. Allow to cool slightly before serving. Garnish with fresh basil or grated Parmesan if desired.

Storage Options:
- Refrigerate: Store leftovers in an airtight container for up to 3 days.
- Freeze: Once cooled, place in a freezer-safe container. Label with the date and freeze for up to 2 months. When ready to eat, thaw in the refrigerator overnight and reheat in the oven.
- Serve with a side salad
- For less prep time, use jarred marinara sauce

Nutritional Information (per serving):
- Calories: 747kcal
- Total Fat: 44.3g
- Monounsaturated Fat: 10.2g
- Polyunsaturated Fat: 1.66g
- Total Carbohydrates: 51.9g
- Dietary Fiber: 4.9g
- Protein: 36.7g
- Sodium: 1344.1mg
- Vitamin A: 288.8mcg
- Vitamin B6: .2mg
- Vitamin B12: 1.1mcg
- Vitamin C: 26.5mg
- Vitamin E: 2.5mg
- Vitamin K: 412.4mcg
- Folate: 20.3mcg
- Iron: 4.1mg
- Calcium: 743mg
- Magnesium: 64.1mg
- Zinc: 1.6mg

Falafel Bowl with Hummus and Tzatziki

VEGETARIAN
A nutrient-rich, Middle Eastern-inspired bowl combining the hearty flavors of falafel with the wholesome goodness of quinoa, vibrant vegetables, creamy hummus, and refreshing tzatziki. This bowl is perfect for pregnant women, providing essential nutrients like protein, fiber, iron, folic acid, and calcium, all crucial for a healthy pregnancy. The diversity of ingredients also ensures a range of vitamins and minerals beneficial for both you and your baby.

Preparation Time: 25 minutes
Cooking Time: 25 minutes
Total Time: 50 minutes
Serves: 2

Ingredients:
For the Falafel:
- 1 can (15 oz.) chickpeas, drained and rinsed
- 1/4 cup fresh parsley, chopped
- 2 garlic cloves, minced
- 1 tsp ground cumin
- 1 tsp ground coriander
- Salt and pepper, to taste
- 2 tbsp olive oil (for frying)
For the Bowl:
- 1 cup quinoa
- 2 cups vegetable broth
- 1/4cup sliced cucumber
- 1/4 cup cherry tomatoes
- 1/2 cup hummus
- 1/2 cup tzatziki

Instructions:
1. In a food processor, combine chickpeas, parsley, garlic, cumin, coriander, salt, and pepper. Process until smooth.
2. Shape the mixture into small patties.
3. Heat olive oil in a skillet over medium heat. Fry the falafel patties for 2-3 minutes on each side or until golden brown. Remove and set aside.
4. Rinse quinoa under cold water until water runs clear.
5. In a pot, combine quinoa and water (or broth). Bring to a boil, then reduce heat, cover, and simmer for 15-20 minutes or until quinoa is cooked and fluffy.
6. Divide quinoa between two bowls.
7. Arrange falafel patties on top of the quinoa.
8. Add the assorted vegetables around the falafel.
9. Dollop hummus and tzatziki on the side or drizzle over the top.

Chef's Notes:
- Add sliced avocados or guacamole for healthy fats.
- Add feta cheese or olives for a Mediterranean touch

Nutritional Information (per serving):
- Calories: 1154kcal
- Total Fat: 50.5g
- Monounsaturated Fat: 9.63g
- Polyunsaturated Fat: 8.96g
- Total Carbohydrates: 136.2g
- Dietary Fiber: 40.1g
- Protein: 37.6g
- Sodium: 1467.8mg
- Vitamin A: 61.6mcg
- Vitamin B6: .6mg
- Vitamin C: 25.7mg
- Vitamin E: 4.1mg
- Vitamin K: 152mcg
- Folate: 529.9mcg
- Iron: 13.5mg
- Calcium: 240.6mg
- Magnesium: 355.6mg
- Zinc: 7mg

Spaghetti Squash Primavera with Seasonal Vegetables

VEGETARIAN

A light, nutritious, and flavorful dish that highlights the best of seasonal vegetables, paired with the mild taste and intriguing texture of spaghetti squash. This primavera is not only delightful to the taste buds but also packs essential nutrients beneficial for pregnancy such as fiber, folic acid and antioxidants.

Preparation Time: 20 minutes
Cooking Time: 60 minutes
Total Time: 80 minutes
Serves: 2

Ingredients:
- 1 medium spaghetti squash
- 2 tbsp olive oil
- 2 garlic cloves, minced
- 1 small onion, diced
- 1 cup cherry tomatoes, halved
- 1 small zucchini, sliced
- 1 small yellow bell pepper, sliced
- 1/2 cup snap peas, trimmed
- Salt and pepper to taste
- 1/4 cup fresh basil, chopped
- 1/4 cup grated Parmesan cheese

Instructions:
1. Preheat the oven to 400°F (200°C). Halve the spaghetti squash lengthwise and scoop out the seeds.
2. Place the halves, cut side down, on a baking sheet. Bake for 40 minutes or until the squash is tender and easily pierced with a fork.
3. Once cooked, use a fork to scrape the squash into spaghetti-like strands. Set aside.
4. In a large skillet, heat olive oil over medium heat. Add the minced garlic and diced onion. Sauté until the onion becomes translucent, about 3 minutes.
5. Add the zucchini, bell pepper, and snap peas. Sauté for another 5-7 minutes or until vegetables are tender.
6. Stir in the cherry tomatoes and cook for an additional 2 minutes, just until they're softened but still hold their shape.
7. Add the spaghetti squash strands to the skillet. Toss well to combine with the vegetables.
8. Season with salt and pepper to taste.
9. Serve in bowls, garnished with fresh basil. Optionally, sprinkle with grated Parmesan cheese.

Chef's Notes:
Ideas for additional toppings:
- Toasted pine nuts or almonds for a crunchy texture
- Shredded chicken or shrimp for additional protein.
- A drizzle of balsamic reduction for a sweet and tangy touch.
- Red pepper flakes for a hint of spice.
- Freshly squeezed lemon juice for added zest.
- Dollops of ricotta cheese for a creamy texture.

Nutritional Information (per serving):
- Calories: 372kcal
- Total Fat: 18.4g
- Monounsaturated Fat: 10.83g
- Polyunsaturated Fat: 2.32g
- Total Carbohydrates: 47.3g
- Dietary Fiber: 10.9g
- Protein: 10.6g
- Sodium: 383.7mg
- Vitamin A: 135.1mcg
- Vitamin B6: .8mg
- Vitamin B12: .2mcg
- Vitamin C: 98.6mg
- Vitamin E: 3.3mg
- Vitamin K: 25.7mcg
- Folate: 83.3mcg
- Iron: 4mg
- Calcium: 274.9mg
- Magnesium: 79.1mg
- Zinc: 1.9mg

Jackfruit Tacos with Avocado Crema

VEGETARIAN

Indulge in these mouth-watering jackfruit tacos that not only bring out a burst of flavors but also cater to the nutritional needs of expecting mothers. Jackfruit provides fiber and vitamins A and C, while avocado is packed with folate, potassium, vitamin E and healthy fats. The plant-based goodness of jackfruit combined with the creaminess of avocado makes this a delightful treat for both taste buds and health.

Preparation Time: 15 minutes
Cooking Time: 25 minutes
Total Time: 40 minutes
Serves: 2

Ingredients:
For the Tacos:
- 1 can (20 oz.) young green jackfruit in water, drained and rinsed
- 1 tbsp olive oil
- 1 small onion, finely chopped
- 2 cloves garlic, minced
- 1 tsp smoked paprika
- 1 tsp ground cumin
- 1/2 tsp chili powder
- Salt and pepper, to taste
- 4 small whole wheat tortillas

For the Avocado Crema:
- 1 ripe avocado, pitted and peeled
- Juice of 1 lime
- 1/4 cup fresh cilantro, chopped
- 1/4 cup unsweetened Greek yogurt (sub coconut yogurt for non-dairy)
- Salt, to taste

Instructions:
1. Using a fork, shred the jackfruit into smaller pieces resembling pulled meat.
2. In a large skillet over medium heat, warm the olive oil. Add the onion and sauté until translucent.
3. Add garlic and sauté for another minute.
4. Mix in the shredded jackfruit, smoked paprika, cumin, chili powder, salt, and pepper. Cook for 20-25 minutes, stirring occasionally, until jackfruit is tender and flavors melded. If the mixture seems dry, add a splash of water.
5. In a blender or food processor, combine avocado, lime juice, cilantro, yogurt, and salt. Blend until smooth. Adjust seasoning if necessary.
6. Warm the tortillas according to package instructions.
7. Place a generous amount of jackfruit filling on each tortilla.
8. Drizzle with avocado crema.
9. Serve with desired toppings and enjoy!

Chef's Notes:
Additional Topping Options:
- Freshly chopped tomatoes
- Sliced red cabbage for crunch and color
- Diced red bell pepper
- Sliced jalapeños for a kick of spice
- Fresh cilantro leaves
- A sprinkle of feta r shredded mexican cheese

Nutritional Information (per serving):
- Calories: 788kcal
- Total Fat: 31.7g
- Monounsaturated Fat: 16.57g
- Polyunsaturated Fat: 3.26g
- Total Carbohydrates: 120.2g
- Dietary Fiber: 19.3g
- Protein: 19.5g
- Sodium: 397.1mg
- Vitamin A: 64.8mcg
- Vitamin B6: 1.4mg
- Vitamin B12: .5mcg
- Vitamin C: 62.4mg
- Vitamin E: 4.7mg
- Vitamin K: 30.3mcg
- Folate: 163.3mcg
- Iron: 3.9mg
- Calcium: 341.6mg
- Magnesium: 127.6mg
- Zinc: 1.5mg

Roasted Vegetable and Quinoa-Stuffed Bell Peppers

MEAL-PREP FRIENDLY
A hearty and nutrient-rich dish perfect for expectant mothers. These stuffed peppers are filled with a flavorful medley of roasted vegetables and quinoa, offering a balanced combination of protein, fiber, vitamins, and minerals such as iron, magnesium, vitamin C and vitamin A which are essential for pregnancy.

Preparation Time: 20 minutes
Cooking Time: 40 minutes
Total Time: 60 minutes
Serves: 2

Ingredients:
- 4 large bell peppers (any color)
- 1 cup quinoa (rinsed and drained)
- 2 cups water
- 1 small zucchini, diced
- 1 small red onion, diced
- 1 cup cherry tomatoes, halved
- 1 medium carrot, diced
- 1/2 cup corn kernels (fresh or frozen)
- 2 cloves garlic, minced
- 2 tbsp olive oil
- Salt and pepper, to taste
- 1 tsp Italian seasoning
- 1/2 cup feta cheese

Instructions:
1. Preheat your oven to 400°F (200°C).
2. In a medium-sized pot, bring the 2 cups of water to a boil. Add quinoa, reduce the heat to low, cover, and simmer for 15 minutes or until the quinoa is cooked and water is absorbed. Fluff with a fork and set aside.
3. While quinoa is cooking, in a large mixing bowl, toss the zucchini, red onion, cherry tomatoes, carrot, corn, and garlic with olive oil, salt, pepper, and dried basil or Italian seasoning.

4. Spread the vegetable mixture on a baking sheet and roast in the preheated oven for 20 minutes, or until vegetables are tender and slightly caramelized.
5. Once the vegetables are roasted, combine them with the cooked quinoa in a large mixing bowl. Adjust seasoning if needed.
6. Cut the tops off the bell peppers and remove the seeds and membranes.
7. Stuff each bell pepper with the quinoa and vegetable mixture, pressing down gently to pack the filling.
8. Place the stuffed peppers in a baking dish and cover loosely with aluminum foil.
9. Bake in the oven for 15-20 minutes, or until the peppers are tender.
10. If using cheese, remove the foil and sprinkle the cheese on top of the peppers. Return to the oven for an additional 5 minutes, or until the cheese is melted and bubbly.
11. Remove from oven and let cool slightly before serving.

Chef's Notes:

- Leftovers can be stored in an airtight container in the refrigerator for up to 3 days. For longer storage, you can freeze the stuffed peppers in individual servings for up to 1 month. When ready to eat, thaw in the refrigerator overnight and reheat in the oven or microwave until heated through.

Nutritional Information (per serving):

- Calories: 348kcal
- Total Fat: 13.9g
- Monounsaturated Fat: 6.54g
- Polyunsaturated Fat: 2.45g
- Total Carbohydrates: 46.3g
- Dietary Fiber: 8.1g
- Protein: 12.3g
- Sodium: 265.9mg
- Vitamin A: 184.3mcg
- Vitamin B6: .8mg
- Vitamin B12: .3mcg
- Vitamin C: 146.7mg
- Vitamin E: 2.8mg
- Vitamin K: 20mcg
- Folate: 121mcg
- Iron: 3.7mg
- Calcium: 162.2mg
- Magnesium: 119.2mg
- Zinc: 2.3mg

Surf and Turf Skewers with Asparagus and Cherry Tomatoes

GLUTEN-FREE

These delightful skewers feature the best of both land and sea. Tender chunks of steak paired with succulent shrimp, juxtaposed with the tang of cherry tomatoes and the crunch of fresh asparagus. A harmonious blend of flavors and textures, they're not only a treat for the palate but also beneficial for expecting mothers. These skewers contain protein and iron as well as folate, healthy fats and vitamins A and C.

Preparation Time: 20 minutes
Cooking Time: 10 minutes
Total Time: 30 minutes
Serves: 2

Ingredients:

- 1/2 pound of beef (sirloin or tenderloin), cut into 1-inch cubes
- 8 large shrimps, peeled and deveined
- 8 cherry tomatoes
- 8 asparagus spears, trimmed and halved
- 2 tbsp olive oil
- 1 tsp garlic powder
- 1 tsp paprika
- Salt and pepper to taste
- Wooden or metal skewers (if wooden, soak in water for at least 30 minutes prior to grilling)

Instructions:

1. In a bowl, combine olive oil, garlic powder, paprika, salt, and pepper. Mix well.
2. Place beef cubes and shrimp in the marinade, ensuring all pieces are well coated. Let them marinate for at least 15 minutes.
3. Preheat grill to medium-high heat.
4. Thread the beef, shrimp, cherry tomatoes, and asparagus onto the skewers, alternating as you like.
5. Place skewers on the grill. Cook for 4-5 minutes on each side or until the shrimp is pink and opaque, and the beef reaches your desired level of doneness.
6. Remove from grill and let rest for a couple of minutes.
7. Serve hot and enjoy!

Chef's Notes:

Side Dish Options:

- Garlic Butter Quinoa: A flavorful and protein-rich grain that complements the skewers and provides additional iron and B vitamins.
- Lemon-Herb Roasted Potatoes: Adds a touch of zestiness and provides essential carbohydrates.
- Green Salad with Vinaigrette: Light, refreshing, and packed with various vitamins and minerals.

Nutritional Information (per serving):

- Calories: 392kcal
- Total Fat: 18.7g
- Monounsaturated Fat: 12.02g
- Polyunsaturated Fat: 2.21g
- Total Carbohydrates: 12.4g
- Dietary Fiber: 5g
- Protein: 43.6g
- Sodium: 372.9mg
- Vitamin A: 137.3mcg
- Vitamin B6: 1.2mg
- Vitamin B12: 3mcg
- Vitamin C: 15.9mg
- Vitamin E: 4.7mg
- Vitamin K: 45.9mcg

- Folate: 54.9mcg
- Iron: 7.8mg
- Calcium: 109mg
- Magnesium: 45.9mg
- Zinc: 6.8mg

Seitan and Mushroom Bourguignon

VEGAN

A delicious and hearty stew that combines the meaty textures of seitan with the earthy flavors of mushrooms in a rich wine sauce. This dish is a vegan take on the classic French Bourguignon and is perfect for warming up during colder months. The incorporation of protein-rich seitan and B vitamin-packed mushrooms makes it a great option for pregnant individuals seeking wholesome and nourishing meals.

Preparation Time: 20 minutes
Cooking Time: 60 minutes
Total Time: 80 minutes
Serves: 4

Ingredients:

- 1 lb seitan, cut into bite-sized chunks
- 1 lb mushrooms, sliced (cremini or button mushrooms work well)
- 1 large onion, diced
- 3 carrots, peeled and chopped
- 3 cloves garlic, minced
- 2 cups red wine (the alcohol will burn off while cooking)
- 2 cups vegetable broth
- 2 tbsp tomato paste
- 1 tsp dried thyme
- 2 bay leaves
- 2 tbsp vegan butter
- Salt and pepper to taste
- Fresh parsley, chopped (for garnish)

Instructions:

1. In a large pot or Dutch oven, heat the olive oil or vegan butter over medium heat.
2. Add the seitan chunks and brown them on all sides. Once browned, remove and set aside.
3. In the same pot, add the onions and carrots. Sauté until the onions become translucent.
4. Add the garlic and mushrooms. Cook until the mushrooms release their moisture and begin to brown.
5. Stir in the tomato paste, mixing well to coat the vegetables.
6. Pour in the red wine, scraping any bits off the bottom of the pot. Allow it to simmer for 5 minutes.
7. Return the seitan to the pot. Add the vegetable broth, thyme, and bay leaves. Season with salt and pepper.
8. Bring the mixture to a boil, then reduce the heat, cover, and let it simmer for 45 minutes or until the vegetables are tender and the flavors meld.
9. Check seasoning and adjust salt and pepper if needed.

10. Remove the bay leaves and serve hot, garnishing with fresh parsley.

Chef's Notes:

- Store leftovers in an airtight container in the refrigerator for up to 4 days or freeze for up to 3 months. To reheat, thaw in the refrigerator overnight and warm on the stovetop.
- Serve over mashed potatoes or mashed cauliflower, rice or pasta and with a side salad.

Nutritional Information (per serving):

- Calories: 330kcal
- Total Fat: 6.2g
- Monounsaturated Fat: 2.81g
- Polyunsaturated Fat: 1.6g
- Total Carbohydrates: 23.2g
- Dietary Fiber: 3.2g
- Protein: 6.1g
- Sodium: 519.9mg
- Vitamin A: 468mg
- Vitamin B6: .4mg
- Vitamin B12: .1mcg
- Vitamin C: 11.1mg
- Vitamin E: .9mg
- Vitamin K: 40mcg
- Folate: 48.9mcg
- Iron: 3mg
- Calcium: 78.3mg
- Magnesium: 52.5mg
- Zinc: 1.8mg

Chickpea and Chorizo Paella with Saffron and Peas

GLUTEN-FREE

This hearty and aromatic dish marries the rich flavors of chorizo with the nutty essence of chickpeas. The delicate aroma of saffron, combined with the sweetness of peas, results in a meal that's not only delectable but also packed with essential nutrition such as fiber, iron, protein, vitamins A and C, and folic acid.

Preparation Time: 15 minutes
Cooking Time: 40 minutes
Total Time: 55 minutes
Serves: 4

Ingredients:

- 1 cup of uncooked paella rice (or Arborio rice)
- 2 cups chicken or vegetable broth
- Λ pinch of saffron threads
- 1 medium onion, finely chopped
- 2 cloves garlic, minced
- 1 cup canned chickpeas
- 150g chorizo, thinly sliced
- 1 cup green peas (frozen or fresh)
- 2 tbsp olive oil
- Salt and pepper, to taste
- 1/4 cup fresh parsley, chopped (for garnish)

Instructions:

1. In a small saucepan, warm the broth over low heat. Add the saffron threads, allowing them to infuse the broth for about 10 minutes. Keep the broth warm.
2. In a large paella pan or wide skillet, heat the olive oil over medium heat. Add the chorizo slices and fry until they release their oils and become slightly crispy. Remove chorizo and set aside.
3. In the same pan, add the chopped onion and sauté until translucent. Add the minced garlic and sauté for another 2 minutes until fragrant.
4. Stir in the rice, ensuring it's well-coated with the oil and onions. Cook for about 2-3 minutes.
5. Slowly pour in the saffron-infused broth. Reduce the heat to low, cover, and let it simmer for about 15-20 minutes. Stir occasionally to prevent sticking.
6. When the rice is halfway cooked, mix in the chickpeas, peas, and fried chorizo. Continue to simmer until the rice is fully cooked and has absorbed most of the broth.
7. Season with salt and pepper to taste. Remove from heat.
8. Garnish with fresh parsley and serve with lemon wedges on the side.

Chef's Notes:

- Leftover paella can be stored in an airtight container in the refrigerator for up to 3 days. To reheat, you can use a microwave or stovetop, adding a bit of water or broth to retain moisture. It's important to reheat it thoroughly before consuming.

Nutritional Information (per serving):

- Calories: 445kcal
- Total Fat: 17.8g
- Monounsaturated Fat: 8.93g
- Polyunsaturated Fat: 2.39g
- Total Carbohydrates: 57.3g
- Dietary Fiber: 9.3g
- Protein: 14.3g
- Sodium: 535.5mg
- Vitamin B6: .3mg
- Vitamin B12: .8mcg
- Vitamin C: 14mg
- Vitamin E: 1.1mg
- Vitamin K: 73.6mcg
- Folate: 98.5mcg
- Iron: 4.4mg
- Calcium: 52.6mg
- Magnesium: 53.5mg
- Zinc: 1.8mg

Grilled Calamari and Roasted Red Pepper Flatbread with Olive Tapenade

MEAL-PREP FRIENDLY

A delectable union of Mediterranean flavors, this flatbread boasts the smoky char of grilled calamari, the sweet depth of roasted red peppers, and the robust savoriness of olive tapenade. This dish is both nutrient-rich and flavorful, packed with protein, iron, healthy fats and vitamins C and E, and therefore designed to cater to the needs of you and your baby.

Preparation Time: 30 minutes
Cooking Time: 15 minutes
Total Time: 45 minutes
Serves: 2

Ingredients:

- 200g fresh calamari, cleaned and cut into rings
- 2 garlic cloves, minced
- 1/4 tsp chili flakes (optional)
- 1 large red bell pepper
- 1 cup pitted Kalamata olives
- 2 tbsp capers, rinsed
- 1 tbsp fresh lemon juice
- 4 tbsp olive oil
- Salt and pepper to taste
- 2 flatbreads

Instructions:

1. Preheat the oven to 475°F (245°C).
2. Place the red bell pepper on a baking sheet and roast for 20-25 minutes, turning occasionally, until the skin is charred.
3. Once roasted, place the pepper in a bowl and cover it with plastic wrap for about 10 minutes. This will steam the pepper and make it easier to peel.
4. Peel the charred skin from the pepper, remove the seeds, and slice it into thin strips.
5. In a food processor, combine olives, garlic, capers, and lemon juice. Pulse until finely chopped.
6. Slowly drizzle in the olive oil while pulsing. Season with salt and pepper. Set aside.
7. Preheat a grill or grill pan over medium-high heat.
8. In a bowl, toss the calamari with olive oil, garlic, chili flakes, salt, and pepper.
9. Grill the calamari for 1-2 minutes on each side or until they become opaque and slightly charred. Be careful not to overcook as calamari can become rubbery.
10. Preheat your oven or grill to medium heat.
11. Lay out the flatbreads and spread a generous amount of olive tapenade on each.
12. Top with the grilled calamari and roasted red pepper strips.
13. Heat the flatbread on the grill or in the oven for 3-5 minutes, just until warmed and slightly crispy.
14. Serve immediately.

Chef's Notes:

- For less prep time, buy premade roasted peppers and olive tapenade.

- Serve with one of the following sides if desired:
  - Greek Salad: A refreshing blend of cucumber, tomatoes, olives, feta cheese, and a light vinaigrette.
  - Lemon-Herb Couscous: Fluffy couscous seasoned with fresh herbs and a hint of lemon zest.
  - Steamed Asparagus: Lightly seasoned with olive oil, salt, and pepper, offering added folate for pregnancy.

Nutritional Information (per serving):
- Calories: 769kcal
- Total Fat: 62.8g
- Monounsaturated Fat: 19.71g
- Polyunsaturated Fat: 2.9g
- Total Carbohydrates: 35.8g
- Dietary Fiber: 2.9g
- Protein: 22g
- Sodium: 1221.6mg
- Vitamin A: 129mcg
- Vitamin B6: .3mg
- Vitamin C: 112.6mg
- Vitamin E: 5.2mg
- Vitamin K: 21.4mcg
- Folate: 40mcg
- Iron: 1.7mg
- Calcium: 131mg

Butternut Squash Mac'n'Cheese

KID FRIENDLY

This creamy and delicious mac and cheese incorporates the sweet and earthy flavors of butternut squash. Not only is it a delightful twist on the classic dish, but it also offers numerous nutritional benefits for pregnancy such as folate, fiber and vitamins A and C. The melding of pasta with the natural sweetness of butternut squash creates a comforting and hearty meal.

Preparation Time: 20 minutes
Cooking Time: 40 minutes
Total Time: 60 minutes
Serves: 4

Ingredients:
- 2 cups butternut squash, peeled and cubed
- 8 oz elbow macaroni or your preferred pasta shape
- 2 cups shredded sharp cheddar cheese
- 1/2 cup whole milk
- 2 tablespoons butter
- 1/2 cup grated Parmesan cheese
- 1/4 teaspoon nutmeg
- 1/2 teaspoon paprika
- Salt and pepper to taste
- 1 tablespoon olive oil

Instructions:
1. Preheat oven to 375°F (190°C).
2. In a large pot, boil the butternut squash until tender, about 15-20 minutes.
3. While the squash is boiling, cook the pasta in another pot following the package instructions until al dente. Drain and set aside.
4. Once the squash is tender, drain and transfer it to a blender. Add milk, butter, nutmeg, and half of the cheddar cheese. Blend until smooth.
5. In a large mixing bowl, combine the blended squash mixture with the cooked pasta. Stir in the remaining cheddar cheese, Parmesan cheese, paprika, salt, and pepper.
6. Transfer the mixture to a baking dish.
7. Bake in the preheated oven for 20-25 minutes, or until the top is golden brown and bubbly.
8. Serve hot and enjoy!

Chef's Notes:
- Side Dish Options:
  - Steamed green beans with a touch of lemon zest
  - A crisp mixed green salad with a light vinaigrette
  - Garlic roasted asparagus
- Store leftovers in an airtight container in the refrigerator for up to 3-4 days or in a freezer-safe container, leaving an inch of space at the top for expansion. Freeze for up to 1 month.

Nutritional Information (per serving):
- Calories: 611kcal
- Total Fat: 32g
- Monounsaturated Fat: 5.23g
- Polyunsaturated Fat: .84g
- Total Carbohydrates: 55.3g
- Dietary Fiber: 4.1g
- Protein: 26.1g
- Sodium: 593mg
- Vitamin A: 472.7mcg
- Vitamin B6: .1mg
- Vitamin B12: .3mcg
- Vitamin C: 14.7
- Vitamin E: 1.8mg
- Iron: 2.2mg
- Calcium: 571.5mg
- Magnesium: 31.7mg
- Zinc: .7mg

Mediterranean Stuffed Sweet Potatoes

VEGETARIAN

Mediterranean Stuffed Sweet Potatoes offer a flavorful and nutritious twist to the usual baked sweet potato. This dish combines the earthy sweetness of the sweet potato with the freshness of Mediterranean ingredients. With its rich nutrients, it's particularly beneficial for pregnant women, offering essential vitamins and minerals for both the you and your baby such as protein, vitamins A and C, iron and calcium.

Preparation Time: 15 minutes
Cooking Time: 45 minutes
Total Time: 60 minutes
Serves: 2

Ingredients:

- 2 medium-sized sweet potatoes
- 1/2 cup cooked canned chickpeas
- 1/2 cup cherry tomatoes, halved
- 1/4 cup crumbled feta cheese
- 2 tbsp chopped Kalamata olives
- 2 tbsp chopped fresh parsley
- 1/4 cup diced cucumber
- 2 tbsp olive oil
- 1 tsp lemon zest
- 2 tbsp lemon juice
- 1 garlic clove, minced
- Salt and pepper, to taste
- 1/4 tsp dried oregano
- 1/4 tsp ground cumin

Instructions:

1. Preheat oven to 400°F (205°C).
2. Wash and scrub the sweet potatoes. Using a fork, prick the potatoes a few times to allow steam to escape.
3. Place the sweet potatoes on a baking sheet and bake for about 40-45 minutes, or until they're tender and can easily be pierced with a fork.
4. While the sweet potatoes are baking, prepare the filling. In a medium-sized mixing bowl, combine chickpeas, cherry tomatoes, cucumber, olives, and feta cheese.
5. In a separate smaller bowl, whisk together olive oil, lemon juice, lemon zest, minced garlic, salt, pepper, and if using, oregano and cumin. Pour this dressing over the chickpea mixture and toss to combine.
6. Once the sweet potatoes are done, let them cool for a few minutes. Then, slice them in half lengthwise.
7. Use a fork to slightly mash the insides of the potatoes, creating a small well for the filling.
8. Spoon the Mediterranean mixture into the sweet potatoes.
9. Garnish with fresh parsley and serve immediately.

Chef's Notes:

Side Dish Options:

- A simple green salad with a lemon vinaigrette.
- Grilled asparagus or zucchini drizzled with olive oil and a sprinkle of salt.
- A light quinoa tabbouleh.

Nutritional Information (per serving):

- Calories: 431kcal
- Total Fat: 5.4g
- Monounsaturated Fat: 1.49g
- Polyunsaturated Fat: .19g
- Total Carbohydrates: 86.4g
- Dietary Fiber: 13.8g
- Protein: 6.7g
- Sodium: 622.3mg
- Vitamin A: 962.4mcg
- Vitamin B6: .4mg
- Vitamin B12: .3mcg
- Vitamin C: 13mg
- Vitamin K: 67.9mcg

- Folate: 59.2mcg
- Iron: 2.5mg
- Calcium: 182.4mg
- Magnesium: 52.8mg
- Zinc: 1.3mg

Slow-cooker Beef Bone Broth

ONE-POT MEAL

Bone broth, a nutrient-dense liquid, is made by simmering animal bones and connective tissues for extended periods. It has been consumed for centuries for its rich flavor and myriad health benefits. Especially for pregnant women, this broth is a source of essential nutrients such as calcium, magnesium, phosphorous, collagen, and amino acids which can support both you and your baby. Additionally, it's easily digestible if you are still experiencing nausea. Using a slow cooker makes the process easier and ensures a deeply flavored and nutritious broth.

Preparation Time: 10 minutes
Cooking Time: 24 hours
Total Time: 24 hours, 10 minutes
Serves: 8
Ingredients:

- 3-4 pounds beef bones (preferably a mix of marrow bones and bones with a bit of meat on them, like oxtail, short ribs, or knuckle bones)
- 2 medium carrots, chopped
- 2 celery stalks, chopped
- 1 medium onion, chopped
- 2 cloves garlic, minced
- 1 bay leaf
- 1 tablespoon apple cider vinegar (helps extract nutrients from the bones)
- Salt and pepper, to taste
- Water

Instructions:

1. Roast the Bones: Preheat the oven to 400°F (200°C). Place the bones on a baking sheet and roast for 30 minutes. Turn the bones over and roast for an additional 30 minutes. Roasting enriches the flavor of the broth.
2. Slow Cooker Preparation: Transfer the roasted bones to your slow cooker. Add the chopped carrots, celery, onion, garlic, bay leaf, and apple cider vinegar. Season with salt and pepper.
3. Water: Fill the slow cooker with water until the bones and vegetables are fully submerged.
4. Cooking: Cover the slow cooker and set it to low. Let the broth simmer for 24-48 hours. The longer it cooks, the richer and more flavorful the broth will be.
5. Strain: After cooking, remove and discard the bones and vegetables. Strain the broth through a fine-mesh strainer to remove any small bone fragments or impurities.
6. Cool: Allow the broth to cool slightly before transferring to storage containers.

Chef's Notes:

Storage Information:

- Refrigeration: Store the broth in airtight containers in the refrigerator for up to 5 days.
- Freezing: For longer storage, pour the broth into freezer-safe containers or ice cube trays (for easy portioning) and freeze. The broth can be stored in the freezer for up to 6 months. Always label containers with the date.
- You can drink the broth as is, use it as a base for soups and stews, or cook grains and vegetables in it for added flavor and nutrition.

Nutritional Information (per serving):

- Calories:15 kcal
- Total Fat: .1g
- Monounsaturated Fat: .01g
- Polyunsaturated Fat: .03g
- Total Carbohydrates: 3.4g
- Dietary Fiber: .9g
- Protein: .4g
- Sodium: 179.1mg
- Vitamin A: 130.9mcg
- Vitamin C: 2.6mg

Mushroom Burger and Oven-baked Green Been Fries

VEGAN

This delectable mushroom burger is rich in flavors and nutrients, perfect for expectant mothers. Paired with crisp oven-baked green bean fries, it offers a balanced meal with proteins, vitamins, and minerals. During pregnancy, maintaining a nutritious diet is crucial, and this dish provides folate, iron, and fiber – all vital nutrients for both mom and baby.

Preparation Time: 15 minutes
Cooking Time: 30 minutes
Total Time: 45 minutes
Serves: 2

Ingredients:

For the Mushroom Burgers:

- 2 large portobello mushroom caps, cleaned and stemmed
- 2 tbsp olive oil
- 2 cloves garlic, minced
- Salt and pepper, to taste
- 2 whole wheat buns
- 1 small red onion, thinly sliced
- 2 lettuce leaves
- 2 slices of tomato
- 2 tbsp hummus

For the Green Bean Fries:

- 2 cups green beans, washed and trimmed
- 1 tbsp olive oil
- 2 tbsp parmesan cheese, grated (optional)
- Salt and pepper, to taste

Instructions:

1. Preheat the oven to 400°F (200°C).
2. In a large bowl, toss the portobello caps with olive oil, garlic, salt, and pepper.
3. Place the mushrooms on a baking sheet, gill side up, and roast for 20-25 minutes until they're tender.
4. Toast the whole wheat buns in the oven for the last 3-4 minutes of the mushroom's cooking time.
5. Assemble the burger by placing a lettuce leaf on the bottom half of the bun, followed by a roasted mushroom cap, a slice of tomato, some red onion slices, and a dollop of hummus. Top with the other half of the bun.
6. While the mushrooms are baking, in a bowl, toss green beans with olive oil, salt, and pepper.
7. Spread the green beans in a single layer on a baking sheet.
8. Bake in the oven for 15-20 minutes or until they're golden and crispy, turning halfway through.
9. Sprinkle with grated parmesan cheese if desired and serve immediately.
10. Serve the mushroom burger hot alongside the green bean fries

Nutritional Information (per serving):

- Calories: 585 kcal
- Total Fat: 34.6g
- Monounsaturated Fat: 18g
- Polyunsaturated Fat: 4.21g
- Total Carbohydrates: 52.2g
- Dietary Fiber: 10.5g
- Protein: 21.6g
- Sodium: 974.3mg
- Vitamin A: 157.1mg
- Vitamin B6: .3mg
- Vitamin B12: .5mcg
- Vitamin C: 22.9mg
- Vitamin E: 3.5mg
- Vitamin K: 32.3mcg
- Folate: 99.5mcg
- Iron: 2.8mg
- Calcium: 379mg
- Magnesium: 30.6mg
- Zinc: 2.2mg

CRAVING-KILLING SNACKS

Quinoa and Black Bean Stuffed Mini Peppers

VEGETARIAN

Stuffed mini peppers are not only visually appealing but also packed with nutrients. This delightful combination of quinoa and black beans makes the dish protein-rich and flavorful, ideal for expecting mothers. The vibrant mini peppers add a touch of sweetness and are an excellent source of vitamin C.

Preparation Time: 20 minutes
Cooking Time: 25 minutes
Total Time: 45 minutes
Serves: 6

Ingredients:

- 18 mini bell peppers
- 1 cup cooked quinoa
- 1 can (15 oz.) black beans, drained and rinsed
- 1 cup corn kernels (frozen or fresh)
- 1 small red onion, finely chopped
- 2 garlic cloves, minced
- 1 tsp cumin
- 1 tsp smoked paprika
- 1/4 cup chopped fresh cilantro
- 1 lime, juiced
- Salt and pepper, to taste
- 1 cup shredded cheese (optional, e.g., cheddar or Monterey Jack)
- 1 tbsp olive oil

Instructions:

1. Preheat the oven to 375°F (190°C).
2. Wash the mini bell peppers, cut off the tops, and remove the seeds.
3. In a large mixing bowl, combine cooked quinoa, black beans, corn, red onion, minced garlic, cumin, smoked paprika, lime juice, and chopped cilantro. Mix well.
4. Season the mixture with salt and pepper to taste.
5. Gently stuff each mini pepper with the quinoa and black bean mixture.
6. If using cheese, sprinkle or stuff some into each pepper on top of the filling.
7. Place the stuffed peppers in a baking dish, drizzle with olive oil, and cover with foil.
8. Bake for 20 minutes. Remove the foil and bake for an additional 5 minutes or until the peppers are tender and the cheese (if using) is melted and slightly golden.
9. Remove from the oven and let cool for a few minutes before serving.

Chef's Notes:

- Store any leftover stuffed peppers in an airtight container in the refrigerator for up to 3 days. They can also be frozen for up to a month. To reheat, thaw in the refrigerator overnight and bake in a preheated oven at 350°F (175°C) until warmed throughout.

Nutritional Information (per serving):

- Calories: 299kcal
- Total Fat: 9.8g
- Monounsaturated Fat: 1.872g
- Polyunsaturated Fat: .84g
- Total Carbohydrates: 39.6g
- Dietary Fiber: 11.2g
- Protein: 14.6g
- Sodium: 138.8mg
- Vitamin B6: .1mg
- Vitamin C: 162.5mg
- Vitamin E: 1.2mg
- Folate: 132.4mcg
- Iron: 2.7mg
- Calcium: 198mg
- Magnesium: 80mg
- Zinc: 1.3mg

Tahini and Date Smoothie

VEGAN

A creamy and naturally sweetened smoothie blending the nutty flavors of tahini with the caramel-like sweetness of dates. This drink is not only delightful to the palate but also packed with essential nutrients beneficial for pregnancy such as fiber, calcium and iron. It's a perfect treat for moms-to-be or anyone seeking a wholesome pick-me-up.

Preparation Time: 5 minutes
Cooking Time: 1 minute (blend time)
Total Time: 6 minutes
Serves: 1

Ingredients:

- 2 large Medjool dates, pitted
- 1 tablespoon tahini (sesame seed paste)
- 1 cup unsweetened almond milk (or any milk of your choice)
- 1/2 ripe banana
- Ice cubes (optional, if you prefer your smoothie cold)

Instructions:

1. Ensure that the dates are pitted. If your dates are dry or hard, soak them in warm water for 10-15 minutes to soften, then drain.
2. In a blender, combine the dates, tahini, almond milk, banana (if using), salt, and vanilla extract.
3. Blend until smooth. If the consistency is too thick for your liking, add more milk and blend again until you reach the desired texture.
4. If desired, add ice cubes and blend once more until smooth and chilled.
5. Pour into a glass and enjoy immediately!

Chef's Notes:

Recipe Variations:

- Protein Boost: Add a scoop of your favorite protein powder (vanilla or unflavored would work best).
- Omega-3 Boost: Add a tablespoon of chia seeds or flaxseeds. Allow the mixture to sit for a few minutes after blending for the seeds to gel and thicken the smoothie.
- Chocolate Twist: Add a tablespoon of cocoa powder or cacao nibs for a chocolatey flavor.
- Green Boost: Add a handful of spinach or kale. The mild flavor of these greens won't overpower the smoothie but will add a dose of vitamins and minerals.

Nutritional Information (per serving):

- Calories: 314kcal
- Total Fat: 10.8g
- Monounsaturated Fat: 4.61g
- Polyunsaturated Fat: 4.2g
- Total Carbohydrates: 56.1g
- Dietary Fiber: 6.7g
- Protein: 5.1g
- Sodium: 207mg
- Vitamin B6: .4mg

- Vitamin C: 5.1mg
- Vitamin D: 2.6mcg
- Vitamin E: 16.7mg
- Folate: 36.3mcg
- Iron: 2.7mg
- Calcium: 579.7mg
- Potassium: 782.9mg
- Phosphorus: 176.1mg
- Magnesium: 71.8mg
- Zinc: 1.1mg

Coconut Yogurt Parfait with Kiwi and Flaxseeds

VEGAN

A refreshing and nutritious layered parfait that brings together the creamy goodness of coconut yogurt, the tangy sweetness of fresh kiwis, and the nutty crunch of flaxseeds. This delightful treat not only satisfies the taste buds but also packs a punch in terms of health benefits for you and your baby, such as fiber, vitamin C and omega-3 fatty acids.

Preparation Time: 10 minutes
Cooking Time: 0 minutes
Total Time: 10 minutes
Serves: 1

Ingredients:

- 1 cup coconut yogurt (unsweetened or lightly sweetened, as per preference)
- 1 ripe kiwi, peeled and sliced
- 2 tablespoons ground flaxseeds (for better absorption)

Instructions:

1. Begin by layering a few spoonfuls of coconut yogurt at the bottom of a glass or jar.
2. Add a layer of kiwi slices on top of the yogurt.
3. Sprinkle a tablespoon of ground flaxseeds over the kiwi layer.
4. Repeat the layers until all the ingredients are used up, finishing with a sprinkle of flaxseeds on top.
5. Enjoy immediately or refrigerate for later. The parfait tastes best when chilled for about 30 minutes before serving.

Chef's Notes:

Recipe Variations:

- Fruit Alternatives: Replace kiwi with fruits like mango, berries, or pineapple for a different taste profile.
- Seeds and Nuts: Chia seeds, hemp seeds, or toasted almonds can be a great addition or alternative to flaxseeds.
- Sweeteners: If you prefer a sweeter parfait, drizzle a bit of honey, or agave nectar between the layers.
- Spice it up: A dash of cinnamon or cardamom can elevate the flavor profile.

Nutritional Information (per serving):
- Calories: XXX kcal
- Total Fat: XX g
- Monounsaturated Fat: XX g
- Polyunsaturated Fat: XX g (indicate omega-3 fatty acids if applicable)
- Total Carbohydrates: XX g
- Dietary Fiber: XX g
- Protein: XX g
- Sodium: XX mg
- Vitamins: indicate relevant vitamins
- Minerals: indicate relevant minerals

Zucchini Rolls Stuffed with Ricotta and Spinach
Preparation Time: 20 minutes
Cooking Time: 40 minutes
Total Time: 60 minutes
Serves: 4

Nutritional Information (per serving):
- Calories: 1053kcal
- Total Fat: 97g
- Monounsaturated Fat: 1.59g
- Polyunsaturated Fat: 6.11g
- Omega-3 Fatty Acids: 4.73g
- Total Carbohydrates: 40.1g
- Dietary Fiber: 19.6g
- Protein: 12.5g
- Sodium: 79.6mg
- Vitamin B6: .1mg
- Vitamin C: 64.1mg
- Vitamin K: 28.7mcg
- Folate: 35.2mcg
- Iron: 5mg
- Magnesium: 92.5mg
- Zinc: 1mg

Mango and Turkey Jerky

MEAL-PREP FRIENDLY

This savory yet sweet jerky combines the lean protein of turkey with the tropical flavor of mango. Perfect for on-the-go snacking, it is nutrient-dense and provides essential vitamins and minerals beneficial during pregnancy, such as protein, iron, folate, and vitamins A and B6.

Preparation Time: 15 minutes
Cooking Time: 4-6 hours
Total Time: 4-6 hours and 15 minutes
Serves: 8

Ingredients:

- 2 lbs turkey breast, thinly sliced
- 1 ripe mango, peeled and finely pureed
- 2 tbsp soy sauce or tamari (for a gluten-free option)
- 1 tbsp honey
- 1 tsp fresh ginger, grated
- 1 clove garlic, minced
- 1/2 tsp black pepper

- 1/4 tsp red pepper flakes (optional for a bit of heat)
- 1 tsp salt

Instructions:
1. Combine mango puree, soy sauce, honey, ginger, garlic, black pepper, red pepper flakes, and salt in a bowl. Mix well.
2. Place the thinly sliced turkey in a zip-top bag or shallow dish. Pour the mango mixture over the turkey, ensuring all pieces are coated well. Seal or cover and marinate for at least 6 hours or overnight in the refrigerator.
3. Preheat your oven to its lowest setting, usually around 150°F (65°C). If your oven doesn't go this low, set it as low as possible and keep the oven door slightly open.
4. Line a baking sheet with parchment paper. Place the marinated turkey slices on the sheet, ensuring they don't overlap.
5. Bake for 4-6 hours, or until the turkey jerky is dried but still pliable. The cooking time will vary depending on your oven and the thickness of the slices.
6. Remove from the oven and let cool completely.

Chef's Notes:
- Instead of baking in the oven, you can use a dehydrator if you have one.
- Storage Information:
  - Store the mango & turkey jerky in an airtight container or zip-top bag.
  - For short term storage (up to a week), keep it in a cool, dark place.
  - For longer storage (up to a month), refrigerate the jerky.
  - For extended storage (several months), consider vacuum sealing and freezing the jerky. Just remember to let it come to room temperature before consuming.

Nutritional Information (per serving):
- Calories: 203kcal
- Total Fat: 2.5g
- Monounsaturated Fat: .77g
- Polyunsaturated Fat: .64g
- Total Carbohydrates: 8.9g
- Dietary Fiber: .8g
- Protein: 34.9g
- Sodium: 623.3mg
- Vitamin B6: 1mg
- Vitamin B12: .4mcg
- Vitamin C: 15.4mg
- Folate: 30.1mcg
- Potassium: 376.1mg
- Phosphorus: 274.3mg
- Magnesium: 43.9mg
- Zinc: 2mg

Olive and Sun-dried Tomato Tapenade on Rye Crispbread

VEGAN

This tapenade combines the deep flavors of olives and sundried tomatoes with aromatic herbs, creating a Mediterranean-inspired spread that is both delicious and nutritious. Perfectly paired with rye crisps, this dish offers a crunchy and savory treat that can be enjoyed as an appetizer or snack. For expecting mothers, this tapenade offers an array of essential nutrients beneficial during pregnancy, such as vitamins C, E, K and potassium.

Preparation Time: 15 minutes
Cooking Time: 00 minutes
Total Time: 15 minutes
Serves: 8

Ingredients:
- 1 cup pitted Kalamata olives
- 1 cup sundried tomatoes (drained, if oil-packed)
- 2 cloves garlic, minced
- 2 tablespoons capers, drained
- 1 tablespoon fresh lemon juice
- 1 teaspoon lemon zest
- 2 tablespoons fresh basil or parsley, chopped
- 2 tablespoons extra virgin olive oil
- Salt and pepper, to taste
- 16 rye crisps

Instructions:
1. In a food processor, combine the Kalamata olives, sundried tomatoes, garlic, capers, lemon juice, and lemon zest. Process until finely chopped, but still a little chunky.
2. Add the fresh basil or parsley and the olive oil. Pulse a few times to combine, ensuring the mixture retains some texture.
3. Taste and adjust seasoning with salt and pepper as necessary. Remember, olives and capers can be salty, so be cautious when adding additional salt.
4. Spread the tapenade on rye crisps and serve immediately.

Chef's Notes:
- Store leftover tapenade in an airtight container in the refrigerator for up to a week. If the tapenade appears to be drying out, you can drizzle a little extra olive oil on top before sealing to retain moisture.

Nutritional Information (per serving):
- Calories: 82kcal
- Total Fat: 5.9g
- Monounsaturated Fat: 4.18g
- Polyunsaturated Fat: .51g
- Total Carbohydrates: 6.5g
- Dietary Fiber: 2.1g
- Protein: 1.5g
- Sodium: 316.1mg
- Vitamin E: .9mg
- Vitamin K: 5.7mcg
- Iron: 1.8mg

Cucumber Slices with Hummus and Pomegranate Seeds

SO FAST!

A refreshing and nutritious snack that combines the coolness of cucumber, the creaminess of hummus, and the sweet crunch of pomegranate seeds. This dish is not only visually appealing but also packed with essential nutrients beneficial during pregnancy such as fiber, protein, potassium, folic acid and vitamins C and K. The combination offers a harmonious blend of flavors and textures, making it a delightful treat for expectant mothers.

Preparation Time: 10 minutes
Cooking Time: 0 minutes
Total Time: 10 minutes
Serves: 0

Ingredients:

- 1 medium cucumber
- 3 tablespoons of hummus (store-bought or homemade)
- 2 tablespoons of pomegranate seeds
- A pinch of salt (optional)
- A sprinkle of paprika (for garnish, optional)

Instructions:

1. Wash the cucumber and cut it into about 1/4-inch-thick slices. You should get about 8-10 slices.
2. Lay the cucumber slices flat on a plate or platter.
3. Spoon a dollop of hummus onto each cucumber slice.
4. Sprinkle the pomegranate seeds over the hummus-topped cucumber slices.
5. If desired, season with a pinch of salt and garnish with a sprinkle of paprika or sumac for added color and a hint of flavor.
6. Serve immediately and enjoy!

Nutritional Information (per serving):

- Calories: 167kcal
- Total Fat: 8.5g
- Monounsaturated Fat: 2.42g
- Polyunsaturated Fat: 4.06g
- Total Carbohydrates: 20.9g
- Dietary Fiber: 4.7g
- Protein: 5.7g
- Sodium: 197.7mg
- Vitamin B6: .2mg
- Vitamin C: 10.3mg
- Vitamin K: 29.6mcg
- Folate: 42.7mcg
- Iron: 2mg
- Calcium: 71.8mg
- Potassium: 624.2mg
- Magnesium: 72.9mg
- Zinc: 1.3mg

Miso Soup with Tofu and Seaweed

ONE-POT MEAL

A soothing and nourishing Japanese soup, miso soup with tofu and seaweed embodies the gentle balance of umami flavors and healthful ingredients. When tailored for expectant mothers, this soup can be a nutrient-packed elixir, offering a comforting blend of flavors and essential nutrients vital for pregnancy such as probiotics for gut health, protein, iron, calcium and iodine.

Preparation Time: 10 minutes
Cooking Time: 20 minutes
Total Time: 30 minutes
Serves: 4

Ingredients:

- 4 cups water
- 1 sheet nori or wakame seaweed, torn into small pieces
- 3 tablespoons miso paste (white or red)
- 1/2 block firm tofu, cut into small cubes
- 2 green onions, thinly sliced
- 1 small piece of ginger (about 1 inch), finely grated (optional for added flavor)

Instructions:

1. In a large pot, bring the 4 cups of water to a boil. Reduce to a simmer.
2. Add the seaweed pieces to the simmering water and let them hydrate for about 5 minutes.
3. While the seaweed simmers, in a separate bowl, mix the miso paste with a little warm water to create a smoother mixture. This will ensure it dissolves properly in the soup without clumping.
4. Add the tofu cubes to the pot and let them cook for another 5 minutes.
5. Move some liquid from the pot to the bowl with the miso mixture and stir until smooth. Pour this miso mixture back into the pot, making sure not to boil the miso as boiling can reduce its health benefits.
6. Add grated ginger if using.
7. Simmer the soup for another 2-3 minutes, ensuring it doesn't come to a boil.
8. Turn off the heat and add the sliced green onions.
9. Serve immediately in bowls.

Chef's Notes:

- Miso soup is best enjoyed fresh. However, if you need to store it, let the soup cool to room temperature and transfer to an airtight container. Refrigerate and consume within 1-2 days. When reheating, gently warm the soup without bringing it to a boil to retain its benefits and flavors.

Nutritional Information (per serving):

- Calories: 345kcal
- Total Fat: 17.2g
- Monounsaturated Fat: 3.13g
- Polyunsaturated Fat: 7.99g
- Total Carbohydrates: 20.1g

- Dietary Fiber: 8.6g
- Protein: 35.6g
- Sodium: 2517.7mg
- Vitamin B6: .2mg
- Vitamin C: 8.5mg
- Vitamin K: 62.1mcg
- Folate: 66.4mcg
- Iron: 5.8mg
- Calcium: 1128.4mg
- Magnesium: 100.9mg
- Zinc: 2.7mg

Watermelon and Feta Skewers

SO FAST!

These refreshing skewers combine the juicy sweetness of watermelon with the savory creaminess of feta cheese, creating a delightful contrast that's perfect for summer gatherings or as a quick snack. Not only are they delicious, but they also offer various benefits for pregnancy such as calcium and vitamins A, C and B6.

Preparation Time: 10 minutes
Cooking Time: 0 minutes
Total Time: 10 minutes
Serves: 1

Ingredients:
- 4 small watermelon cubes (about 1 inch each)
- 4 small pieces of feta cheese (about 1/2-inch cubes)
- 4 fresh mint leaves (optional)
- 1 small skewer or toothpick

Instructions:
1. Begin by cutting the watermelon into 1-inch cubes. You'll need 4 cubes for one serving.
2. Cut the feta cheese into 1/2-inch cubes.
3. If you're using mint leaves, make sure they're washed and dried.
4. To assemble, take a skewer or toothpick and carefully thread a piece of watermelon, followed by a piece of feta, and then a mint leaf if using.
5. Repeat with the remaining ingredients until the skewer is full.
6. Serve immediately and enjoy!

Nutritional Information (per serving):
- Calories: 150kcal
- Total Fat: 7.3g
- Monounsaturated Fat: 1.57g
- Polyunsaturated Fat: .2g
- Total Carbohydrates: 13.4g
- Dietary Fiber: 0g
- Protein: 4.8g
- Sodium: 387.3mg
- Calcium: 180.7mg
- Vitamin A: 42.9mcg
- Vitamin B6: .1mg
- Vitamin B12: .6mcg
- Zinc: 1mg

Balsamic Glazed Brussels Sprouts with Almonds

VEGAN

Tender and caramelized Brussels sprouts, kissed with a sweet and tangy balsamic glaze, and garnished with crunchy almonds. This dish is not only a treat for the tastebuds but also a nutritional powerhouse, especially beneficial for mom and baby since it includes fiber, folate, protein, healthy fats, and vitamins C, E and K.

Preparation Time: 10 minutes
Cooking Time: 20 minutes
Total Time: 30 minutes
Serves: 1

Ingredients:
- 1 cup brussels sprouts, halved
- 2 tbsp almonds, roughly chopped
- 1 tbsp balsamic vinegar
- 1 tsp honey
- 1 tbsp olive oil
- Salt, to taste
- Black pepper, to taste
- 1 garlic clove, minced

Instructions:
1. Clean the Brussels sprouts by removing any yellow or damaged outer leaves. Slice off the stem end and then halve each sprout.
2. Preheat your oven to 400°F (205°C). In a mixing bowl, toss the halved Brussels sprouts with olive oil, minced garlic (if using), salt, and pepper. Spread them out on a baking sheet in a single layer, ensuring the cut sides are facing down for better caramelization.
3. Roast in the preheated oven for about 15-20 minutes or until the sprouts are golden brown on the edges. A fork should easily pierce the sprouts when they are done.
4. While the Brussels sprouts are roasting, prepare the balsamic glaze. In a small saucepan, combine the balsamic vinegar and honey. Simmer on low heat until the mixture reduces by half and becomes syrupy (about 5 minutes).
5. Once the Brussels sprouts are roasted, transfer them to a serving bowl. Drizzle the balsamic glaze over the sprouts and toss to coat them evenly.
6. Sprinkle the chopped almonds on top.

Nutritional Information (per serving):
- Calories: 306kcal
- Total Fat: 19.5g
- Monounsaturated Fat: 13.5g
- Polyunsaturated Fat: 2.98g
- Total Carbohydrates: 31.4g
- Dietary Fiber: 4.9g
- Protein: 5.7g
- Sodium: 182.4mg
- Vitamin B6: .3mg
- Vitamin C: 75.8mg
- Vitamin E: 5.7mg

- Vitamin K: 162.9mcg
- Folate: 59.3mcg
- Iron: 2mg
- Calcium: 79.1mg
- Potassium: 467.7mg
- Phosphorus: 124.5mg
- Magnesium: 54.4mg
- Zinc: .8mg

Spicy Choco-Latte

SO FAST!

A warming, delectable blend of rich cocoa, mild spices, and creamy milk. This Spicy Choco Latte is perfect for expecting mothers who crave a sweet, comforting drink with a hint of heat. With a good balance of cocoa, which is known to contain flavonoids, and gentle spices like cinnamon that can aid digestion, as well as the protein and calcium in milk, this latte can be a great addition to your diet. Enjoy it on chilly mornings or as an afternoon treat!

Preparation Time: 5 minutes
Cooking Time: 5 minutes
Total Time: 10 minutes
Serves: 1

Ingredients:

- 1 cup full fat milk
- 2 tbsp unsweetened cocoa powder
- 1/4 tsp ground cinnamon
- A pinch of cayenne pepper (adjust according to your heat preference)
- 1-2 tsp honey (adjust sweetness as per preference)
- A tiny pinch of salt

Instructions:

1. In a small saucepan, combine milk, cocoa powder, cinnamon, cayenne pepper, and salt. Whisk continuously over medium heat until all ingredients are well combined and the mixture is hot, but not boiling.
2. Once hot, remove from the heat and stir in honey. Adjust sweetness according to preference.
3. Pour the spicy choco latte into a mug.
4. Serve immediately and enjoy your comforting treat!

Chef's Notes:

- For a non-dairy option, use almond, soy, oat, hemp or coconut milk.

Nutritional Information (per serving):

- Calories: 223kcal
- Total Fat: 10g
- Monounsaturated Fat: 2g
- Polyunsaturated Fat: .5g
- Total Carbohydrates: 25g
- Dietary Fiber: 4.4g
- Protein: 9.8g
- Sodium: 183mg
- Vitamin A: 117mcg
- Vitamin B6: .1mg
- Vitamin B12: 1.1mcg
- Vitamin D: 3.2mcg
- Iron: 3.2mg
- Calcium: 283.2mg
- Potassium: 794.9mg
- Magnesium: 25.3mg
- Zinc: .9mg

Third Trimester Cookbook

Physical Discomfort: As the fetus grows larger, many mothers experience backaches, swollen feet, leg cramps, and general discomfort. The baby's increasing weight can put strain on the mother's back and pelvis.

III TRIMESTER

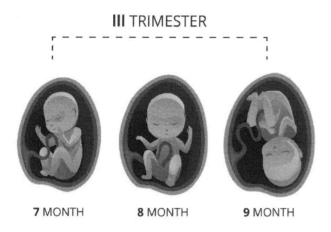

7 MONTH   **8 MONTH**   **9 MONTH**

Unique Challenges of the Third Trimester

Breathing & Heartburn: With the uterus pushing against the diaphragm, shortness of breath can become an issue. Additionally, the relaxed valve between the stomach and esophagus can allow stomach acid to leak, leading to heartburn.

Fatigue: Despite the need for rest, many women find it hard to sleep due to discomfort, frequent urination, and anxiety about the impending birth.

Mood Fluctuations: Hormonal changes can result in mood swings, irritability, and anxiety.

Braxton Hicks Contractions: These "practice" contractions can sometimes be mistaken for real labor.

Essential Nutrients for the Third Trimester

Protein: Aids in the growth of fetal tissue, supports brain development, and increases maternal blood volume. Good sources include lean meats, tofu, beans, and lentils.

Calcium: Essential for the baby's bone development. Mothers who don't consume enough calcium might experience a depletion from their own bones. Dairy products, fortified plant-based milk, green leafy vegetables, and sesame seeds are good sources.

Iron: Vital to support the mother's increased blood volume and to provide the baby with an iron reserve for the first six months of life. Sources include lean meats, spinach, and iron-fortified cereals.

Folic Acid: Continues to be crucial to prevent neural tube defects and aids in the production of red blood cells.

Green leafy vegetables, citrus fruits, and legumes are rich in folic acid.

Omega-3 Fatty Acids: Essential for the baby's brain and eye development. Sources include fatty fish like salmon, walnuts, and flaxseeds.

Fiber: Helps combat constipation, a common problem in the third trimester. Whole grains, fruits, and vegetables are high in fiber.

Helpful Notes:

- Stay Hydrated: Drink plenty of water to support amniotic fluid levels and to reduce swelling.
- Engage in Gentle Exercise: Activities like prenatal yoga or walking can help ease some discomfort and prepare the body for labor.
- Maintain a Balanced Diet: Prioritize the nutrients listed above, but also focus on a comprehensive, well-rounded diet.
- Rest: Listen to your body and rest when necessary. Consider using pillows to support your body during sleep.

Do's:

- Do attend regular prenatal check-ups.
- Do perform pelvic floor exercises to strengthen muscles for delivery.
- Do consume a diverse range of nutrient-rich foods.
- Do listen to your body and rest when needed.

Don'ts:

- Don't take any medication or supplement without consulting your healthcare provider.
- Don't indulge in foods high in sugar and unhealthy fats.
- Don't consume caffeine or alcohol in excess.
- Don't ignore persistent pain or any unusual symptoms; consult your healthcare provider immediately.

While the third trimester is fraught with challenges, it's also a time of intense bonding and preparation for the arrival of the baby. By being informed and making mindful choices, mothers can ensure both their own well-being and the healthy development of their baby.

Heartburn During the Third Trimester

Heartburn, which is a burning sensation in the chest, is a common symptom many women experience during pregnancy, especially in the third trimester. Several factors contribute to this.

Hormonal Changes: Pregnancy hormones, especially progesterone, can cause the valve between the stomach and esophagus to relax, allowing stomach acid to flow back into the esophagus, leading to heartburn.

Growing Baby: As the baby grows, there's increasing pressure on the mother's stomach. This pressure can push stomach contents, including the acid, upward into the esophagus.

Delayed Gastric Emptying: Pregnancy hormones can also slow the digestive process, causing food to stay in the stomach longer, which can increase the risk of heartburn.

How to Fight Heartburn

Eat Smaller Meals: Instead of three large meals a day, try eating five or six smaller meals. This ensures the stomach isn't too full, reducing the likelihood of acid reflux.

Avoid Trigger Foods: Certain foods can exacerbate heartburn. These can include spicy, acidic, and fried foods, as well as caffeine and chocolate. It's beneficial to identify and avoid personal trigger foods.

Stay Upright After Eating: After a meal, try to stay upright for at least an hour. Lying down can cause stomach acid to flow back into the esophagus.

Elevate the Upper Body: When sleeping or resting, use pillows to elevate the upper body. This can prevent acid from flowing up into the esophagus.

Wear Loose Clothing: Tight clothing, especially around the waist, can put extra pressure on the stomach, which can contribute to acid reflux.

Stay Hydrated: Drink plenty of water throughout the day, but try to limit the amount during meals. Too much liquid during a meal can fill the stomach quickly, increasing the risk of reflux.

Avoid Carbonated Beverages: Carbonated drinks can cause bloating and exacerbate heartburn.

Some herbal teas can help, such as:

Chamomile Tea: Known for its soothing properties, chamomile can help neutralize stomach acid and reduce inflammation.

Ginger Tea: Ginger has been used for centuries as a remedy for various gastrointestinal discomforts, including heartburn.

Constipation During Pregnancy

Constipation is another common complaint during pregnancy, especially in the third trimester. Factors contributing to constipation include the following.

Hormonal Changes: Increased levels of progesterone during pregnancy can cause the muscles in the intestines to relax, leading to slower digestion and constipation.

Pressure from the Growing Uterus: As the uterus expands, it can put pressure on the intestines, potentially affecting bowel movements.

Iron Supplements: Many prenatal vitamins contain iron, which can contribute to constipation.

Strategies to Alleviate Constipation

Increase Fiber Intake: Eating foods high in fiber, like whole grains, fruits, and vegetables, can help stimulate bowel movements. Consider adding foods like prunes or bran cereal to your diet.

Stay Hydrated: Drinking plenty of water can help soften stool, making it easier to pass.

Regular Physical Activity: Engaging in light exercises, such as walking or prenatal yoga, can promote healthy digestion and alleviate constipation.

Avoid Iron Supplements if Possible: If iron supplements are causing constipation, speak to your healthcare provider about possible alternatives or adjustments.

Over-the-counter Remedies: If natural methods aren't helping, consider over-the-counter stool softeners. However, always consult with a healthcare provider before taking any medication during pregnancy.

Establish a Routine: Try to have a regular routine for bowel movements, like going at the same time every day. This can train your body to have more regular movements.

Limit Intake of Refined Foods: Processed and refined foods can exacerbate constipation. Limit foods like white bread, pastries, and certain snack foods.

Herbal Teas Recommended for Constipation

Peppermint Tea: This tea can help relax the muscles of the gastrointestinal tract and stimulate bile flow, potentially easing constipation.

Dandelion Root Tea: This is a mild laxative and can promote digestion.

Senna Tea: A stronger herbal laxative, senna should only be used occasionally and under the guidance of a healthcare provider.

WHOLESOME BREAKFASTS

Spiced Apple and Walnut Quinoa Bowl

MIX-AND-MATCH RECIPE

This nutritious and flavorful bowl combines the earthy richness of quinoa, the sweet crispness of apples, and the delightful crunch of walnuts. Perfect for expectant mothers, this dish provides essential nutrients such as fiber, protein, iron, magnesium, healthy fats and B vitamins and vitamin C to support a healthy pregnancy. It's a harmonious blend of textures and tastes that is both satisfying and healthful.

Preparation Time: 10 minutes
Cooking Time: 15 minutes
Total Time: 25 minutes
Serves: 1

Ingredients:
- 1/2 cup uncooked quinoa
- 1 cup water
- 1 medium apple
- 1/4 cup walnuts, roughly chopped
- 1 tablespoon honey
- 1/2 teaspoon ground cinnamon
- Pinch of salt

Instructions:
1. Rinse the quinoa under cold water using a fine mesh strainer.
2. In a medium saucepan, bring 1 cup of water to a boil. Add the rinsed quinoa and a pinch of salt. Reduce the heat to low, cover, and let simmer for 15 minutes or until the quinoa is cooked and water is absorbed.
3. While the quinoa is cooking, slice the apple into thin pieces, discarding the core.
4. Once quinoa is done, remove from heat and fluff it with a fork. Transfer to a bowl.
5. Top the quinoa with sliced apples and chopped walnuts.
6. Drizzle with honey and sprinkle with ground cinnamon.
7. Mix everything well and serve warm.

Chef's Notes:
Mix it up by adding different ingredients each time, such as:
- Dried Fruits: Add raisins, dried cranberries, or dried apricots for an added chew and sweetness.
- Seeds: Mix in chia seeds, flaxseeds, or sunflower seeds for an extra crunch and a boost in nutrients.
- Yogurt: A dollop of Greek yogurt or your favorite plant-based yogurt can add creaminess and additional protein.
- Spices: Experiment with nutmeg or cardamom for a unique flavor twist.

Nutritional Information (per serving):
- Calories: 666kcal
- Total Fat: 24.6g
- Monounsaturated Fat: 4g
- Polyunsaturated Fat: 16.69g
- Omega-3 Fatty Acids: 2.9g
- Total Carbohydrates: 102g
- Dietary Fiber: 13g
- Protein: 17g
- Sodium: 162.7mg
- Vitamin B6: .7mg
- Vitamin C: 8.9mg
- Vitamin E: 2.6mg
- Folate: 191mcg
- Iron: 5.2mg
- Calcium: 93.9mg
- Potassium: 818.8mg
- Phosphorus: 511.3mg
- Magnesium: 224mg
- Zinc: 3.7mg

Moroccan Lentil Soup with Whole Wheat Pita

MEAL-PREP FRIENDLY

Moroccan Lentil Soup is a hearty, flavorful, and nutritious dish brimming with warming spices, vegetables, and iron and protein-rich lentils. Paired with a side of whole wheat pita, this soup offers a balanced meal ideal for expectant mothers and anyone looking for a healthy, comforting dish.

Preparation Time: 15 minutes
Cooking Time: 45 minutes
Total Time: 60 minutes
Serves: 4

Ingredients:
- 1 cup dried green or brown lentils, rinsed and drained
- 1 large onion, finely chopped
- 2 carrots, diced
- 2 celery stalks, diced
- 3 garlic cloves, minced
- 1 teaspoon ground cumin
- 1/2 teaspoon ground turmeric
- 1/2 teaspoon ground cinnamon
- 1/2 teaspoon paprika
- 1/4 teaspoon ground ginger
- 4 cups vegetable broth
- 1 (14.5 oz) can diced tomatoes
- 2 tablespoons olive oil
- Salt and pepper, to taste
- Fresh cilantro or parsley, chopped (for garnish)
- Juice of 1 lemon
- 4 whole wheat pitas

Instructions:
1. In a large pot, heat the olive oil over medium heat. Add the onions, carrots, and celery. Sauté until the vegetables are softened, about 5-7 minutes.
2. Add the minced garlic, cumin, turmeric, cinnamon, paprika, and ginger to the pot. Stir well and cook for another 2 minutes until the spices are fragrant.

3. Add the lentils, vegetable broth, and diced tomatoes (with their juices) to the pot. Bring the mixture to a boil, then reduce to a simmer.
4. Cover and let the soup simmer for about 30-40 minutes or until the lentils are tender. Season with salt and pepper to taste.
5. Once cooked, add the lemon juice and stir well. Adjust seasonings if necessary.
6. Warm the whole wheat pitas in the oven or on a skillet just before serving.
7. Serve the soup hot, garnished with fresh cilantro or parsley. Pair with a side of whole wheat pita.

Chef's Notes:
- Store leftover soup in an airtight container in the refrigerator for up to 3-4 days.
- For longer storage, freeze the soup in portion-sized containers. It can be frozen for up to 2-3 months. Thaw overnight in the fridge before reheating.
- Whole wheat pitas are best consumed fresh. If storing, keep them in a sealed plastic bag at room temperature for 1-2 days. They can also be frozen for up to a month. Thaw at room temperature before warming and serving.

Nutritional Information (per serving):
- Calories: 392kcal
- Total Fat: 8.2g
- Monounsaturated Fat: 5.16g
- Polyunsaturated Fat: 1.39g
- Total Carbohydrates: 65.6g
- Dietary Fiber: 12.5g
- Protein: 18.2g
- Sodium: 991.1mg
- Vitamin A: 342.5mcg
- Vitamin B6: .5mg
- Vitamin C: 46mg
- Vitamin E: 1.8mg
- Vitamin K: 23.1mcg
- Folate: 267.8mcg
- Iron: 5.5mg
- Calcium: 80.3mg
- Magnesium: 59.6mg
- Zinc: 2.3mg

Roasted Root Vegetable Hash with Farm Fresh Eggs

VEGETARIAN

Savor the earthy flavors and rich nutrients of roasted root vegetables paired with creamy, farm-fresh eggs. This dish not only tantalizes the palate but is also packed with essential nutrients beneficial for pregnancy. Root vegetables offer essential vitamins and minerals like folate, vitamin C, and potassium, while eggs provide a high-quality protein source rich in choline and omega-3s. Together, they create a balanced meal to nourish both mother and baby.

Preparation Time: 10 minutes
Cooking Time: 30 minutes

Total Time: 40 minutes
Serves: 1

Ingredients:
- 1 small beet, peeled and diced
- 1 small carrot, peeled and diced
- 1 small potato, peeled and diced
- 1 small parsnip, peeled and diced
- 2 tsp olive oil
- Salt and pepper to taste
- 1 farm-fresh egg
- Fresh herbs for garnish (optional, e.g., parsley or chives)

Preparation:
1. Preheat the oven to 425°F (220°C).
2. In a mixing bowl, toss the diced root vegetables with olive oil, salt, and pepper until well-coated.
3. Spread the vegetables on a baking sheet in a single layer.
4. Roast the vegetables in the preheated oven for about 25-30 minutes, or until they are tender and lightly browned, stirring occasionally to ensure even cooking.
5. In the last 5 minutes of roasting, heat a skillet over medium heat. Crack the farm-fresh egg into the skillet and cook to your desired doneness (sunny side up, over easy, etc.).
6. Place the roasted root vegetable hash on a plate and top with the cooked egg.
7. Garnish with fresh herbs if desired.

Chef's Notes:
- Top with a sprinkle of feta or parmesan cheese if desired
- Add sauteed spinach for extra nutrition
- Add a tablespoon of chopped walnuts for extra protein and healthy fats

Nutritional Information (per serving):
- Calories: 427kcal
- Total Fat: 14.6g
- Monounsaturated Fat: 8.58g
- Polyunsaturated Fat: 2.16g
- Total Carbohydrates: 64g
- Dietary Fiber: 12.7g
- Protein: 12.8g
- Sodium: 354.5mg
- Vitamin A: 500.5mcg
- Vitamin B6: .6mg
- Vitamin B12: .4mcg
- Vitamin C: 47mg
- Vitamin D: 1mcg
- Vitamin E: 4.3mg
- Vitamin K: 46.1mcg
- Folate: 248.8mcg
- Iron: 3.5mg
- Calcium: 118.1mg
- Potassium: 1746.5mg
- Phosphorus: 343.1mg
- Magnesium: 108.1mg
- Zinc: 2.4mg

Turmeric and Ginger Smoothie with Hemp Hearts

GLUTEN-FREE

A vibrant and refreshing smoothie that harnesses the natural benefits of turmeric and ginger. Perfect for expectant mothers, this drink aids in digestion, reduces inflammation, and may help in alleviating nausea associated with morning sickness. The addition of other nutritious ingredients like bananas and chia seeds makes it a wholesome drink to boost your nutrition for the upcoming day.

Preparation Time: 5 minutes
Cooking Time: 0 minutes
Total Time: 5 minutes
Serves: 1

Ingredients:
- 1 ripe banana
- 1 cup of almond milk (or any milk of your choice)
- 1/2 tsp of fresh turmeric, grated (or 1/4 tsp of turmeric powder)
- 1/2 tsp of fresh ginger, grated
- 1 tbsp hemp hearts
- Ice cubes (optional)

Instructions:
1. Start by peeling and slicing the banana.
2. In a blender, combine the banana slices, almond milk, grated turmeric, grated ginger, and chia seeds.
3. If you're adding sweetness, put in the honey.
4. Add the pinch of black pepper.
5. Blend on high until the smoothie is creamy and smooth. If the consistency is too thick for your liking, you can add a bit more milk.
6. If you prefer a colder drink, toss in some ice cubes and blend again until smooth.
7. Pour into a glass and enjoy immediately!

Chef's Notes:
- Add frozen pineapple and/or mango instead of ice cubes for extra nutrition and sweetness
- Can use whole dairy milk or other non-dairy alternatives such as oat, coconut, hemp or soy milks.

Nutritional Information (per serving):
- Calories: 195kcal
- Total Fat: 7g
- Monounsaturated Fat: 1.6g
- Polyunsaturated Fat: .73g
- Total Carbohydrates: 32g
- Dietary Fiber: 4.1g
- Protein: 5g
- Sodium: 190.3mg
- Vitamin B6: .4mg
- Vitamin C: 10.3mg
- Vitamin D: 2.6mcg
- Vitamin E: 16.7mg
- Folate: 26.5mcg
- Iron: 2.4mg
- Calcium: 490.3mg
- Magnesium: 51.1mg

Wild Rice and Mushroom Pilaf with Steamed Greens

VEGAN

A wholesome dish that combines the nutty flavor of wild rice with earthy mushrooms, accompanied by lightly steamed greens. It's a comforting, nourishing meal that's especially beneficial during pregnancy due to its rich combination of essential nutrients such as folic acid, B vitamins, magnesium, fiber, iron and calcium.

.

Preparation Time: 15 minutes
Cooking Time: 50 minutes
Total Time: 65 minutes
Serves: 2

Ingredients:
- 1/2 cup wild rice
- 1 cup water (for rice)
- 1 tbsp olive oil
- 1/2 cup finely chopped onions
- 1 garlic clove, minced
- 1 cup mushrooms, sliced
- 1/2 cup vegetable broth
- Salt and pepper to taste
- 1 cup spinach
- 1 cup kale
- Lemon zest (optional)

Instructions:
- Rinse the wild rice under cold water using a fine mesh strainer.
- In a saucepan, bring 1 cup of water to a boil. Add the wild rice, reduce the heat to low, cover, and simmer for 40-50 minutes or until the rice is tender and the grains have burst open.
- While the rice is cooking, heat the olive oil or butter in a skillet over medium heat. Add onions and sauté until translucent.
- Add garlic and mushrooms. Cook until mushrooms are browned and have released their moisture.
- Once the rice is cooked, combine it with the mushroom mixture. Pour in the vegetable broth and cook until most of the liquid is absorbed. Season with salt and pepper.
- In a steamer or a pot with a steaming basket, bring a small amount of water to a boil.
- Add greens to the steamer or basket. Cover and steam for 3-5 minutes or until tender but still bright green.
- Season with a pinch of salt and optionally, some lemon zest for an extra burst of flavor.

Chef's Notes:
- Serve the wild rice and mushroom pilaf alongside the steamed greens.

- Add additional vegetables such as steamed broccoli or cherry tomatoes for extra flavor and nutrition
- Drizzle with a touch of olive oil or a squeeze of fresh lemon juice for added flavor.
- Store leftovers in an airtight container in the refrigerator for up to 3 days.
- Reheat in a microwave or on the stovetop, adding a splash of water or broth to prevent the pilaf from drying out. Steamed greens are best consumed when freshly made but can also be reheated gently.

Nutritional Information (per serving):
- Calories: 237kcal
- Total Fat: 7.6g
- Monounsaturated Fat: 5g
- Polyunsaturated Fat: 1.13g
- Total Carbohydrates: 36.7g
- Dietary Fiber: 4.2g
- Protein: 8.3g
- Sodium: 186.2mg
- Vitamin A: 96.7mcg
- Vitamin B6: .3mg
- Vitamin C: 16.1mg
- Vitamin E: 1.7mg
- Vitamin K: 109mcg
- Folate: 85.7mcg
- Iron: 1.7mg
- Potassium: 468.6mg
- Phosphorus: 230.6mg
- Magnesium: 93.4mg
- Zinc: 2.8mg

Pomegranate and Pistachio Overnight Oats

MIX-AND-MATCH RECIPE

A refreshing blend of creamy oats, the tang of pomegranate seeds, and the crunch of pistachios. This no-cook recipe is not only a visual delight with its vibrant colors but also packs a nutritional punch, especially beneficial during pregnancy. The synergy of essential nutrients such as fiber, magnesium, potassium, vitamin C, calcium, protein and healthy fats support both the mother's and baby's health, making it an ideal breakfast or snack.

Preparation Time: 10 minutes
Cooking Time: 0 minutes (requires overnight refrigeration)
Total Time: 10 minutes
Serves: 1

Ingredients:
- 1/2 cup rolled oats
- 2/3 cup unsweetened almond milk (or any milk of your choice)
- 1/2 tsp chia seeds
- 1 tbsp honey
- 1/4 cup pomegranate seeds
- 1 tbsp crushed pistachios
- A pinch of salt
- 1/4 tsp vanilla extract (optional)

Instructions:
1. In a jar or a bowl, mix together the rolled oats, chia seeds, almond milk, honey, vanilla extract (if using), and a pinch of salt. Stir well to combine.
2. Seal the jar or cover the bowl with a lid or plastic wrap. Place it in the refrigerator and allow it to sit overnight.
3. The next morning, give the oats a good stir. If the mixture is too thick, you can add a splash more milk to reach your desired consistency.
4. Top with pomegranate seeds and crushed pistachios.
5. Enjoy your delightful bowl of pomegranate and pistachio overnight oats!

Chef's Notes:
Recipe Variations:
- Dairy-Free: Substitute almond milk with coconut milk, oat milk, or any dairy-free alternative.
- Nut-Free: Replace pistachios with sunflower seeds or pumpkin seeds.
- Additional Fruits: Add sliced bananas, berries, or kiwi for extra flavor and nutrients.
- Spice it up: Incorporate a sprinkle of cinnamon or cardamom for added warmth and flavor.
- Sweeteners: Swap out honey with maple syrup or coconut sugar for a different taste profile.

Nutritional Information (per serving):
- Calories: 311kcal
- Total Fat: 8.5g
- Monounsaturated Fat: 2.07g
- Polyunsaturated Fat: 1.95g
- Total Carbohydrates: 56g
- Dietary Fiber: 7.4g
- Protein: 8.1g
- Sodium: 155.7mg
- Vitamin C: 4.2mg
- Vitamin D: 1.7mcg
- Vitamin E: 11mg
- Iron: 2.8mg
- Calcium: 363.6mg
- Magnesium: 18.4mg

Warm Farro Salad with Roasted Beet and Goat Cheese

VEGETARIAN

A delightful mixture of chewy farro, earthy beets, and creamy goat cheese, this warm salad is both delicious and nutritious. It's perfect for expectant mothers, boasting ingredients rich in vital nutrients to support a healthy pregnancy. Farro provides whole grains and fiber, beets supply folate and antioxidants, and goat cheese offers a good dose of calcium. This dish not only supports maternal health but also satisfies cravings with its mix of flavors and textures.

Preparation Time: 10 minutes
Cooking Time: 45 minutes
Total Time: 55 minutes
Serves: 1

Ingredients:

- 1 medium-sized beet, peeled and diced
- 1/2 cup farro
- 1 1/2 cups vegetable broth
- 1 oz goat cheese, crumbled
- 1 tbsp olive oil
- 1 tbsp balsamic vinegar
- Salt and pepper to taste
- Fresh parsley or microgreens for garnish (optional)
- 1 small garlic clove, minced

Instructions:

1. Preheat your oven to 400°F (200°C). In a bowl, toss the diced beets with a half tablespoon of olive oil, salt, and pepper. Transfer to a baking sheet lined with parchment paper or aluminum foil. Roast for about 30-35 minutes or until the beets are tender and slightly caramelized. Turn them once or twice during cooking for even roasting.

2. While the beets are roasting, rinse the farro under cold water. In a pot, bring water or vegetable broth to a boil. Add the farro and a pinch of salt. Reduce heat, cover, and simmer for about 25-30 minutes or until the grains are tender but still chewy. Drain any excess liquid.

3. In a small bowl, whisk together the remaining olive oil, balsamic vinegar, minced garlic (if using), salt, and pepper until well combined.

4. In a serving bowl, mix the warm cooked farro with the roasted beets. Drizzle the dressing over the top and gently toss to combine. Crumble the goat cheese on top. Garnish with fresh parsley or microgreens, if desired.

5. Serve warm and enjoy!

Chef's Notes:

- Add additional vegetables for flavor and nutrition, such as broccoli, asparagus or sauteed spinach
- Add chopped almonds, walnuts or pistachios for crunch and extra protein and healthy fats
- Add apple slices at the end for additional crunch, sweetness and nutrition.

Nutritional Information (per serving):

- Calories: 658kcal
- Total Fat: 26g
- Monounsaturated Fat: 12.2g
- Polyunsaturated Fat: 1.73g
- Total Carbohydrates: 79.3g
- Dietary Fiber: 8.4g
- Protein: 25g
- Sodium: 1189.8mg
- Vitamin A: 179.4mcg
- Vitamin B6: .14mg
- Vitamin C: 6.3mg
- Vitamin E: 2.1mg
- Vitamin K: 11.5mcg
- Folate: 90.6mcg
- Iron: 2.3mg
- Calcium: 327.2mg
- Magnesium: 20.2mg
- Zinc: .89mg

Chia Seed Pudding Infused with Matcha and Topped with Mango

MIX-AND-MATCH RECIPE

This refreshing and nutrient-packed pudding combines the subtle earthiness of matcha with the sweet tropical notes of mango. A perfect treat for expecting mothers, it offers a wealth of health benefits such as fiber, protein, healthy fats and vitamins A and C, and is sure to satisfy those pregnancy cravings.

Preparation Time: 10 minutes
Cooking Time: 0 minutes (must be refrigerated for 3 hours to overnight)
Total Time: 10 minutes
Serves: 1

Ingredients:

- 3 tbsp chia seeds
- 1 cup almond milk (or any milk of your choice)
- 1 tsp matcha green tea powder
- 1 tbsp honey
- 1/2 ripe mango, diced

Instructions:

1. In a mixing bowl, whisk together almond milk, matcha powder, and honey until the matcha is fully dissolved.
2. Stir in the chia seeds, ensuring they're well dispersed and not clumping.
3. Transfer the mixture to a serving bowl or jar, cover, and refrigerate for at least 3 hours or overnight. The pudding will thicken as the chia seeds absorb the liquid.
4. Once set, give the pudding a good stir to break up any lumps.
5. Top with diced mango before serving. Enjoy!

Chef's Notes:

Recipe Variations:

- Tropical Delight: Swap mango for a mix of tropical fruits such as kiwi, pineapple, and passion fruit.
- Berry Burst: Replace mango with a medley of berries like strawberries, blueberries, and raspberries.
- Creamy Indulgence: Mix in a spoonful of coconut milk or yogurt for a creamier texture.
- Nutty Crunch: Add a sprinkle of crushed nuts, such as almonds or walnuts, for an added crunch and boost of omega-3.
- Sweetness Swap: If you'd like to avoid added sugars, try blending dates into the milk for a natural sweetness.

Nutritional Information (per serving):

- Calories: 211kcal
- Total Fat: 3.2g
- Monounsaturated Fat: 1.78g
- Polyunsaturated Fat: .75g
- Total Carbohydrates: 45.9g

- Dietary Fiber: 3.3g
- Protein: 2.5g
- Sodium: 191.2mg
- Vitamin A: 90.7mcg
- Vitamin B6: .2mg
- Vitamin C: 61.3mg
- Vitamin D: 2.6mcg
- Vitamin E: 18.1mg
- Vitamin K: 7.1mcg
- Folate: 75.3mcg
- Iron: 1.4mg
- Calcium: 507.8mg
- Magnesium: 32.9mg

Apple and Cinnamon Overnight Oats with Collagen

SO FAST!

This nourishing and flavorful recipe combines the wholesome goodness of oats with the crispiness of apples and the warm hint of cinnamon. By adding collagen, you're giving your breakfast an extra boost of protein that has been touted for its benefits for skin, hair, nails, and joints. It's especially beneficial during pregnancy as it can support the skin's elasticity and hydration, making it a wonderful addition to your diet. With minimal preparation time, this is a fantastic way to ensure a hearty and nutritious start to your day.

Preparation Time: 10 minutes
Cooking Time: 0 minutes (overnight refrigeration)
Total Time: 10 minutes
Serves: 1

Ingredients:
- 1/2 cup rolled oats
- 1 apple, diced (preferably organic, and you can keep the skin on for added fiber)
- 3/4 cup whole milk (you can use almond, soy, cow's, or any milk of your choice)
- 1 tsp ground cinnamon
- 1 tbsp chia seeds (optional, for extra texture and nutrition)
- 1 tbsp honey
- 1-2 scoops of collagen powder (based on your preference and product recommendation)

Instructions:
1. In a jar or bowl, combine the rolled oats, diced apple, cinnamon, and chia seeds.
2. Add the milk and stir until everything is well-mixed.
3. Mix in the collagen powder until it's fully dissolved.
4. Sweeten with honey according to your taste.
5. Seal the jar with a lid or cover the bowl.
6. Place it in the refrigerator overnight.
7. In the morning, give it a good stir. If it's too thick, add a little more milk until it reaches your preferred consistency.
8. Top with more diced apples, a sprinkle of cinnamon, or any other toppings you like before serving.

Chef's Notes
Recipe Variations:
- For a non-dairy option, use any plant-based milk
- Berry Bliss: Replace apple with a mix of berries like blueberries, strawberries, and raspberries.
- Tropical Twist: Use diced mango or pineapple and coconut flakes.
- Chocolate Delight: Add a tablespoon of cocoa powder and top with chocolate chips.
- Nutty Nourishment: Incorporate almond butter or peanut butter for a creamy texture and added protein.

Nutritional Information (per serving):
- Calories: 508kcal
- Total Fat: 13.1g
- Monounsaturated Fat: 2.83g
- Polyunsaturated Fat: 4.79g
- Omega-3 Fatty Acids: 2.63g
- Total Carbohydrates: 81.7g
- Dietary Fiber: 13.9g
- Protein: 23.7g
- Vitamin A: 89mcg
- Vitamin B6: .14mg
- Vitamin B12: .82mcg
- Vitamin C: 7.3mg
- Vitamin D: 2.4mcg
- Folate: 21.2mcg
- Calcium: 374.6mg
- Potassium: 621.9mg
- Magnesium: 75.3mg
- Zinc: 1.5mg

Baked Oatmeal with Blueberries

MEAL-PREP FRIENDLY

A warm, wholesome, and satisfying breakfast, this baked oatmeal combines the natural sweetness of blueberries with hearty oats. It's not just delicious – it's also packed with nutrients that are beneficial for expecting moms, such as fiber, vitamin C, folic acid, protein and calcium.

Preparation Time: 10 minutes
Cooking Time: 35-40 minutes
Total Time: 45-50 minutes
Serves: 6
Ingredients:
- 2 cups old-fashioned rolled oats
- 1 teaspoon baking powder
- 1/2 teaspoon salt
- 1 teaspoon cinnamon
- 2 cups whole milk
- 1/4 cup honey
- 2 large eggs
- 1 teaspoon vanilla extract
- 2 cups fresh blueberries

Instructions:
1. Preheat the oven to 375°F (190°C). Grease a 9x9-inch baking dish or similar size.

2. In a large bowl, mix together the oats, baking powder, salt, and cinnamon.
3. In a separate bowl, whisk together the milk, honey, eggs, and vanilla extract.
4. Combine the wet and dry ingredients. Gently fold in the blueberries.
5. Pour the mixture into the prepared baking dish.
6. Optional: Sprinkle with additional toppings if desired.
7. Bake for 35-40 minutes, or until the top is golden and the oatmeal is set.
8. Remove from the oven and let it cool for a few minutes. Serve warm.

Chef's Notes:
- For a non-dairy option, use any plant-based milk
- Add chopped nuts, banana slices or any other fruits for additional flavors and nutrients

Storage Information:
- Refrigerating: Allow the baked oatmeal to cool completely. Cover the baking dish with plastic wrap or transfer to an airtight container. Store in the refrigerator for up to 4 days.
- Freezing: Once cooled, cut the baked oatmeal into servings and place them on a baking sheet. Freeze until solid, then transfer to airtight containers or freezer bags. Properly stored, it will maintain the best quality for 1 to 2 months.
- Reheating: Microwave individual servings for 1-2 minutes until warm. If reheating from frozen, add an additional minute or two.

Nutritional Information (per serving):
- Calories: 298kcal
- Total Fat: 7.1g
- Monounsaturated Fat: 2.38g
- Polyunsaturated Fat: 1.64g
- Total Carbohydrates: 52.3g
- Dietary Fiber: 5.8g
- Protein: 10.5g
- Vitamin A: 65mcg
- Vitamin B6: .09mg
- Vitamin B12: .51mcg
- Vitamin C: 4.8mg
- Vitamin D: 1.4mcg
- Vitamin K: 9.8mcg
- Folate: 15mcg
- Iron: 2.4mg
- Calcium: 130.3mg
- Potassium: 330.2mg
- Zinc: .63mg

Salsa Verde Baked Eggs

GLUTEN-FREE

A savory, spicy, and nutritious breakfast dish that combines the zesty flavors of salsa verde with perfectly baked eggs. Ideal for a morning boost, especially for expectant mothers, this recipe is rich in protein, choline and vitamin C.

Preparation Time: 5 minutes

Cooking Time: 15 minutes
Total Time: 20 minutes
Serves: 1

Ingredients:
- 1 large egg
- 1/3 cup salsa verde (store-bought or homemade)
- 1 tbsp olive oil
- 1 clove garlic, minced
- 1 tbsp onion, finely chopped
- Salt and pepper, to taste
- Fresh cilantro, for garnish
- 1 tbsp shredded mexican cheese

Instructions:
1. Preheat your oven to 375°F (190°C).
2. In a small oven-safe skillet or ramekin, heat the olive oil over medium heat. Add the minced garlic and chopped onion. Sauté until fragrant and translucent, around 2-3 minutes.
3. Pour the salsa verde into the skillet, stirring well to combine with the garlic and onion.
4. Create a small well in the center of the salsa mixture using a spoon.
5. Crack the egg into the well, ensuring the yolk remains intact.
6. Season with salt and pepper to your liking.
7. Place the skillet or ramekin into the preheated oven and bake for 10-12 minutes, or until the egg whites are set but the yolk remains runny. For a firmer yolk, bake an additional 3-5 minutes.
8. Remove from the oven and garnish with fresh cilantro and shredded cheese if desired.
9. Serve hot and enjoy!

Chef's Notes:
Side Dish Recommendations:
- Avocado Toast: Avocado is rich in folate, which is beneficial during pregnancy. Simply mash a ripe avocado on a toasted slice of whole grain bread, sprinkle with salt, pepper, and a dash of lemon juice.
- Quinoa Salad: Quinoa is a complete protein and rich in iron. Toss cooked quinoa with chopped veggies like bell peppers, cucumbers, and tomatoes. Drizzle with olive oil and lemon juice.
- Fruit Salad: Fresh fruits like berries, oranges, and bananas provide necessary vitamins and natural sugars for energy. Mix your favorites for a refreshing side.

Nutritional Information (per serving):
- Calories: 264kcal
- Total Fat: 20.5g
- Monounsaturated Fat: 11.68g
- Polyunsaturated Fat: 2.39g
- Total Carbohydrates: 7.6g
- Dietary Fiber: 2.7g
- Protein: 8.4g
- Sodium: 687.7mg
- Vitamin A: 83.4mcg

- Vitamin B6: .14mg
- Vitamin B12: .45mcg
- Vitamin D: 1mcg
- Vitamin E: 2.5mg
- Vitamin K: 11.5mcg
- Folate: 26.1mcg
- Iron: 2mg
- Calcium: 83.8mg
- Zinc: .7mg

HEARTY LUNCHES AND DINNERS

Roasted Cauliflower Salad

VEGAN

A deliciously hearty salad that combines the nutty flavors of roasted cauliflower with fresh greens and tangy dressing. This dish offers a multitude of nutrients beneficial for pregnancy including fiber, calcium, iron, folate, protein and healthy fats.

Preparation Time: 10 minutes
Cooking Time: 25 minutes
Total Time: 35 minutes
Serves: 2

Ingredients:

- 1 small cauliflower, cut into florets
- 2 tablespoons olive oil
- Salt and pepper, to taste
- 1 cup spinach
- 1 cup arugula
- 1/4 cup walnuts
- 1/4 cup pumpkin seeds
- 1/4 cup crumbled feta cheese
- 2 tablespoons balsamic vinegar
- 1 tablespoon honey
- 1 tablespoon Dijon mustard
- 2 tablespoons extra virgin olive oil

Instructions:

1. Roast the Cauliflower: Preheat the oven to 425°F (220°C). Toss the cauliflower florets with olive oil, salt, and pepper. Spread them out on a baking sheet and roast for 20-25 minutes, or until golden brown and tender. Remove from the oven and let them cool.
2. Prepare the Dressing: In a small bowl, whisk together balsamic vinegar, honey, Dijon mustard, and extra virgin olive oil. Season with salt and pepper to taste.
3. Assemble the Salad: In a large bowl, combine the roasted cauliflower, mixed greens, nuts, seeds, and feta cheese (if using). Drizzle the dressing over the salad and toss gently to combine.
4. Serve: Divide the salad between two plates and serve immediately.

Chef's Notes/Recipe Variations:

- **Protein Boost:** Add grilled chicken or tofu for added protein.
- **Fruity Twist:** Incorporate dried fruits like cranberries or fresh fruits like pomegranate seeds or apple slices.
- **Herbal Touch:** Sprinkle with fresh herbs like parsley, dill, or basil for a burst of flavor.
- **Spicy Kick:** Add a pinch of red pepper flakes or a drizzle of spicy oil for those who like a bit of heat.
- **Dairy-Free:** Skip the feta or replace with a dairy-free alternative like vegan feta or nutritional yeast for a cheesy flavor.

Nutritional Information (per serving):
- Calories: 533kcal
- Total Fat: 45.8g
- Monounsaturated Fat: XX g
- Polyunsaturated Fat: XX g (indicate omega-3 fatty acids if applicable)
- Total Carbohydrates: 24.6g
- Dietary Fiber: 4.6g
- Protein: 11.2g
- Sodium: 676.8mg
- Vitamin A: 105.8mcg
- Vitamin B6: .44mg
- Vitamin B12: .32mcg
- Vitamin C: 69.8mg
- Vitamin E: 4.5mg
- Vitamin K: 120.8mcg
- Folate: 134.9mcg
- Iron: 2.7mg
- Calcium: 189.2mg
- Magnesium: 65.2mg
- Zinc: 1.5mg

Roast Chicken with Garlic and Herb Root Vegetables

MEAL-PREP FRIENDLY

This heartwarming recipe combines the rich flavors of roasted chicken with the earthy tones of root vegetables, enhanced by aromatic herbs and garlic. Not only is this dish delectable, but it's also nutrient-rich with fiber, protein and vitamin A, making it especially beneficial for you and your baby.

Preparation Time: 20 minutes
Cooking Time: 1 hour, 20 minutes
Total Time: 1 hour, 40 minutes
Serves: 4

Ingredients:
- 1 whole chicken (about 4-5 pounds)
- 4 large carrots, peeled and chopped
- 4 parsnips, peeled and chopped
- 2 large potatoes, scrubbed and chopped
- 1 turnip, peeled and chopped
- 8 cloves of garlic, minced
- 2 tablespoons olive oil
- 2 teaspoons fresh rosemary, finely chopped

- 2 teaspoons fresh thyme, finely chopped
- Salt and pepper to taste

Instructions:

1. Preheat the oven to 425°F (220°C). Ensure the chicken is cleaned, and the giblets are removed.
2. In a large mixing bowl, combine the chopped root vegetables. Add half of the minced garlic, one tablespoon of olive oil, rosemary, thyme, salt, and pepper. Mix until the vegetables are well-coated.
3. Rub the chicken with the remaining tablespoon of olive oil. Sprinkle the remaining garlic inside the chicken cavity and season with salt and pepper.
4. Place the chicken breast-side up in a large roasting pan. Scatter the seasoned root vegetables around the chicken.
5. Place the roasting pan in the oven and roast for about 1 hour and 20 minutes or until the chicken's internal temperature reaches 165°F (74°C) and the vegetables are tender.
6. Once cooked, let the chicken rest for 10 minutes before carving. Serve the chicken slices with a generous helping of the roasted vegetables.

Chef's Note:
- Make extra and store leftovers in an airtight container in the refrigerator for up to 3-4 days.

Nutritional Information (per serving):
- Calories: 985kcal
- Total Fat: 59g
- Monounsaturated Fat: 5.08g
- Polyunsaturated Fat: .87g
- Total Carbohydrates: 46.3g
- Dietary Fiber: 9.1g
- Protein: 67.9g
- Sodium: 437.6mg
- Vitamin B6: .41mg
- Vitamin C: 49.6mg
- Vitamin E: 3mg
- Vitamin K: 36.5mcg
- Folate: 127.3mcg
- Iron: 6.1mg
- Calcium: 140.7mg
- Magnesium: 67.7mg
- Zinc: 1.3mg

Veggie-Stuffed Portobello Mushrooms with Lentils

GLUTEN-FREE

This hearty and nutritious dish combines the meaty texture of portobello mushrooms with a rich filling of cooked lentils and vegetables. Perfect for a wholesome dinner, this recipe boasts a variety of essential nutrients beneficial for pregnancy, such as folic acid, iron, and protein. It's a delicious way to nourish both you and your baby.

Preparation Time: 15 minutes
Cooking Time: 30 minutes

Total Time: 45 minutes
Serves: 2
Ingredients:
- 2 large portobello mushrooms, stems removed
- 1/2 cup dried lentils (preferably green or brown), rinsed and drained
- 1 1/2 cups vegetable broth
- 1 small onion, finely chopped
- 1 small carrot, diced
- 1 clove garlic, minced
- 1/2 bell pepper, diced (any color)
- 1 tbsp olive oil
- 1/4 tsp dried thyme
- Salt and pepper, to taste
- 2 tbsp grated Parmesan cheese or nutritional yeast (for a dairy-free option)
- Fresh parsley, for garnish

Instructions:

1. In a medium saucepan, combine the lentils and vegetable broth or water. Bring to a boil, reduce heat, cover, and simmer for 20-25 minutes, or until lentils are tender but not mushy. Drain any excess liquid and set aside.
2. While the lentils are cooking, heat the olive oil in a skillet over medium heat. Add onions and garlic and sauté until translucent, about 2-3 minutes. Add carrots and bell peppers, and cook for another 5 minutes until they start to soften.
3. Once the lentils are done, add them to the skillet with the vegetables. Stir in the thyme, salt, and pepper, and cook for an additional 2-3 minutes. Remove from heat and set aside.
4. Preheat the oven to 375°F (190°C). Clean the portobello mushrooms with a damp cloth and place them on a baking sheet, gill side up.
5. Divide the lentil-vegetable mixture between the two mushrooms, pressing down to pack the filling. Sprinkle with Parmesan cheese or nutritional yeast.
6. Place the stuffed mushrooms in the preheated oven and bake for about 15 minutes, or until the mushrooms are tender and the filling is heated through.
7. Garnish with fresh parsley and serve immediately.

Chef's Notes:
- You can pair this dish with a side salad or steamed greens for added nutrients.

Nutritional Information (per serving):
- Calories: 208kcal
- Total Fat: 9.8g
- Monounsaturated Fat: 5.01g
- Polyunsaturated Fat: 1.14g
- Total Carbohydrates: 22.8g
- Dietary Fiber: 7g
- Protein: 10.7g
- Sodium: 609.5mg
- Vitamin A: 275.6mcg
- Vitamin B6: .41mg
- Vitamin C: 44mg

- Vitamin E: 1.7mg
- Vitamin K: 13.1mcg
- Folate: 138.6mcg
- Iron: 2.5mg
- Calcium: 130.4mg
- Magnesium: 30.2mg
- Zinc: 1.3mg

Moroccan Chickpea Stew with Whole Grain Couscous

MEAL-PREP FRIENDLY

A hearty and flavorful Moroccan-inspired stew, this dish combines nutrient-rich chickpeas with a blend of spices and vegetables. Served over whole grain couscous, it's not only delicious but also particularly beneficial for pregnancy, offering a good balance of protein, fiber, iron, folate, and vitamins C and E.

Preparation Time: 15 minutes
Cooking Time: 35 minutes
Total Time: 50 minutes
Serves: 6

Ingredients:

- 2 cans (15 oz each) chickpeas, drained and rinsed
- 1 large onion, diced
- 3 garlic cloves, minced
- 2 bell peppers (any color), diced
- 1 can (14 oz) diced tomatoes (with juice)
- 3 cups baby spinach
- 2 tsp ground cumin
- 2 tsp ground coriander
- 1 tsp turmeric
- 1/2 tsp ground cinnamon
- 1/2 tsp paprika
- 1/4 cup chopped almonds
- 4 cups whole grain couscous
- 5 cups vegetable broth or water
- 2 tbsp olive oil
- Salt and pepper to taste
- Fresh cilantro or parsley for garnish (optional)
- Lemon wedges for serving

Instructions:

1. In a large pot, heat olive oil over medium heat. Add the diced onion and sauté until translucent, about 5 minutes.
2. Add garlic, bell peppers, and all the spices (cumin, coriander, turmeric, cinnamon, paprika). Cook for another 5 minutes until the bell peppers soften slightly.
3. Stir in the chickpeas, diced tomatoes with their juice, and 3 cups of vegetable broth. Bring to a simmer and let cook for 20 minutes.
4. In a separate pot, bring 2 cups of vegetable broth or water to a boil. Add the whole grain couscous, cover and remove from heat. Let it sit for 5 minutes, then fluff with a fork.

5. Towards the last 5 minutes of the stew's cooking time, fold in the baby spinach and chopped almonds. Season with salt and pepper.
6. Serve the chickpea stew over a bed of whole grain couscous. Garnish with fresh cilantro or parsley and a squeeze of lemon, if desired.

Chef's Notes/Storage Information:

This is a great dish to prepare in a large batch and store for future meals.

- Refrigerator: Store the stew and couscous separately in airtight containers for up to 3 days.
- Freezer: The stew can be frozen for up to 2 months in an airtight container. It's best to store couscous separately and make fresh when needed. Thaw in the refrigerator overnight and reheat thoroughly before serving.

Nutritional Information (per serving):

- Calories: 813kcal
- Total Fat: 11.6g
- Monounsaturated Fat: 3.42g
- Polyunsaturated Fat: .88g
- Total Carbohydrates: 142.4g
- Dietary Fiber: 30.6g
- Protein: 30.9g
- Sodium: 591.2mg
- Vitamin A: 159.4mcg
- Vitamin B6: .34mg
- Vitamin C: 78.7mg
- Vitamin E: 1.7mg
- Vitamin K: 82mcg
- Folate: 295.2mcg
- Iron: 7.2mg
- Calcium: 173.6mg
- Magnesium: 160.4mg
- Zinc: 3.4mg

Grilled Sea Bass with Avocado and Mango Salsa

GLUTEN-FREE

A refreshing and nutritious summer dish, this grilled sea bass pairs perfectly with the tropical flavors of avocado and mango. The omega-3 fatty acids in the sea bass, combined with vitamins A, C and B6 in the mango and folic acid avocado, make this a great option for pregnant women looking to support their baby's brain development and their own overall health.

Preparation Time: 15 minutes
Cooking Time: 10 minutes
Total Time: 25 minutes
Serves: 2

Ingredients:

- 2 sea bass fillets
- Salt and pepper, to taste
- 1 tbsp olive oil
- 1 ripe avocado, diced

- 1 ripe mango, diced
- 1 small red onion, finely chopped
- 1 small red chili, deseeded and finely chopped (optional)
- Juice of 1 lime
- 2 tbsp fresh cilantro, chopped
- 1 tbsp olive oil (for salsa)

Instructions:

1. Salsa Preparation: In a bowl, combine diced avocado, mango, red onion, chili (if using), lime juice, cilantro, and 1 tbsp of olive oil. Mix well and season with salt and pepper. Set aside to let the flavors meld.
2. Preheat the grill to medium-high heat.
3. Drizzle the sea bass fillets with olive oil and season both sides with salt and pepper.
4. Place the fillets skin-side down on the grill. Cook for about 4-5 minutes on each side, or until the fish is opaque and flakes easily with a fork.
5. Remove the fillets from the grill and let them rest for a couple of minutes.
6. To serve, place each sea bass fillet on a plate and top generously with the avocado and mango salsa.

Chef's Notes/Side Dish Suggestions:

- Quinoa Salad: Mix cooked quinoa with diced bell peppers, cherry tomatoes, cucumber, olive oil, lemon juice, and fresh herbs. This side provides essential proteins and fiber.
- Steamed Green Beans: Lightly seasoned with salt, pepper, and a drizzle of olive oil, they offer a crisp contrast and added nutritional value.
- Roasted Sweet Potatoes: High in fiber and vitamin A, they complement the tropical flavors of the salsa and support eye health for both mother and baby.

Nutritional Information (per serving):

- Calories: 620kcal
- Total Fat: 32.6g
- Monounsaturated Fat: 20.55g
- Polyunsaturated Fat: 4.89g
- Omega-3 Fatty Acids: 1.21g
- Total Carbohydrates: 60.4g
- Dietary Fiber: 14.4g
- Protein: 32.1g
- Sodium: 119.6mg
- Vitamin A: 274.4mcg
- Vitamin B6: 2.1mg
- Vitamin B12: .3mcg
- Vitamin C: 407.1mg
- Vitamin E: 7.2mg
- Vitamin K: 71.2mcg
- Folate: 221.4mcg
- Iron: 3.9mg
- Calcium: 95.1mg
- Potassium: 1916.1mg
- Phosphorus: 439.7mg
- Magnesium: 157mg
- Zinc: 2mg

Tofu and Broccoli Stir-Fry with Brown Rice

VEGAN

This nutritious stir fry pairs protein-packed tofu with iron and vitamin-rich broccoli, served alongside wholesome brown rice. It's a balanced, easy-to-prepare dish that's rich in protein, fiber, folate, vitamin C and magnesium. The combination supports fetal development and can help manage blood sugar levels during pregnancy.

Preparation Time: 20 minutes
Cooking Time: 30 minutes
Total Time: 50 minutes
Serves: 4

Ingredients:

- 2 cups uncooked brown rice
- 4 cups water (for rice)
- 1 lb (450g) firm tofu, pressed and cubed
- 4 cups broccoli florets
- 3 tablespoons sesame oil
- 4 cloves garlic, minced
- 2 tablespoons soy sauce (or tamari for a gluten-free option)
- 1 tablespoon sesame oil
- 1 tablespoon ginger, grated
- 2 green onions, sliced
- 1 tablespoon sesame seeds
- Red pepper flakes (to taste, optional)

Instructions:

1. In a medium pot, bring the 4 cups of water to a boil. Add the brown rice, reduce heat to low, cover, and simmer for 25-30 minutes, or until the rice is cooked through and the water is absorbed. Remove from heat and let it sit for a few minutes before fluffing with a fork.
2. While the rice is cooking, in a large skillet or wok, heat 2 tablespoons of vegetable oil over medium heat. Add the tofu cubes, frying them until they are golden brown on all sides. Once done, transfer the tofu to a plate.
3. In the same skillet, add the remaining tablespoon of oil, and sauté the garlic and ginger for about 1 minute, until fragrant. Add the broccoli florets and stir fry for about 5-7 minutes, or until they turn vibrant green and are slightly tender.
4. Return the tofu to the skillet. Drizzle with soy sauce and sesame oil, stirring well to ensure all ingredients are evenly coated. Continue to cook for another 2-3 minutes.
5. Dish out the brown rice onto plates or in bowls. Top with the tofu and broccoli stir fry. Garnish with green onions, sesame seeds, and red pepper flakes (if using).

Chef's Notes/Storage Information:

- Store any leftovers in an airtight container in the refrigerator for up to 3 days. This dish can be reheated in a microwave or on the stove. If considering freezing, it's best to store the tofu and broccoli stir fry separate from the rice for up to 1 month. Thaw in the refrigerator and reheat thoroughly before serving.

Nutritional Information (per serving):
- Calories: 432kcal
- Total Fat: 22.5g
- Monounsaturated Fat: 7g
- Polyunsaturated Fat: 10.76g
- Total Carbohydrates: 37.7g
- Dietary Fiber: 7.2g
- Protein: 26.1g
- Sodium: 491.3mg
- Vitamin C: 83.8mg
- Iron: 4.8mg
- Calcium: 846.4mg
- Potassium: 724.1mg
- Phosphorus: 412.2mg
- Magnesium: 140.2mg
- Zinc: 3.2mg

Pumpkin and Black Bean Enchiladas with Cashew Cream

VEGAN

This nutritious enchilada dish combines the rich flavors of pumpkin and black beans, both of which are powerhouse foods for pregnancy. Pumpkin is packed with Vitamin A, essential for the development of the baby's organs, while black beans are a great source of protein and fiber to keep the digestive system in good shape. The cashew crema offers a dairy-free alternative that's high in magnesium and healthy fats. This meal is not only a delight to the taste buds but also aids in the overall well-being of expecting mothers.

Preparation Time: 20 minutes
Cooking Time: 35 minutes
Total Time: 55 minutes
Serves: 2

Ingredients:

For the Enchiladas:
- 1 cup pumpkin puree (fresh or canned)
- 1 cup cooked black beans, rinsed and drained
- 1 small onion, finely chopped
- 2 garlic cloves, minced
- 2 medium-sized tortillas
- 1 cup enchilada sauce (store-bought or homemade)
- 1 tsp ground cumin
- 1/2 tsp smoked paprika
- Salt and pepper, to taste
- Olive oil, for sautéing
- Fresh cilantro, chopped (for garnish)

For the Cashew Crema:
- 1/2 cup raw cashews (soaked for 4 hours or quick-soaked in hot water for 20 minutes)
- 1/2 cup water
- 1 garlic clove
- 1 tsp lemon or lime juice
- Salt, to taste

Instructions:
1. Preparation of Cashew Crema: a. Drain the soaked cashews and place them in a blender. b. Add water, garlic, lemon or lime juice, and salt. c. Blend until smooth and creamy. If needed, add more water to achieve the desired consistency. Set aside.
2. For the Enchilada Filling: a. In a skillet over medium heat, add a splash of olive oil. Once hot, add the onions and sauté until translucent. b. Add garlic, cumin, and smoked paprika. Cook for another 2 minutes. c. Stir in pumpkin puree and black beans. Season with salt and pepper. Cook for 5-7 minutes until heated through.
3. Assembling the Enchiladas: a. Preheat the oven to 375°F (190°C). b. Spread a thin layer of enchilada sauce at the bottom of a baking dish. c. Divide the pumpkin and black bean mixture between the two tortillas. Roll them up and place seam-side down in the baking dish. d. Pour the remaining enchilada sauce over the tortillas. e. Bake in the preheated oven for 20-25 minutes or until the enchiladas are bubbly and slightly golden.
4. Serving: a. Drizzle the enchiladas with the prepared cashew crema. b. Garnish with chopped cilantro. c. Serve hot and enjoy!

Chef's Notes:
- This recipe is highly adaptable. You can add other veggies or use different types of beans. The cashew crema can be stored in the refrigerator for up to a week.

Nutritional Information (per serving):
- Calories: 501kcal
- Total Fat: 18.1g
- Monounsaturated Fat: XX g
- Polyunsaturated Fat: XX g (indicate omega-3 fatty acids if applicable)
- Total Carbohydrates: 70.8g
- Dietary Fiber: 14.3g
- Protein: 19.9g
- Sodium: 565.3mg
- Vitamin B6
- Vitamin C: 47.5mg
- Vitamin E: 1.5mg
- Vitamin K: 24mcg
- Folate: 154.7mcg
- Iron: 8.9mg
- Calcium: 162.7mg
- Magnesium: 89.6mg
- Zinc: 1.4mg

Stuffed Bell Peppers with Bison and Wild Rice

MEAL-PREP FRIENDLY

This nourishing and hearty stuffed peppers recipe combines the lean protein of bison with the wholesomeness of wild rice. Perfect for expectant mothers, it provides essential nutrients beneficial during pregnancy such as iron, protein, vitamins B6, B12 and C, zinc, and fiber. With its rich, earthy flavors and colorful presentation, this dish is not only a healthy choice but also a feast for the eyes. If you're meal prepping, these stuffed peppers store well, making them an excellent option for fuss-free future meals.

Preparation Time: 20 minutes
Cooking Time: 75-80 minutes
Total Time: 95-100 minutes
Serves: 4

Ingredients:

- 4 large bell peppers (any color of choice)
- 1 cup wild rice
- 2 cups beef bone broth for cooking the rice
- 1 lb ground bison meat
- 1 medium onion, finely chopped
- 2 cloves garlic, minced
- 1 can (14.5 oz) diced tomatoes, drained
- 1 tsp olive oil
- Salt and pepper to taste

Instructions:

1. In a medium pot, bring 2 cups of water or broth to a boil. Add the wild rice, reduce heat to low, cover, and simmer for 45 minutes or until rice is tender and has absorbed the liquid. Remove from heat and set aside.
2. In a large skillet, heat the olive oil over medium heat. Add the chopped onions and garlic and sauté until translucent. Add the ground bison, breaking it apart as it cooks. Cook until the meat is browned and fully cooked. Season with salt and pepper.
3. Combine the cooked wild rice and the can of drained diced tomatoes with the bison mixture in the skillet, stirring well.
4. Preheat your oven to 375°F (190°C). Wash the bell peppers and cut off their tops. Remove the seeds and membranes, creating a hollow cavity.
5. Stuff each bell pepper with the bison and wild rice mixture, pressing down gently to pack the filling.
6. Place the stuffed peppers in a baking dish, upright. Cover the dish with aluminum foil.
7. Bake in the preheated oven for 30-35 minutes, or until the peppers are tender. If desired, in the last 5-10 minutes of baking, you can remove the foil and sprinkle some shredded cheese on top of the peppers, returning them to the oven until the cheese is melted and slightly golden.
8. Once done, remove from oven and let it cool slightly before serving. Garnish with optional toppings if desired.

Chef's Notes:

- Optional toppings: shredded cheese, chopped parsley, or sour cream
- Refrigeration: Store any leftover stuffed peppers in an airtight container in the refrigerator for up to 3-4 days.
- Freezing: For longer storage, place the stuffed peppers (without cheese) in a single layer on a baking sheet and freeze until solid. Once frozen, transfer the peppers to a freezer bag or container. Properly stored, they can last for up to 2 months. To reheat, thaw in the refrigerator overnight and bake in a 375°F oven until heated through, adding cheese in the last 10 minutes if desired.

Nutritional Information (per serving):

- Calories: 399kcal
- Total Fat: 10.1g
- Monounsaturated Fat: 4.03g
- Polyunsaturated Fat: .881g
- Total Carbohydrates: 46.6g
- Dietary Fiber: 8.2g
- Protein: 33.4g
- Sodium: 511.8mg
- Vitamin B6: 1mg
- Vitamin B12: 2.2mcg
- Vitamin C: 159.6mg
- Vitamin E: 1.3mg
- Vitamin K: 15.1mcg
- Folate: 73.3mcg
- Iron: 4.9mg
- Calcium: 46.3mg
- Magnesium: 114.2mg
- Zinc: 7.9mg

Butternut Squash Risotto with Sage and Pecorino

ONE-POT MEAL

This creamy butternut squash risotto with sage and pecorino is a delightful blend of autumn flavors. Packed with essential nutrients, the squash provides an array of vitamins and minerals beneficial for pregnancy, like Vitamin A for baby's eye development and fiber for digestion. Pecorino adds a touch of calcium, and sage not only brings an aromatic essence but also may help in digestion. Serve this heartwarming dish with your choice of protein and vegetables for a wholesome meal.

Preparation Time: 15 minutes
Cooking Time: 30 minutes
Total Time: 45 minutes
Serves: 2

Ingredients:

- 1/2 medium-sized butternut squash, peeled and diced
- 1 small onion, finely chopped
- 1 cup Arborio rice
- 2 1/2 cups vegetable broth (warm)
- 2 tbsp olive oil
- 1/4 cup freshly grated pecorino cheese
- 8 fresh sage leaves, finely chopped
- Salt and pepper, to taste

Instructions:

1. In a medium-sized pot or deep pan, heat the olive oil over medium heat. Add the chopped onions and sauté until translucent.
2. Add the diced butternut squash and sauté for another 5 minutes or until the squash begins to soften.
3. Stir in the Arborio rice, ensuring it's coated well with the oil. Toast for about 2 minutes.
4. Start adding the warm broth, one ladle at a time, stirring consistently. Allow each ladle of broth to be mostly absorbed before adding the next.

5. Continue adding broth and stirring until the rice is cooked through and has a creamy consistency. This should take about 18-20 minutes.
6. Stir in the chopped sage, pecorino cheese, salt, and pepper. Mix well until cheese is melted and everything is combined.
7. Taste and adjust seasonings if needed.
8. Serve immediately, garnishing with additional pecorino cheese if desired.

Chef's Notes/Side Dish Suggestions:
- Proteins: Grilled chicken breast with a hint of lemon and rosemary, pan-seared salmon with a drizzle of olive oil and dill, or a tenderloin steak with a touch of garlic butter.
- Vegetables: Steamed asparagus with a sprinkle of sea salt, sautéed Brussels sprouts with a touch of balsamic glaze, or roasted green beans tossed in olive oil and almond slivers.

Nutritional Information (per serving):
- Calories: 577 kcal
- Total Fat: 17g
- Monounsaturated Fat: 9.88g
- Polyunsaturated Fat: 1.5g
- Total Carbohydrates: 94.5g
- Dietary Fiber: 5.7g
- Protein: 11.4g
- Sodium: 948.1mg
- Vitamin A: 867.3mg
- Vitamin B6: .3mg
- Vitamin C: 36.6mg
- Vitamin E: 4.2mg
- Vitamin K: 11.9mcg
- Folate: 49mcg
- Iron: 1.4mg
- Calcium: 161.7mg
- Magnesium: 59.6mg

Lamb Tagine with Apricots and Almonds

GLUTEN-FREE

A sumptuous and exotic Moroccan dish, this Lamb Tagine combines the rich flavors of tender lamb with sweet apricots and crunchy almonds. Enhanced with warm spices, it creates a comforting and nutritious dish. Especially beneficial for pregnancy, this dish is packed with protein for fetal development, iron for preventing anemia, as well as healthy fats, zinc, and vitamins B12, C and E. Serve alongside vegetable or protein side dishes to create a balanced and delightful meal.

Preparation Time: 15 minutes
Cooking Time: 2 hours
Total Time: 2 hours, 15 minutes
Serves: 2

Ingredients:
- 300g lamb shoulder, diced
- 1 medium onion, finely chopped
- 2 garlic cloves, minced
- 1 tsp ginger, grated
- 1 tsp ground cinnamon
- 1 tsp ground cumin
- 1 tsp ground coriander
- 1/2 tsp ground turmeric
- ¾ cup chicken or vegetable stock
- ⅓ cup dried apricots, chopped
- 3 tbsp blanched almonds
- 1 tbsp honey
- 2 tbsp olive oil
- Salt and pepper to taste

Instructions:
1. In a tagine or heavy-bottomed pot, heat olive oil over medium-high heat. Add lamb pieces and brown on all sides. Remove lamb and set aside.
2. In the same pot, add the chopped onions. Sauté until translucent. Add garlic and ginger, and cook for another minute until fragrant.
3. Stir in the ground cinnamon, cumin, coriander, turmeric, salt, and pepper. Mix well until the onions are well-coated with the spices.
4. Return the browned lamb to the pot. Add stock, bring to a simmer, then reduce heat to low. Cover and let it cook for about 1.5 hours, or until the lamb is tender.
5. Stir in the chopped apricots, almonds, and honey. Let it simmer for another 20 minutes.
6. Check seasoning and adjust if necessary.

Chef's Notes/Side Dish Suggestions:
- Protein: A side of chickpea salad or lentil soup complements the dish and adds more protein, fiber, and nutrients beneficial during pregnancy.
- Vegetables: Serve with roasted vegetables like carrots, zucchini, and bell peppers drizzled with olive oil and seasoned with cumin and paprika. Alternatively, a side of sautéed greens with garlic and a sprinkle of lemon juice pairs beautifully with the tagine.

Nutritional Information (per serving):
- Calories: 834kcal
- Total Fat: 47.7g
- Monounsaturated Fat: 27.26g
- Polyunsaturated Fat: 6.01g
- Total Carbohydrates: 37.1g
- Dietary Fiber: 6.7g
- Protein: 65.9g
- Sodium: 807.7mg
- Vitamin B6: .37mg
- Vitamin B12: 4mcg
- Vitamin C: 7.1mg
- Vitamin E: 9.8mg
- Vitamin K: 13.6mcg
- Folate: 58.3mcg
- Iron: 7mg
- Calcium: 166.7mg
- Magnesium: 131mg
- Zinc: 12.1mg

Spicy Shrimp Tacos with Cilantro Lime Slaw

Indulge in the perfect fusion of fiery flavors and zesty freshness with these spicy shrimp tacos accompanied by a crisp cilantro-lime slaw. Shrimps, packed with lean protein and omega-3 fatty acids, support fetal brain and eye development, making this recipe a fantastic choice for expectant mothers. Cilantro contributes a dash of antioxidants, and lime gives a hit of vitamin C, making every bite both healthful and delightful. Pair it with our suggested toppings to customize it just the way you like!

Preparation Time: 20 minutes
Cooking Time: 10 minutes
Total Time: 30 minutes
Serves: 2

Ingredients:

For the Spicy Shrimp:
- 10-12 large shrimps, peeled and deveined
- 1 tablespoon olive oil
- 1 teaspoon smoked paprika
- 1/2 teaspoon chili powder
- 1/2 teaspoon cumin
- 1/4 teaspoon cayenne pepper (adjust according to spice preference)
- Salt and pepper to taste

For the Cilantro Lime Slaw:
- 2 cups shredded cabbage (mix of green and red for color)
- 1/4 cup fresh cilantro, chopped
- Juice of 1 lime
- 2 tablespoons Greek yogurt
- Salt and pepper to taste

For Assembling:
- 4 small whole wheat tortillas

Instructions:

1. In a medium bowl, mix the shrimp with olive oil, smoked paprika, chili powder, cumin, cayenne pepper, salt, and pepper. Allow it to marinate for 10 minutes.
2. In a separate bowl, combine the shredded cabbage, cilantro, lime juice, Greek yogurt, salt, and pepper. Mix well and set aside, allowing the flavors to meld.
3. Heat a large skillet over medium-high heat. Once hot, add the marinated shrimp in a single layer. Cook for 2-3 minutes on each side or until the shrimp are opaque and cooked through.
4. Warm the tortillas according to package directions. Lay a tortilla flat, place a generous helping of cilantro lime slaw, then add 2-3 shrimps on top. Add your choice of optional toppings.
5. Serve immediately with your favorite side dish or salsa. A refreshing lime wedge on the side is also a great touch!

Chef's Notes/Topping Suggestions:

- Avocado: Offers healthy fats, fiber, and a range of vitamins.
- Feta Cheese: For a tangy touch and a calcium boost.
- Tomatoes: They are rich in antioxidants, vitamins, and provide a refreshing bite.
- Hot Sauce: For those who like an extra kick! (Make sure it's pregnancy-safe and doesn't contain too much sodium.)
- Sour Cream: Adds creaminess and a cooling effect against the spices.

Nutritional Information (per serving):
- Calories: 342kcal
- Total Fat: 13.1g
- Monounsaturated Fat: 5.26g
- Polyunsaturated Fat: 1.12g
- Total Carbohydrates: 43.7g
- Dietary Fiber: 9.4g
- Protein: 15.6g
- Sodium: 689.2mg
- Vitamin A: 81.3mcg
- Vitamin B6: .23mg
- Vitamin B12: .6mcg
- Vitamin C: 36mg
- Vitamin E: 2.5mg
- Vitamin K: 65.5mcg
- Folate: 43.2mcg
- Iron: 2.8mg
- Calcium: 248mg
- Magnesium: 27.1
- Zinc: .83mg

Sautéed Spinach and Feta-Stuffed Chicken Breast

GLUTEN-FREE

This scrumptious dish is not only a delight for the taste buds but also offers numerous nutritional benefits suitable for pregnancy. Spinach is packed with iron and folic acid, vital for fetal neural development, while chicken is a great source of lean protein. The addition of feta brings a creamy texture and calcium. Perfect for expectant mothers looking for a health boost!

Preparation Time: 15 minutes
Cooking Time: 30 minutes
Total Time: 45 minutes
Serves: 2

Ingredients:
- 2 boneless, skinless chicken breasts
- 1 cup fresh spinach, finely chopped
- 1/2 cup feta cheese, crumbled
- 1 clove garlic, minced
- 1 tbsp olive oil, plus extra for sautéing
- Salt and pepper, to taste
- 1/2 tsp dried oregano
- 1/2 tsp dried basil
- 2 toothpicks or kitchen twine (for securing)

Instructions:

1. Using a sharp knife, butterfly the chicken breasts without cutting all the way through, creating a pocket for the filling.
2. In a medium skillet over medium heat, warm 1 tbsp of olive oil. Add the minced garlic and sauté until fragrant, about 1 minute. Add the spinach and sauté until wilted, around 2-3 minutes. Remove from heat and let it cool slightly. Mix in the crumbled feta cheese. Season with salt, pepper, dried oregano, and dried basil.
3. Carefully spoon the spinach and feta mixture into each chicken pocket. Secure the open sides with toothpicks or tie with kitchen twine to keep the filling inside.
4. In the same skillet, add a bit more olive oil over medium heat. Place the stuffed chicken breasts in the skillet and cook for about 7-8 minutes on each side or until the chicken is golden brown and cooked through (internal temperature of 165°F or 74°C).
5. Once cooked, remove the toothpicks or twine from the chicken breasts. Place on plates and serve immediately.

Chef's Notes/Side Dish Suggestions:

- Quinoa Salad: Mix cooked quinoa with cherry tomatoes, cucumbers, and a lemon vinaigrette. This grain is protein-rich and provides essential amino acids.
- Steamed Broccoli: A powerhouse of vitamins and fiber, it complements the chicken's flavor and boosts the dish's nutritional value.
- Mashed Sweet Potatoes: A sweet and creamy side that's rich in beta-carotene, essential for the baby's vision, growth, and immune system development.

Nutritional Information (per serving):

- Calories: 497kcal
- Total Fat: 22.1g
- Monounsaturated Fat: 8.56g
- Polyunsaturated Fat: 2.2g
- Total Carbohydrates: 3.2 g
- Dietary Fiber: .81g
- Protein: 67.7g
- Sodium: 562.7mg
- Vitamin A: 197.9mcg
- Vitamin B6: 2.4mg
- Vitamin B12: 1.2mcg
- Vitamin C: 8.5mg
- Vitamin E: 3.1mg
- Vitamin K: 166.7mcg
- Folate: 80.6mcg
- Iron: 2.5mg
- Calcium: 257.6mg
- Potassium: 1087.2mg
- Phosphorus: 727.6mg
- Magnesium: 109.8mg
- Zinc: 3.2mg

Thai Beef Salad with Mixed Greens and Lime Dressing

GLUTEN-FREE

This refreshing Thai Beef Salad combines tender slices of beef with mixed greens, topped with a zesty lime dressing. Ideal for expecting mothers, this dish offers a good balance of iron and protein from the beef and essential folate and vitamin C from the greens. Its light and tangy flavor profile can also help with nausea often associated with pregnancy. You can further customize this salad with various toppings to suit your taste buds.

Preparation Time: 20 minutes
Cooking Time: 10 minutes
Total Time: 30 minutes
Serves: 2

Ingredients:

- 200g beef steak (sirloin or tenderloin)
- Salt and pepper, to season
- 4 cups mixed greens (e.g., romaine, arugula, spinach)
- 1/2 red onion, thinly sliced
- 1/2 cucumber, sliced
- 1 carrot, julienned or grated
- 1 red bell pepper, thinly sliced
- Fresh coriander leaves, for garnish
- Fresh mint leaves, for garnish

Lime Dressing:

- Juice of 2 limes
- 2 tablespoons fish sauce (or soy sauce for a vegetarian alternative)
- 1 tablespoon honey
- 1 garlic clove, minced
- 1 red chili, deseeded and finely chopped (optional for heat)
- 1 teaspoon grated ginger

Instructions:

1. Season the beef steak with salt and pepper. Heat a skillet or grill pan over medium-high heat. Once hot, cook the steak for 3-4 minutes on each side for medium-rare or until your preferred doneness. Remove from heat and let it rest for 5 minutes before slicing thinly.
2. In a small bowl, combine the lime juice, fish sauce, honey, minced garlic, chili (if using), and grated ginger. Whisk together until the sugar is dissolved.
3. In a large bowl, toss the mixed greens, red onion, cucumber, carrot, and bell pepper. Divide the salad onto two plates. Top with the sliced beef.
4. Drizzle the lime dressing over the salads. Garnish with fresh coriander and mint leaves.

Chef's Notes/Topping Suggestions:

- Roasted peanuts or cashews for a crunchy texture.
- Cherry tomatoes for added freshness.
- Sliced avocado for creamy texture and beneficial fats.

- Toasted sesame seeds for a nutty flavor.
- Fresh mango slices for a sweet and tangy complement.

Nutritional Information (per serving):
- Calories: 550kcal
- Total Fat: 11.2g
- Monounsaturated Fat: .03g
- Polyunsaturated Fat: .2g
- Total Carbohydrates: 68.2g
- Dietary Fiber: 16.6g
- Protein: 46.4g
- Sodium: 3691.4mg
- Vitamin A: 399.3mcg
- Vitamin B6: .33mg
- Vitamin C: 102.3mg
- Vitamin E: 1.4mg
- Vitamin K: 20.5mcg
- Folate: 50.3mcg
- Iron: 12.9mg
- Calcium: 369.2mg
- Magnesium: 28.9mg
- Zinc: .53mg

Curried Lentils with Spinach and Tomatoes

MEAL-PREP FRIENDLY

This nutritious and flavorful dish combines the earthy taste of lentils with the richness of spinach and the heartiness of potatoes, creating a balanced and delicious meal. Lentils provide essential proteins and iron, spinach is packed with folic acid and calcium, and potatoes offer beneficial carbohydrates and fiber – all of which are vital for expecting mothers. The warm spices not only tantalize the taste buds but also aid in digestion. It's a perfect dish for pregnancy and can be made in batches for future meals.

Preparation Time: 20 minutes
Cooking Time: 40 minutes
Total Time: 60 minutes
Serves: 4

Ingredients:
- 1 cup dried lentils, rinsed and drained
- 3 medium-sized potatoes, peeled and diced into 1-inch cubes
- 2 cups fresh spinach, roughly chopped
- 1 large onion, finely chopped
- 3 garlic cloves, minced
- 1 inch ginger, minced or grated
- 2 tablespoons curry powder (adjust to taste)
- 1 teaspoon turmeric powder
- 1 teaspoon cumin seeds
- 1/2 teaspoon red chili powder (optional, for added heat)
- 3 cups vegetable broth
- 2 tablespoons olive oil or coconut oil
- Salt, to taste
- 1 can (14 oz) diced tomatoes or 2 fresh tomatoes, chopped

Instructions:
1. In a large pot or Dutch oven, heat the oil over medium heat. Add cumin seeds and let them splutter.
2. Add onions and sauté until translucent, about 4-5 minutes.
3. Stir in the minced garlic and ginger, and sauté for another 2 minutes, until fragrant.
4. Sprinkle in the curry powder, turmeric, and red chili powder (if using). Sauté for another minute, allowing the spices to toast slightly.
5. Add the diced tomatoes to the pot and stir well. Let the mixture cook for about 5 minutes until the tomatoes are soft.
6. Incorporate the diced potatoes, ensuring they're well-coated with the tomato-spice mixture.
7. Add lentils and pour in the vegetable broth or water. Season with salt.
8. Bring the mixture to a boil, then reduce the heat to low and let it simmer. Cover and cook for about 20-25 minutes or until the lentils and potatoes are tender.
9. Once the lentils and potatoes are cooked, fold in the chopped spinach. Let it wilt in the heat for 2-3 minutes.
10. Taste and adjust seasonings if necessary.
11. Remove from heat and serve warm with your choice of accompaniments.

Chef's Notes:
- Can be served on its own, or over quinoa or brown rice.
- Store leftovers in an airtight container in the refrigerator for up to 3-4 days. This dish also freezes well; when reheating, add a splash of water or broth to refresh the consistency. It's best to freeze in portioned containers for easier future meals.

Nutritional Information (per serving):
- Calories: 384kcal
- Total Fat: 8.2g
- Monounsaturated Fat: 5.4g
- Polyunsaturated Fat: 1.2g
- Total Carbohydrates: 63.3g
- Dietary Fiber: 10.8g
- Protein: 16.6g
- Sodium: 671.8mg
- Vitamin A: 96.6mcg
- Vitamin B6: .69mg
- Vitamin C: 33.7mg
- Vitamin E: 2.5mg
- Vitamin K: 86.1mcg
- Folate: 278.5mcg
- Iron: 6.1mg
- Calcium: 95.2mg
- Magnesium: 75.1mg
- Zinc: 2.3mg

Minestrone

MEAL-PREP FRIENDLY

This hearty and nutritious Minestrone Soup is a fantastic meal for expectant mothers. Bursting with essential vitamins and minerals, its ingredients like beans, vegetables, and whole grains help support a healthy pregnancy. It's rich in folate from the beans, spinach, and other vegetables, beneficial for preventing neural tube defects. It's also a good source of iron, necessary for increasing blood volume during pregnancy. Apart from being a comforting meal, this soup can be made in large batches, making it perfect for meal prepping and ensuring you always have a healthy meal on hand.

Preparation Time: 20 minutes
Cooking Time: 40 minutes
Total Time: 60 minutes
Serves: 12

Ingredients:

- 3 tablespoons olive oil
- 1 large onion, diced
- 3 cloves garlic, minced
- 3 carrots, diced
- 3 celery stalks, diced
- 1 zucchini, diced
- 1 cup fresh green beans, chopped
- 1 cup spinach or kale, chopped
- 1 can (28 ounces) diced tomatoes
- 1 can (15 ounces) kidney beans, drained and rinsed
- 1 can (15 ounces) cannellini beans, drained and rinsed
- 8 cups vegetable broth or chicken broth
- 1 cup whole grain pasta (like small shells or ditalini)
- 2 teaspoons dried oregano
- 2 teaspoons dried basil
- Salt and black pepper to taste
- 1/4 cup fresh parsley, chopped
- 1/2 cup grated Parmesan cheese (optional)
- Juice of 1 lemon

Instructions:

1. In a large pot, heat the olive oil over medium heat. Add the onion and garlic and sauté until translucent, about 3-4 minutes.
2. Add the carrots, celery, zucchini, and green beans. Continue to cook, stirring occasionally, for another 5-7 minutes or until the vegetables start to soften.
3. Stir in the diced tomatoes with their juices, kidney beans, cannellini beans, and vegetable broth.
4. Add the oregano, basil, salt, and black pepper. Bring the soup to a boil, then reduce the heat and let it simmer.
5. Add the pasta and let the soup simmer for about 10-15 minutes, or until the pasta is al dente.
6. About 5 minutes before the pasta is done, stir in the spinach or kale.
7. Once cooked, remove the soup from heat and stir in the fresh parsley, lemon juice, and grated Parmesan cheese if using.
8. Adjust seasonings to taste, then serve hot.

Chef's Notes:

Storage for Meal Prepping:

- Allow the soup to cool to room temperature.
- Divide the soup into individual portion-sized containers or into larger containers if you prefer.
- Store in the refrigerator for up to 4 days. For longer storage, you can freeze the soup for up to 3 months.
- To reheat, microwave the soup in intervals, stirring in between, or warm on the stove over medium heat.

Nutritional Information (per serving):

- Calories: 196kcall
- Total Fat: 5.3g
- Monounsaturated Fat: 2.79gg
- Polyunsaturated Fat: .65g
- Total Carbohydrates: 29.7g
- Dietary Fiber: 7.9g
- Protein: 8.8g
- Sodium: 647mg
- Vitamin A: 204.9mcg
- Vitamin B6: .16mg
- Vitamin C: 26.4mg
- Vitamin E: .85mg
- Vitamin K: 531.mcg
- Folate: 79.7mcg
- Iron: 2.3mg
- Calcium: 92.8mg
- Magnesium: 31.5mg
- Zinc: .78mg

Cod and Summer Vegetable Foil Packets

GLUTEN-FREE

This simple yet flavorful cod and summer vegetable foil packet is an ideal choice for expectant mothers. Rich in omega-3 fatty acids from the cod, which support fetal brain development, and packed with essential vitamins and minerals from the vibrant summer vegetables such as vitamins A, B6 and E, this dish promotes maternal and fetal health. As a bonus, the foil packet preparation makes for a quick cleanup and ensures all the nutritious juices are retained. Pair with whole grains or a leafy green salad for a complete, balanced meal.

Preparation Time: 10 minutes
Cooking Time: 20 minutes
Total Time: 30 minutes
Serves: 2

Ingredients:

- 2 fresh cod fillets (4-6 oz)
- 1 zucchini, thinly sliced
- 1 yellow bell pepper, thinly sliced
- 12-16 cherry tomatoes, halved
- 2 cloves garlic, minced
- 2 tablespoons olive oil
- Salt and pepper, to taste
- 1 teaspoon dried herbs (like oregano, thyme, or basil) or fresh herbs if available
- 2 lemon wedges

Instructions:

1. Preheat your oven to 400°F (200°C).
2. Cut a large piece of aluminum foil, ensuring it's large enough to encase the cod and vegetables.
3. In a mixing bowl, combine zucchini, bell pepper, cherry tomatoes, garlic, olive oil, salt, pepper, and dried herbs. Toss well to coat.
4. Place the cod fillet in the center of the foil. Season with a bit more salt and pepper. Surround the cod with the seasoned vegetable mixture. Squeeze the lemon wedge over the top.
5. Fold the foil around the fish and vegetables, sealing it to create a packet. Ensure no juices will escape.
6. Place the foil packet on a baking sheet and bake in the preheated oven for about 20 minutes, or until the cod easily flakes with a fork and the vegetables are tender.
7. Carefully open the foil packet (be cautious of the steam). Transfer the contents to a plate and enjoy!

Chef's Notes/Side Dish Suggestions:

- Quinoa Salad: A protein-rich grain, quinoa pairs well with the delicate flavors of cod and provides added minerals beneficial during pregnancy.
- Leafy Green Salad: Spinach, arugula, and other leafy greens can boost your iron and calcium intake.
- Steamed Brown Rice: A whole grain option that complements the lightness of the fish and provides sustained energy.
- Whole Grain Bread: Ideal for sopping up the delicious juices from the foil packet.

Nutritional Information (per serving):

- Calories: 822kcal
- Total Fat: 42g
- Monounsaturated Fat: 10g
- Polyunsaturated Fat: .16g
- Omega-3 Fatty Acids: .18mg
- Total Carbohydrates: 68.2g
- Dietary Fiber: 10.4g
- Protein: 38g
- Sodium: 1320.4mg
- Vitamin A: 103mcg
- Vitamin B6: .38mg
- Vitamin C: 120.8mg
- Vitamin E: 3mg
- Vitamin K: 15mcg
- Folate: 51mcg
- Iron: 5mg
- Calcium: 106mg

Grilled Eggplant Parmesan with Zucchini Noodles

GLUTEN-FREE

This delicious and nutritious Grilled Eggplant Parmesan is a lighter twist on the classic dish. Perfectly charred eggplant slices layered with rich tomato sauce and melted cheese create a hearty, yet light meal. The dish is a good source of essential vitamins and minerals, including folic acid, calcium, and vitamin C which is beneficial during pregnancy. It's a delightful way to enjoy the flavors of traditional eggplant parmesan without the heaviness of frying.

Preparation Time: 20 minutes
Cooking Time: 25 minutes
Total Time: 45 minutes
Serves: 2

Ingredients:

- 1 medium eggplant, sliced into 1/2-inch-thick rounds
- 1 cup of your favorite marinara or tomato sauce
- 1 cup shredded mozzarella cheese
- 1/4 cup freshly grated Parmesan cheese
- 1/4 cup fresh basil leaves, for garnish
- 2 tsp olive oil (for brushing)
- Salt and pepper, to taste
- 1/4 tsp red pepper flakes (optional)

Instructions:

1. Preheat your grill to medium-high heat.
2. Brush both sides of each eggplant slice with olive oil. Season with salt and pepper.
3. Place the eggplant slices on the grill. Cook for about 3-4 minutes on each side, until they have nice grill marks and are tender.
4. In a grill-safe dish or a foil pan, start layering the dish. Begin with a spoonful of tomato sauce at the bottom, then a layer of grilled eggplant, more sauce, a sprinkle of mozzarella and Parmesan cheese. Repeat the layers until all ingredients are used up, finishing with a generous layer of cheese on top.
5. Place the dish on the grill, close the lid, and let it cook for another 8-10 minutes, or until the cheese is melted and bubbly.
6. Remove from the grill and let it sit for a couple of minutes. Garnish with fresh basil leaves and red pepper flakes if you like a little heat. Serve hot.

Chef's Notes:

Side Dish Suggestions:

- Grilled Chicken: Packed with protein and you can easily throw this on the grill with the eggplant.
- Green Salad: A fresh green salad with a lemon vinaigrette is a refreshing side to balance out the rich flavors of the main dish.
- Quinoa Salad: Packed with protein and fiber, a Mediterranean quinoa salad would complement the dish and further enhance its nutritional profile for expecting mothers.

Nutritional Information (per serving):
- Calories: 456kcal
- Total Fat: 29.5g
- Monounsaturated Fat: 11.172g
- Polyunsaturated Fat: 2.66g
- Total Carbohydrates: 27g
- Dietary Fiber: 11.3g
- Protein: 19.7g
- Sodium: 1227.2mg
- Vitamin A: 79.3mcg
- Vitamin B6: .43mg
- Vitamin B12: .18mcg
- Vitamin C: 7.9mg
- Vitamin E: 5.9mg
- Vitamin K: 39.9mcg
- Folate: 69.1mcg
- Iron: 1.7mg
- Calcium: 563.7mg
- Magnesium: 60.9mg
- Zinc: 1.2mg

Creamy Polenta with Roasted Cherry Tomatoes and Basil

VEGETARIAN

This dish combines the creamy texture of polenta with the bursting flavor of roasted cherry tomatoes and aromatic basil. Not only is it delicious and comforting, but it's also nutritious. The polenta offers a good source of complex carbohydrates, which provide energy during pregnancy, while tomatoes are rich in essential vitamins, especially vitamin C and lycopene. Basil adds a touch of freshness, and its anti-inflammatory properties can be beneficial for expecting mothers. This dish can be a perfect main course or pair it with the side dishes suggested below for a wholesome meal.

Preparation Time: 10 minutes
Cooking Time: 40 minutes
Total Time: 50 minutes
Serves: 2

Ingredients:
- 1 cup coarse polenta (or cornmeal)
- 4 cups low-sodium vegetable broth
- 1 cup cherry tomatoes
- 1/4 cup freshly grated Parmesan cheese
- 2 tbsp olive oil
- Salt and pepper, to taste
- 1/4 cup fresh basil leaves, roughly torn
- 1 tbsp olive oil (for roasting)
- 2 cloves garlic, minced

Instructions:
1. Preheat the oven to 400°F (205°C). Toss cherry tomatoes with olive oil, minced garlic, salt, and pepper in a mixing bowl. Spread the tomatoes on a baking sheet in a single layer. Roast in the oven for 15-20 minutes or until tomatoes are softened and slightly charred. Remove from oven and set aside.

2. In a medium saucepan, bring the broth to a boil. Gradually whisk in the polenta, ensuring no lumps form. Reduce heat to low and simmer, frequently stirring, until the polenta is soft and thickened, about 20-25 minutes. If it becomes too thick, you can add a bit more water or broth to achieve the desired consistency.

3. Once the polenta is cooked, stir in the or olive oil and Parmesan cheese until melted and creamy. Season with salt and pepper to taste.

4. Pour the creamy polenta onto plates, top with roasted cherry tomatoes, and garnish with fresh basil leaves. Drizzle with a bit more olive oil if desired.

Chef's Notes/Side Dish Suggestions:
- Steamed Asparagus: Lightly seasoned with olive oil, salt, and lemon zest.
- Mixed Green Salad: Tossed with a vinaigrette dressing, containing baby spinach, arugula, and walnuts for an added dose of omega-3s beneficial for brain development during pregnancy.
- Grilled Zucchini: Seasoned with a touch of garlic powder and freshly ground black pepper.
- Salmon or Chicken: Seasoned with olive oil, salt and lemon.

Nutritional Information (per serving):
- Calories: 343kcal
- Total Fat: 24.4g
- Monounsaturated Fat: 15.7g
- Polyunsaturated Fat: 2.3g
- Total Carbohydrates: 24.1g
- Dietary Fiber: 2.7g
- Protein: 8.2g
- Sodium: 1787.4mg
- Vitamin A: 89.1mcg
- Vitamin B6: .08mcg
- Vitamin B12: .18mcg
- Vitamin C: 15.1mg
- Vitamin E: 3mb
- Vitamin K: 20.7mcg
- Iron: 2.2mg
- Calcium: 181.2mg
- Zinc: .7mg

Pulled Pork with Cabbage and Apple Slaw

GLUTEN-FREE

This delectable pulled pork dish, accompanied by a fresh cabbage and apple slaw, is not only a culinary delight but also beneficial for expectant mothers. The protein from the pork supports fetal development and muscle growth, while the cabbage and apples provide vitamins C and K, and fiber that aids digestion and boosts overall health. When paired together, this combination makes for a well-rounded meal.

Preparation Time: 30 minutes
Cooking Time: 8 hours (in slow cooker)
Total Time: 8 hours, 30 minutes
Serves: 4

Ingredients:

For the Pulled Pork:
- 2 lbs pork shoulder or butt
- 1 cup of BBQ sauce (your favorite brand or homemade)
- 1/2 cup of chicken stock or water
- 2 cloves garlic, minced
- 1 onion, thinly sliced
- 1 tsp smoked paprika
- Salt and pepper to taste

For the Cabbage and Apple Slaw:
- 2 cups of shredded green cabbage
- 1 cup of shredded red cabbage
- 2 large apples, thinly sliced or julienned
- 1/4 cup of mayonnaise
- 2 tbsp of apple cider vinegar
- 1 tbsp of honey
- Salt and pepper to taste

Instructions:

For the Pulled Pork:
1. Season the pork shoulder with salt, pepper, and smoked paprika.
2. Place the sliced onion and minced garlic at the bottom of a slow cooker.
3. Lay the pork shoulder on top of the onions and garlic.
4. Pour the chicken stock or water and BBQ sauce over the pork.
5. Cover and cook on low for 7-8 hours until the pork is tender and easily shreds with a fork.
6. Once cooked, shred the pork using two forks, discarding any fat. Mix the shredded pork with the juices in the slow cooker until well-coated with the sauce.

For the Cabbage and Apple Slaw:
7. In a large bowl, combine the shredded green and red cabbage with the sliced apples.
8. In a separate small bowl, whisk together the mayonnaise, apple cider vinegar, honey, salt, and pepper to taste.
9. Pour the dressing over the cabbage and apple mixture and toss until everything is well combined and coated.

To Serve:
10. Place a generous amount of pulled pork on a plate or bun and top with the cabbage and apple slaw. Enjoy!

Chef's Notes/Storage Information:
- Store leftover pulled pork and cabbage & apple slaw separately in airtight containers in the refrigerator.
- The pulled pork can be refrigerated for up to 3-4 days.
- The slaw is best enjoyed within 1-2 days for optimal freshness and crunch, but can be stored for up to 3 days.

Nutritional Information (per serving):
- Calories: 629kcal
- Total Fat: 23.5 g
- Monounsaturated Fat: 8.62g
- Polyunsaturated Fat: 8.14g
- Total Carbohydrates: 62.7g
- Dietary Fiber: 4.7g
- Protein: 39.8g
- Sodium: 1613.9mg
- Vitamin B6: .18mg
- Vitamin C: 26.9mg
- Vitamin K: 43mcg
- Folate: 32.3mcg
- Iron: 2.1mg

Beet and Walnut Pesto Pasta with Grilled Chicken

MEAL-PREP FRIENDLY

This nutrient-dense dish is a delightful fusion of earthy beets, crunchy walnuts, and savory grilled chicken served atop protein-rich pasta. Especially beneficial for pregnant women, the recipe is packed with folate from beets, omega-3 fatty acids from walnuts, and high-quality protein from both the pasta and chicken. Not only is it tasty, but it's also a powerhouse of essential nutrients to support the health of both you and your growing baby.

Preparation Time: 20 minutes
Cooking Time: 30 minutes
Total Time: 50 minutes
Serves: 4

Ingredients:
- 2 medium-sized beets, peeled and diced
- 1/2 cup walnuts, toasted
- 2 garlic cloves, minced
- 1/2 cup grated Parmesan cheese
- 1/4 cup extra virgin olive oil
- Salt and pepper, to taste
- Juice of 1 lemon
- 12 oz protein pasta (like chickpea or lentil pasta)
- 4 boneless, skinless chicken breasts
- 2 tbsp olive oil (for grilling)
- Fresh basil or parsley (optional, for garnish)

Instructions:
1. In a food processor, combine the diced beets, toasted walnuts, minced garlic, Parmesan cheese, and lemon juice. Pulse until the mixture forms a paste. While the processor is running, slowly add the olive oil until the

pesto reaches your desired consistency. Season with salt and pepper to taste.

2. In a large pot of boiling salted water, cook the protein pasta according to the package instructions until al dente. Drain and set aside.

3. Season chicken breasts with salt and pepper. Heat 2 tablespoons of olive oil in a grill pan over medium-high heat. Once hot, add the chicken breasts and grill for 6-8 minutes on each side or until fully cooked and the internal temperature reaches 165°F (74°C). Once done, let the chicken rest for a few minutes before slicing.

4. Toss the cooked pasta with the beet and walnut pesto. Divide the pasta among four plates. Top each serving with sliced grilled chicken. Garnish with fresh basil or parsley if desired.

Chef's Notes/Storage Information:

- Store any leftovers in an airtight container in the refrigerator for up to 3 days.
- The beet and walnut pesto can be stored separately in a jar with a thin layer of olive oil on top to preserve freshness. It can be refrigerated for up to a week.

Nutritional Information (per serving):

- Calories: 853kcal
- Total Fat: 27.7g
- Monounsaturated Fat: 12.5g
- Polyunsaturated Fat: 5.54g
- Total Carbohydrates: 68.2g
- Dietary Fiber: 7.7g
- Protein: 86.8g
- Sodium: 264.3mg
- Vitamin A: 41.6mcg
- Vitamin B6: 2.3mg
- Vitamin B12: .66mcg
- Vitamin C: 30.6mg
- Vitamin E: 3.6mg
- Vitamin K: 8.3mcg
- Folate: 81.3mcg
- Iron: 8.1mg
- Calcium: 115.1mg
- Potassium: 1723mg
- Magnesium: 101.7mg
- Zinc: 2.5mg

Roasted Chickpeas with Turmeric and Black Pepper

MIX-AND-MATCH RECIPE

A crunchy, savory snack, roasted chickpeas offer a protein-packed bite that's perfect for satisfying pregnancy cravings. Turmeric, with its anti-inflammatory properties, combined with black pepper which helps in its absorption, is beneficial for overall health. It's a delightful blend of earthy and spicy flavors, and this snack is also rich in fiber, which can aid in digestion, especially crucial during pregnancy.

Preparation Time: 10 minutes
Cooking Time: 30 minutes
Total Time: 40 minutes
Serves: 1

Ingredients:

- 1/2 cup canned chickpeas, drained, rinsed, and patted dry
- 1 tbsp olive oil
- 1/4 tsp ground turmeric
- 1/4 tsp freshly ground black pepper
- Salt, to taste

Instructions:

1. Preheat the oven to 400°F (200°C). Line a baking sheet with parchment paper.
2. In a bowl, mix chickpeas with olive oil, ensuring they are well-coated. Sprinkle turmeric, black pepper, and salt, and toss again to coat evenly.
3. Spread the chickpeas in a single layer on the baking sheet. Roast for 25-30 minutes or until crispy and golden brown, shaking the pan or stirring occasionally to ensure even cooking.
4. Remove from the oven and let them cool on the baking sheet for about 10 minutes. They will get crunchier as they cool.

Chef's Notes:

- Prepare in an air fryer for a quicker cooking time
- Recipe Variations:
  - Spicy Kick: Add a pinch of cayenne or chili powder.
  - Herby Touch: Mix in dried rosemary or thyme before roasting.
  - Garlic Lover: Add 1/4 tsp garlic powder for a garlicky twist.
  - Cheesy Flavor: Sprinkle nutritional yeast before roasting for a cheesy, vegan touch.
  - Sweet and Savory: Add a pinch of salt and cinnamon and a drizzle of honey.

Nutritional Information (per serving):

- Calories: 258kcal
- Total Fat: 15.7g
- Monounsaturated Fat: 10.34g

- Polyunsaturated Fat: 2.3g
- Total Carbohydrates: 23.4g
- Dietary Fiber: 6.5g
- Protein: 7.4g
- Sodium: 161.4mg
- Iron: 2.9mg
- Calcium: 44.2mg
- Vitamin B6: .12mg
- Vitamin E: 2.3mg
- Vitamin K: 12.4mcg
- Folate: 141.3mcg
- Potassium: 262mg
- Phosphorus: 140.9mg
- Magnesium: 41.9mg
- Zinc: 1.3mg

Almond Butter and Banana-Stuffed Dates

SO FAST!

These Almond Butter and Banana Stuffed Dates are a delightful, nutrient-packed snack. Rich in natural sugars from the dates, they provide an immediate energy boost, while the almond butter adds a dose of protein and healthy fats. Bananas chip in potassium and vitamin B6, essential for nerve health and the development of the baby's nervous system. This snack is a delicious way to support both energy and nutritional needs during pregnancy.

Preparation Time: 10 minutes
Cooking Time: 0 minutes
Total Time: 10 minutes
Serves: 1

Ingredients:
- 3 Medjool dates
- 1-2 tablespoons almond butter
- 1/2 ripe banana, sliced
- A pinch of sea salt (optional)

Instructions:
1. Carefully slit each date lengthwise to create an opening, ensuring not to cut all the way through. Remove the pit from each date.
2. Fill each date cavity with about a teaspoon (or more, depending on the size of the date) of almond butter.
3. Place a slice of banana on top of the almond butter in each date.
4. Sprinkle a tiny pinch of sea salt over the top, if desired, to enhance flavors.
5. Serve immediately and enjoy this nutritious, energy-boosting snack.

Chef's Notes:
- Sprinkle a few chia or hemp seeds on top for a crunch an additional nutrient.

Nutritional Information (per serving):
- Calories: 399kcal
- Total Fat: 13.6g
- Monounsaturated Fat: 7.8g

- Polyunsaturated Fat: 3.3g
- Total Carbohydrates: 72g
- Dietary Fiber: 8.8g
- Protein: 7g
- Sodium: 158mg
- Vitamin B6: .42mg
- Vitamin C: 5.1mg
- Vitamin E: 5.9mg
- Folate: 35.3mcg
- Iron: 1.6mg
- Calcium: 132.4mg
- Potassium: 891.9mg
- Phosphorus: 179.5mg
- Magnesium: 121.8mg
- Zinc: 1.2mg

Spicy Tuna and Avocado Lettuce Wraps

SO FAST!

These spicy tuna and avocado lettuce wraps are a delectable fusion of flavors, offering a healthy alternative for those pregnancy cravings. Tuna provides essential omega-3 fatty acids which aid in baby's brain and eye development. Avocado is packed with folate and the lettuce wrap ensures a low-carb, hydrating base. Together, they offer a mix of taste and nutrition that's perfect during pregnancy.

Preparation Time: 10 minutes
Cooking Time: 0 minutes
Total Time: 10 minutes
Serves: 1

Ingredients:
- 1 can (5 oz.) light tuna in water, drained
- 1 ripe avocado, peeled, pitted, and diced
- 1 small red chili pepper, finely chopped (adjust to desired spiciness)
- 1 tsp. fresh lime juice
- 1 tbsp. chopped fresh cilantro
- 1 green onion, thinly sliced
- 1/4 tsp. salt (or to taste)
- 1/8 tsp. black pepper (or to taste)
- 3-4 large lettuce leaves (such as iceberg, romaine or butter lettuce)

Instructions:
1. In a medium-sized mixing bowl, flake the drained tuna with a fork. Add the diced avocado, chopped red chili pepper, lime juice, cilantro, and green onion. Mix gently until combined.
2. Sprinkle the mixture with salt and black pepper. Give it a gentle stir until seasonings are well-distributed.
3. Take a lettuce leaf and place a generous spoonful of the tuna and avocado mixture in the center. Fold the sides of the lettuce over, similar to a taco, or roll it up like a burrito depending on the size and flexibility of your lettuce.
4. Enjoy your spicy tuna and avocado lettuce wrap immediately!

Chef's Notes:
- Use store-bought, spicy guacamole for shorter prep time.
- While tuna offers great benefits, it's vital to ensure that you consume tuna in moderation during pregnancy due to concerns about mercury levels. Opt for light tuna, which typically has less mercury than albacore tuna, and limit your intake as per your doctor's advice.

Nutritional Information (per serving):
- Calories: 527kcal
- Total Fat: 33.3g
- Monounsaturated Fat: XX g
- Polyunsaturated Fat: XX g (indicate omega-3 fatty acids if applicable)
- Total Carbohydrates: 25.4g
- Dietary Fiber: 23g
- Protein: 42.9g
- Sodium: 311.3mg
- Vitamin A: 412.9mcg
- Vitamin B6: .82mg
- Vitamin C: 92.7mg
- Vitamin E: 4.7mg
- Vitamin K: 168.8mcg
- Folate: 298.1mcg
- Iron: 3.8mg
- Calcium: 104.3
- Potassium: 1613.4mg
- Magnesium: 84mg
- Zinc: 1.7mg

Cantaloupe and Prosciutto Skewers

GLUTEN-FREE

These refreshing skewers marry the sweet, juicy flavor of cantaloupe with the savory touch of prosciutto. Not only are they a visually appealing appetizer or snack, but they're also beneficial for expecting mothers. Cantaloupes are rich in vitamins A and C, which support immune function, and folic acid, crucial for fetal development. Prosciutto, while indulgent, provides protein. When paired together, you get a delightful combination of taste and nutrition.

Preparation Time: 15 minutes
Cooking Time: 2-4 minutes (if grilling)
Total Time: 15-19 minutes
Serves: 4

Ingredients:
- 1 ripe cantaloupe
- 8 slices of prosciutto, thinly sliced
- Fresh mint leaves (optional for garnish)
- 8-12 wooden skewers

Instructions:
1. Begin by soaking the wooden skewers in water for about 30 minutes to prevent them from burning if you choose to grill or toast them.

2. Slice the cantaloupe in half and scoop out the seeds. Using a melon baller or just a knife, cut the cantaloupe into bite-sized cubes or balls.

3. Cut each prosciutto slice into long, 1-inch-wide strips. Depending on the size, you may want to cut each strip in half.

4. Gently wrap a strip of prosciutto around a cantaloupe piece, ensuring it's snug but not too tight. Slide the prosciutto-wrapped cantaloupe onto the skewer. Repeat until the skewer is filled, leaving about an inch on each end for handling.

5. If you desire a warm, crisp touch to the prosciutto, lightly grill the skewers on medium heat for about 1-2 minutes each side. This step is purely optional as the skewers are delicious cold.

6. Before serving, you can adorn each skewer with a fresh mint leaf for an extra touch of freshness and color.

Chef's Notes:
- Store any leftover skewers in an airtight container in the refrigerator. They are best consumed within 1-2 days for optimal freshness. If storing for longer, consider keeping the cantaloupe and prosciutto separate and assembling just before eating to maintain the best texture and taste.

Nutritional Information (per serving):
- Calories: 441kcal
- Total Fat: 17.8g
- Monounsaturated Fat: .013 g
- Polyunsaturated Fat: .36g
- Total Carbohydrates: 36g
- Dietary Fiber: 4g
- Protein: 37.7g
- Sodium: 2596.1mg
- Vitamin A: 745.3mcg
- Vitamin B6: .32mg
- Vitamin C: 161.8mg
- Vitamin K: 11mcg
- Folate: 92.6mcg
- Iron: 2.7mg
- Calcium: 39.7mg
- Magnesium: 52.9mg
- Zinc: .79mg

Guacamole-Stuffed Cherry Tomatoes

SO FAST!

These guacamoles stuffed cherry tomatoes are a vibrant, refreshing appetizer perfect for a light snack or as part of a larger meal. Packed with beneficial nutrients, they are especially wonderful for pregnancy. Avocados, the primary ingredient in guacamole, are rich in folate which is crucial for fetal brain development. They also contain potassium, which can help reduce leg cramps, a common pregnancy symptom. Cherry tomatoes add a burst of juicy flavor and are also a great source of vitamins A, C, and K. Together, these ingredients offer a tasty and nutrient-packed bite!

Preparation Time: 10 minutes
Cooking Time: 0 minutes
Total Time: 10 minutes
Serves: 1

Ingredients:

- 5-6 cherry tomatoes
- 1 ripe avocado
- 1 tablespoon chopped red onion
- 1 clove garlic, minced
- 1 tablespoon chopped fresh cilantro
- Juice of half a lime
- Salt and pepper to taste
- Optional: a dash of cayenne pepper or chopped jalapeño for some heat

Instructions:

- Rinse the cherry tomatoes and pat dry.
- Using a sharp knife, cut off the tops and carefully scoop out the insides of each cherry tomato to create a small hollow. Set aside.
- Cut the avocado in half, remove the pit, and scoop the flesh into a bowl.
- Mash the avocado using a fork until mostly smooth but with some small chunks remaining.
- Add the chopped red onion, minced garlic, cilantro, and lime juice to the bowl. Mix well.
- Season with salt and pepper. If you'd like a little heat, add cayenne pepper or chopped jalapeño to taste.
- Carefully spoon the guacamole mixture into each hollowed-out cherry tomato until full.
- Arrange the stuffed cherry tomatoes on a plate. They can be enjoyed immediately or refrigerated for a short time to let the flavors meld together.

Chef's Notes:

- You can garnish with extra cilantro or a sprinkle of crumbled feta cheese if desired. Enjoy your nutritious and tasty treat!
- You can use store-bought guacamole to save prep time.

Nutritional Information (per serving):

- Calories: 364kcal
- Total Fat: 29.6g
- Monounsaturated Fat: 19.7g
- Polyunsaturated Fat: 3.68g
- Total Carbohydrates: 27.1g
- Dietary Fiber: 16.1g
- Protein: 6.1g
- Sodium: 71mg
- Vitamin B6: .58mg
- Vitamin C: 40.2mg
- Vitamin E: 4.3mg
- Vitamin K: 45.6mcg
- Folate: 168.1mcg
- Iron: 2.5mg
- Calcium: 73.3mg
- Magnesium: 62.3mg
- Zinc: 1.4mg

Yogurt and Dill Dip with Veggie Sticks

MEAL-PREP FRIENDLY

A creamy, refreshing dip made with yogurt and dill, this recipe is not only delightful to the taste buds but also offers several benefits for pregnancy. Yogurt provides essential probiotics that can be beneficial for gut health, and calcium which is crucial for the development of the baby's bones. Dill, a wonderful herb, aids in digestion and can combat bloating. Paired with an assortment of colorful veggie sticks, this snack is a powerhouse of vitamins and minerals that support both mother and baby. Additionally, the vegetables offer dietary fiber, which can help with common pregnancy issues like constipation.

Preparation Time: 10 minutes
Cooking Time: 0 minutes
Total Time: 10 minutes
Serves: 4

Ingredients:

- 1 cup plain Greek yogurt (full-fat for creamier texture)
- 2 tablespoons fresh dill, finely chopped
- 1 clove garlic, minced (optional for added flavor)
- 1 tablespoon lemon juice
- 1/4 teaspoon salt (or to taste)
- 1/8 teaspoon black pepper (or to taste)
- 1 carrot, peeled and cut into sticks
- 1 celery stalk, cut into sticks
- 1 bell pepper, cut into slices
- 1 cucumber, cut into slices

Instructions:

1. In a mixing bowl, combine Greek yogurt, chopped dill, minced garlic (if using), lemon juice, salt, and black pepper. Mix thoroughly until all ingredients are well-incorporated.
2. Give your dip a taste test and adjust the seasonings (salt, pepper, lemon) if necessary.
3. Pour the dip into a serving bowl and surround it with the freshly cut veggie sticks.

Chef's Notes/Storage Information:

- The yogurt and dill dip can be stored in an airtight container in the refrigerator for up to 3 days. It's recommended to keep the veggie sticks separate until serving to maintain their crispness. Before consuming leftovers, give the dip a good stir. If the dip has any off-odors or mold, discard it.

Nutritional Information (per serving):
- Calories: 102kcal
- Total Fat: 3.8g
- Monounsaturated Fat: 1.53g
- Polyunsaturated Fat: .44g
- Total Carbohydrates: 10.8g
- Dietary Fiber: 1.8g
- Protein: 7.5g
- Sodium: 208.2mg
- Vitamin A: 206.7mcg
- Vitamin B6: .21mg
- Vitamin B12: .53mg
- Vitamin C: 47.8mg
- Vitamin E: .68mg
- Vitamin K: 20.9mcg
- Folate: 35mcg
- Calcium: 100.2mg
- Potassium: 392.5mg
- Phosphorus: 134.1mg
- Magnesium: 26.3mg
- Zinc: .68mg

Baked Sweet Potato Fries with Greek Yogurt Dip

GLUTEN-FREE

These baked sweet potato fries are not only delicious but also packed with essential nutrients that can be especially beneficial during pregnancy. Sweet potatoes are rich in vitamins A and C, fiber, and potassium, which can support the health of both you and your baby, while greek yogurt provides protein and calcium. This recipe provides a healthy alternative to traditional deep-fried fries and is easy to prepare.

Preparation Time: 10 minutes
Cooking Time: 25 minutes
Total Time: 35 minutes
Serves: 1

Ingredients:
- 1 medium-sized sweet potato
- 1 tablespoon olive oil
- 1/2 teaspoon paprika
- 1/2 teaspoon garlic powder
- 1/2 teaspoon salt
- 1/2 teaspoon black pepper
- 1/4 cup Greek yogurt
- 1 tablespoon fresh lemon juice
- 1/2 teaspoon fresh dill (chopped)

Instructions:

1. Preheat your oven to 425°F (220°C). This high temperature will help to make your sweet potato fries crispy.
2. Wash and peel the sweet potato.
3. Cut it into evenly-sized fries, about 1/4 to 1/2 inch wide. This ensures they cook evenly.
4. In a mixing bowl, combine the olive oil, paprika, garlic powder, salt, and black pepper.
5. Add the sweet potato fries to the bowl and toss them until they are well coated with the seasoning mixture.
6. Line a baking sheet with parchment paper or lightly grease it with cooking spray. Spread the seasoned sweet potato fries in a single layer on the baking sheet. Make sure they aren't crowded to allow for even cooking.
7. Place the baking sheet in the preheated oven.
8. Bake for about 20-25 minutes, flipping the fries halfway through. They should become golden brown and crispy on the outside.
9. While the fries are baking, prepare the dip. In a small bowl, combine Greek yogurt, fresh lemon juice, chopped dill, garlic powder, salt, and pepper. Mix well.
10. Once the sweet potato fries are done, remove them from the oven and let them cool for a minute.
11. Serve them hot alongside the creamy Greek yogurt dip.

Chef's Notes:

- Cook potatoes in an air fryer for shorter cooking time
- Serve them as a healthy and delicious snack or a side dish with your main meal

Nutritional Information (per serving):
- Calories: 304kcal
- Total Fat: 17g
- Monounsaturated Fat: XX11.27 g
- Polyunsaturated Fat: 1.84g
- Total Carbohydrates: 30.9g
- Dietary Fiber: XX g
- Protein: 8.4g
- Sodium: 1259.4mg
- Vitamin A: 953.3mcg
- Vitamin B6: .37mg
- Vitamin B12: .49mcg
- Vitamin C: 5.9mg
- Vitamin E: 2.6mg
- Vitamin K: 11.4mcg
- Folate: 20.8mcg
- Iron: 1.2mg
- Calcium: 110.3mg
- Potassium: 584.9mg
- Magnesium: 43.6mg
- Zinc: .84mg

Garlic and Rosemary Marinated Olives

MEAL-PREP FRIENDLY

These garlic and rosemary marinated olives can be a delicious and nutritious addition to a pregnancy diet. Olives are a good source of healthy fats, particularly monounsaturated fats, which are essential for the development of the baby's nervous system. They also provide essential vitamins and minerals, including vitamin E and iron, which are important during pregnancy. Garlic adds a savory depth of flavor while offering immune-boosting benefits, and rosemary can provide antioxidants.

Preparation Time: 15 minutes
Cooking Time: 2 hours marinating time
Total Time: 2 hours, 15 minutes
Serves: 8

Ingredients:

- 2 cups mixed olives (such as green and black)
- 4 cloves garlic, thinly sliced
- 2 sprigs fresh rosemary
- 1/2 teaspoon red pepper flakes (adjust to taste)
- Zest of 1 lemon
- 2 tablespoons extra-virgin olive oil
- 1 tablespoon balsamic vinegar
- Salt and freshly ground black pepper to taste

Instructions:

1. Rinse the olives thoroughly under cold running water to remove excess brine. Drain them and place them in a large bowl.
2. Add the sliced garlic, fresh rosemary sprigs, red pepper flakes, and lemon zest to the olives. Toss everything together gently to distribute the flavors.
3. In a separate small bowl, whisk together the extra-virgin olive oil and balsamic vinegar. Season with a pinch of salt and a few cracks of black pepper.
4. Pour the marinade over the olives mixture. Toss well to ensure the olives are evenly coated with the garlic, rosemary, and lemon zest.
5. Cover the bowl with plastic wrap or a lid and refrigerate for at least 2 hours to allow the flavors to meld. You can leave them to marinate longer for a richer taste.
6. When ready to serve, remove the marinated olives from the refrigerator and let them come to room temperature for about 15 minutes before serving. Discard the rosemary sprigs if desired.

Chef's Notes/Storage Information:

- Store any leftover marinated olives in an airtight container in the refrigerator for up to one week. The olives may become more flavorful as they continue to marinate over time. If you need to store them for a longer period, you can freeze the olives in an airtight container for up to three months. Thaw them in the refrigerator before serving.

Nutritional Information (per serving):

- Calories: 73kcal
- Total Fat: 6.9g
- Monounsaturated Fat: 5.06g
- Polyunsaturated Fat: .662g
- Total Carbohydrates: 3.2g
- Dietary Fiber: 1.2g
- Protein: .44g
- Sodium: 290.4mg
- Vitamin E: 1.1mg
- Iron: 1.3mg

Celery Sticks with Almond Ricotta and Chives

VEGAN

These celery sticks with almond ricotta and chives are a delightful and healthy snack, perfect for pregnancy and anyone looking for a nutritious and satisfying treat. Celery provides essential vitamins and minerals, while almond ricotta adds creaminess and plant-based protein. Chives add a burst of flavor and a touch of freshness. This snack is not only delicious but also packed with nutrients including folic acid, calcium, and healthy fats. Plus, it's incredibly easy to prepare and requires no cooking, making it a convenient option for busy moms-to-be.

Preparation Time: 15 minutes
Cooking Time: 0 minutes
Total Time: 15 minutes
Serves: 4

Ingredients:

- 8 celery stalks, washed and trimmed
- 1 cup almond ricotta cheese (store-bought or homemade)
- 2 tablespoons fresh chives, chopped
- Salt and pepper, to taste

Instructions:

1. Cut the washed celery stalks into manageable lengths, about 4-5 inches long. Make sure to trim the ends for a neat presentation.
2. If using store-bought almond ricotta, simply scoop it into a small serving bowl. If making your own, blend soaked and drained almonds with a touch of water, lemon juice, salt, and nutritional yeast until creamy. Adjust the consistency with more water if needed. Transfer the almond ricotta to a serving bowl.
3. Finely chop the fresh chives and set them aside.
4. Take each celery stick and use a small spoon to fill it with almond ricotta. Alternatively, you can spread the almond ricotta onto each celery stick.
5. Sprinkle the chopped chives over the almond ricotta-filled celery sticks. Add a pinch of salt and a dash of pepper to taste.
6. Arrange the filled celery sticks on a serving platter, garnish with extra chives if desired, and serve immediately.

Chef's Notes:

- Use a variety of cut vegetables including carrots, bell peppers and cucumbers.
- Storage Information: These celery sticks are best served fresh for maximum crunch and flavor. If you need to prepare them ahead of time, you can store the celery sticks and almond ricotta separately in airtight containers in the refrigerator. Assemble just before serving to maintain their crispness.

Nutritional Information (per serving):

- Calories: 158kcal
- Total Fat: 30g
- Monounsaturated Fat: .04g
- Polyunsaturated Fat: .11g
- Total Carbohydrates: 8.9g
- Dietary Fiber: 4.1g
- Protein: 5.93g
- Sodium: 332.4mg
- Vitamin B6: .1mg
- Vitamin C: 4.8mg
- Vitamin K: 40.7mcg
- Folate: 47.7mcg
- Calcium: 108.6mg
- Potassium: 411.2mg

Fig and Cashew Energy Bites

KID FRIENDLY

These Fig and Cashew Energy Bites are a delicious and nutritious snack option, perfect for pregnancy and beyond. Loaded with natural sweetness from figs, the creaminess of cashews, and a touch of spice from cinnamon, these bites are not only tasty but also provide essential nutrients for expectant mothers. Packed with fiber, healthy fats, and protein, they offer sustained energy and can help combat pregnancy cravings. Plus, they're easy to make and can be stored for a quick grab-and-go snack whenever hunger strikes.

Preparation Time: 15 minutes
Cooking Time: 0 minutes
Total Time: 15 minutes
Serves: 8

Ingredients:

- 1 cup dried figs, stems removed
- 1 cup raw cashews
- 1/2 cup rolled oats
- 1/2 teaspoon ground cinnamon
- 1/4 teaspoon salt
- 1 tablespoon honey
- 1-2 tablespoons water, as needed
- 1/2 cup unsweetened shredded coconut (for coating, optional)

Instructions:

1. If your dried figs are very dry or hard, soak them in warm water for 10-15 minutes to soften. Drain well before using.
2. In a food processor, add the cashews, rolled oats, ground cinnamon, and salt. Pulse until the mixture becomes fine crumbs.
3. Add the dried figs to the food processor and blend until the mixture starts to come together. If it's too dry, add 1-2 tablespoons of water or more as needed until the mixture holds together when pressed between your fingers. You can also add honey at this stage if you prefer a sweeter taste.
4. Scoop out tablespoon-sized portions of the mixture and roll them into small balls using your hands. If desired, roll each ball in unsweetened shredded coconut to add extra flavor and texture.
5. Place the energy bites on a parchment paper-lined tray or plate and refrigerate for at least 30 minutes to firm up.
6. Once the energy bites have chilled, transfer them to an airtight container.

Chef's Notes/Storage Information:

- Store your Fig and Cashew Energy Bites in an airtight container in the refrigerator for up to two weeks. You can also freeze them for longer storage. Simply place them in a single layer on a tray in the freezer until they're firm, then transfer them to a freezer-safe container or bag. Frozen energy bites can be kept for up to three months. Thaw in the refrigerator before consuming.

Nutritional Information (per serving):

- Calories: 217kcal
- Total Fat: 12.5g
- Monounsaturated Fat: .16g
- Polyunsaturated Fat: .19g
- Total Carbohydrates: 24.6g
- Dietary Fiber: 3.9g
- Protein: 4.8g
- Sodium: 575mg
- Iron: 1.7mg

Homemade Granola Bars

MEAL-PREP FRIENDLY

These homemade nutty granola bars are not only a delicious and convenient snack but also packed with nutrients that are beneficial during pregnancy. Loaded with oats, nuts, seeds, and a touch of sweetness, these bars provide a healthy dose of fiber, protein, and essential vitamins and minerals. They are perfect for satisfying pregnancy cravings while ensuring you get the energy and nutrients needed for a healthy pregnancy. Plus, they are super easy to make and can be stored for a quick grab-and-go snack anytime.

Preparation Time: 15 minutes
Cooking Time: 20 minutes
Total Time: 35 minutes
Serves: 8

Ingredients:

- 1 1/2 cups rolled oats
- 1/4 cup chopped almonds
- 1/4 cup chopped walnuts

- 1/8 cup chia seeds
- 1/8 cup pumpkin seeds
- 1/4 cup honey
- 1/4 cup almond butter
- 1/4 cup raisins
- 1/4 cup dark chocolate chips (optional)
- 1/2 teaspoon vanilla extract
- 1/2 teaspoon cinnamon
- A pinch of salt

Instructions:

1. Preheat your oven to 350°F (175°C) and line an 8x8-inch (20x20 cm) baking pan with parchment paper, leaving some overhang on the sides for easy removal.
2. In a large bowl, combine the rolled oats, chopped nuts, seeds, cinnamon, and a pinch of salt. Mix well.
3. In a microwave-safe bowl, warm the honey and nut butter for about 30 seconds until they are easy to stir together. Stir in the vanilla extract.
4. Pour the honey and nut butter mixture over the dry ingredients. Stir until all the dry ingredients are evenly coated and everything sticks together.
5. Gently fold in the dried fruit and dark chocolate chips if using.
6. Transfer the mixture to the prepared baking pan. Use a spatula or your hands to press it down firmly and evenly.
7. Bake in the preheated oven for about 18-20 minutes or until the edges turn golden brown.
8. Allow the granola bars to cool completely in the pan. Once cooled, use the parchment paper overhang to lift the entire slab out of the pan. Place it on a cutting board and cut it into 8 bars.

Chef's Notes:

- Add a variety of nuts, seeds. nut butter, and dried fruits based on your taste preferences.
- Store the granola bars in an airtight container. For long-term storage, you can individually wrap them in plastic wrap or parchment paper and store them in the freezer for up to 3 months. They can also be kept at room temperature for up to 2 weeks.

Nutritional Information (per serving):

- Calories: 266kcal
- Total Fat: 13.9g
- Monounsaturated Fat: 4.3g
- Polyunsaturated Fat: 4.3g
- Total Carbohydrates: 31.4g
- Dietary Fiber: 4.6g
- Protein: 6.6g
- Sodium: 160.5mg
- Vitamin E: 2.8mg
- Iron: 2.1mg
- Calcium: 74.4.mg
- Magnesium: 38.9mg
- Zinc: .52mg

Fitness By Trimester

Maintaining a fit lifestyle during pregnancy is incredibly important, not just for you, but also for your growing baby. It might sound like a bit of a challenge, but trust me, it's worth it. Let's talk about why it's so crucial to keep active during this special time in your life.

First off, exercise can be a real mood booster. Pregnancy comes with its fair share of emotional ups and downs, thanks to those hormones running wild. But when you exercise, your body releases endorphins, those lovely little chemicals that make you feel happy. So, staying active can help you feel more positive and less stressed during your pregnancy journey.

Now, I know how tired you can get during pregnancy. Your body is working overtime to nurture that little one inside you. But here's the thing: regular exercise can actually give you more energy. It improves your cardiovascular health and boosts your stamina, making you feel more energized overall. It's like a natural pick-me-up that can really come in handy when you're expecting.

But perhaps one of the most compelling reasons to stay active during pregnancy is how it can impact your labor and delivery. Labor is physically demanding, and being fit can make a big difference. When you exercise, you build strength and endurance, which can help you handle the demands of labor more effectively. Strong core muscles, flexibility, and good cardiovascular health can all contribute to a smoother labor experience.

And here's a bonus: staying active can also help you maintain a healthy weight during pregnancy. This can lower the risk of complications like gestational diabetes and hypertension. In some cases, regular exercise during pregnancy can even lead to shorter labor durations and fewer interventions. Who wouldn't want that, right?

Now, before you lace up those sneakers, remember that safety should always be your top priority. It's crucial to consult with your healthcare provider before starting or continuing an exercise routine during pregnancy. They'll help you figure out what's best for your unique circumstances and ensure that you're doing exercises that are safe for both you and your baby.

There are some circumstances where it may be best to not exercise. If you have specific medical issues like asthma, heart disease, or type 1 diabetes, it may not be advisable to engage in exercise. Additionally, if you have the following conditions, check with your doctor first:

- Bleeding or spotting
- A weak cervix:
- Heart or lung disease
- Incompetent cervix/cerclage
- Pregnant with multiples
- Persistent second- or third-trimester bleeding
- Placenta previa
- At-risk of premature labor
- Preeclampsia

In a nutshell, staying active during pregnancy is a game-changer if it is safe. It'll boost your mood, increase your energy levels, and make labor and delivery a bit smoother. So, go ahead, embrace that fit lifestyle during this incredible journey you're on. Your body and your baby will thank you for it! Just be sure to consult with your healthcare provider to make sure you're on the right track.

FITNESS IN THE FIRST TRIMESTER

As you navigate the first trimester, it's essential to adapt your fitness routine to support both you and your growing baby. During this phase, your body undergoes significant hormonal changes, leading to common symptoms like morning sickness, fatigue, and mood swings. These symptoms are entirely normal responses to the pregnancy, and they signal the need to adjust your fitness goals accordingly.

Your primary focus during the first trimester should be on maintaining a healthy pregnancy, rather than pushing yourself to meet ambitious fitness goals. If you were previously training intensely or engaging in high-impact workouts, it may be time to scale things back. Listen to your body and be flexible with your exercise expectations.

Morning sickness can pose a challenge for staying active. To manage this, consider choosing a time of day when your nausea tends to be less severe for your workouts. Opt for low-intensity exercises such as walking, yoga, or swimming, which are gentler on your body. Staying well-hydrated is crucial to combat dehydration-induced nausea, and eating small, frequent meals can help stabilize your blood sugar levels.

Fatigue is another common symptom during the first trimester, making it tempting to skip workouts. However, staying active can actually help boost your energy levels. Instead of long, exhausting sessions, opt for shorter, more frequent workouts. If fatigue strikes hard, it's perfectly acceptable to take short naps throughout the day and prioritize rest.

Mood swings are a normal part of pregnancy, and exercise can be a valuable tool in managing them. Physical activity releases endorphins, which can help stabilize your emotions. Consider joining a prenatal fitness class or working out with a friend to boost your mood and motivation. Activities like prenatal yoga or meditation can also help you feel more grounded and in control of your emotions. To prevent boredom, mix up your exercise routine with various activities.

Safe Exercises

Here's a list of exercises that are safe and beneficial for you and your baby during this early stage:

- **Walking**: Walking is a fantastic way to stay active without overexerting yourself. It's low-impact and easy to incorporate into your daily routine.
- **Swimming**: Consider swimming or water aerobics, as the buoyancy of the water reduces joint impact and supports your growing belly.
- **Pilates**: If you enjoy Pilates, opt for prenatal Pilates classes that emphasize core strength and posture while avoiding exercises that strain your abdomen.
- **Low-Impact Aerobics**: Look for low-impact aerobics classes tailored for expectant mothers, as they offer a cardiovascular workout without the harsh movements associated with high-impact activities.
- **Stationary Cycling**: Riding a stationary bike is a low-impact way to maintain cardiovascular fitness without putting stress on your joints or abdominal muscles.
- **Prenatal Dance**: Enjoyable and low-impact, prenatal dance classes like gentle ballet or dance aerobics can provide a good workout. Ensure your instructor is knowledgeable about prenatal modifications.
- **Tai Chi**: Tai Chi, with its slow, graceful movements, promotes balance and relaxation without any high-impact actions. It's a safe choice for pregnant women.

What to Avoid

Let's start with the obvious one: contact sports. Whether you're a boxing enthusiast, a karate black belt, or an avid rugby player, it's time to take a break from these high-intensity contact activities during the first trimester. While staying active is beneficial, the risk of getting bumped or tackled in these sports can put unnecessary strain on your body and, more importantly, your baby. It's not just about protecting your belly; it's also about safeguarding your overall well-being.

If you've been enjoying exercises that require you to lie flat on your back, like traditional crunches or certain yoga poses, it's time to bid farewell to these moves—at least for now. As your baby grows, the weight of your uterus can put pressure on a major blood vessel called the vena cava. This can potentially reduce blood flow to your heart and brain, causing dizziness, nausea, or even fainting. Instead, opt for exercises in a supported seated or upright position to ensure proper blood circulation.

Now, let's talk about activities that pose a high risk of falling or injury. If you're into extreme sports like downhill skiing, snowboarding, or mountain biking on rugged terrains, it's advisable to take a pause during the first trimester. These activities can be exhilarating but also hazardous, and even a minor mishap can have serious consequences for you and your baby. Remember, your body is undergoing profound changes, and your balance and coordination might not be as sharp as usual. Stick to lower-impact exercises and activities that keep you on stable ground and out of harm's way.

Above all, remember to listen to your body. During the first trimester, fatigue and morning sickness can be common companions. If you're feeling extra tired or nauseous, it's perfectly fine to skip a workout or take it easy. Your body is working hard to nurture your growing baby, and rest is just as important as exercise.

The first trimester of pregnancy is a time for caution and adjustment in your fitness routine. Avoid contact sports, exercises on your back, and activities with a high risk of falling or injury. Instead, focus on safe and gentle workouts that prioritize your well-being and the health of your little one.

FITNESS IN THE SECOND TRIMESTER

In the first trimester, you may have been grappling with nausea, fatigue, and the rollercoaster of hormonal changes. But as you transition into the second trimester, you might notice a remarkable change in your energy levels. It's like a cloud has lifted, and suddenly you feel more like yourself again.

This boost in energy can be a game-changer when it comes to incorporating physical activity into your routine. It's not uncommon to feel more motivated and ready to tackle some exercise during this period. But before we delve into the benefits and precautions of exercising in the second trimester, let's take a moment to acknowledge the unique challenges you might face during this time.

By the time you reach the second trimester, your baby bump becomes more pronounced. It's a beautiful reminder of the life growing inside you, but it can also affect your balance and stability. This means that certain exercises and movements you were comfortable with before may now feel a bit different. Don't worry; we'll explore how to adapt and choose exercises that work best for your changing body.

Additionally, your body is still undergoing significant hormonal shifts, even if some of the more severe symptoms have eased. These changes can affect your joints and ligaments, making them a bit looser and potentially more prone to injury. It's crucial to keep this in mind as you select your exercise routine.

During the second trimester, your body is working overtime to supply blood to both you and your baby. This means that you might experience a faster heart rate and increased circulation, which can impact your exercise capacity and response. Understanding how your body reacts to these changes is essential for a safe and effective workout.

Now, let's turn our attention to the exciting part—the benefits of exercising in the second trimester. With your newfound energy and these unique challenges in mind, you can make the most of this phase in your pregnancy journey.

As we mentioned earlier, this is the time when many women feel a surge of energy. Taking advantage of this can help improve your mood, reduce stress, and boost your overall well-being. Regular, moderate exercise can help you maintain your strength and stamina, making everyday tasks easier as your pregnancy progresses.

With a growing belly, your body's center of gravity shifts. Proper exercises can help you maintain good posture and alleviate some common discomforts like back pain. Additionally, exercising promotes better circulation, which can help reduce swelling in your extremities and keep your heart and circulatory system healthy.

Safe Exercises

In addition to the exercises listed for the first trimester, you can now add these options to your routine.

- **Water Aerobics**: Wand water aerobics is an excellent option as it provides buoyancy and reduces strain on the joints. It's also gentle on the body and can help relieve back pain. To modify, use buoyancy aids if needed for support.
  - Safety precautions include ensuring that the pool water is at a comfortable temperature. Extreme temperatures can cause discomfort, so opt for pools with moderate water temperatures.
- **Prenatal Yoga**: Prenatal yoga can help improve flexibility, strength, and relaxation. It's a popular choice for expecting mothers. To modify poses, use props like yoga blocks or bolsters for support and stability.
  - Safety precautions for prenatal yoga include avoiding poses that involve lying flat on your back after the first trimester. It's important to prioritize your comfort and avoid any poses that cause strain or discomfort.
- **Strength Training**: Strength training with light weights or resistance bands can help maintain muscle tone and strength during pregnancy. To modify, reduce weights as needed and focus on proper form.
  - Safety precautions for strength training involve avoiding exercises that put pressure on the abdomen or require lying flat on your back. Ensure you're breathing properly during each repetition to prevent overexertion.
- **Pelvic Floor Exercises (Kegels)**: Kegel exercises help strengthen the pelvic floor muscles, which can be beneficial for pregnancy and postpartum recovery.
  - Safety cautions involve learning the proper technique from your healthcare provider or physical therapist to be sure you are doing them correctly.

What to Avoid

As your baby bump becomes more noticeable, you'll likely notice some physical changes that affect your mobility and balance. These changes are natural and necessary for the development of your baby, but they do impact your ability to perform certain exercises. Here are some exercises to be cautious about during the second trimester:

1. **Lying Flat on Your Back**: It's worth mentioning again to avoid exercises that require you to lie flat on your back for an extended period, such as traditional crunches. This position can put pressure on the vena cava, a major blood vessel, and reduce blood flow to the uterus and the baby.

2. **Deep Twists and Bends**: As your belly grows, your abdominal muscles stretch and weaken. Deep twisting or bending movements can strain these muscles further and potentially lead to discomfort or injury. Opt for gentler, controlled movements instead.

3. **High-Impact Exercises:** While some women can continue with high-impact exercises like running during the second trimester, it's essential to be cautious. The increased weight and the hormone relaxin, which loosens your joints, can make you more susceptible to injuries. Consider lower-impact alternatives like walking, swimming, or stationary cycling.

4. **Heavy Weightlifting:** As your pregnancy progresses, it's wise to reduce the amount of weight you lift. The hormone relaxin, which loosens your ligaments and joints, can make you more prone to injury. Focus on maintaining strength with lighter weights and higher repetitions.

Avoid Over-Exertion

During the second trimester, it's crucial to listen to your body. Pay close attention to how you feel during and after exercise. If you experience any of the following symptoms, stop exercising immediately and consult your healthcare provider:

- Dizziness or lightheadedness
- Shortness of breath
- Rapid or irregular heartbeat
- Chest pain
- Excessive fatigue
- Contractions or cramping
- Vaginal bleeding

Stay Hydrated and Maintain Good Posture

One aspect that's often overlooked is staying adequately hydrated. Dehydration can lead to overheating, which is particularly concerning during pregnancy. Make sure to drink plenty of water before, during, and after your workouts.

Additionally, focus on maintaining good posture during your exercises. Proper alignment can help alleviate the stress on your back and joints. Engage your core muscles gently and be mindful of your body's alignment throughout your routine.

FITNESS IN THE THIRD TRIMESTER

First, let's address the elephant in the room – the weight gain. By now, your baby bump has grown significantly, and it feels like you're carrying around a bowling ball 24/7. It's completely natural to feel heavier and less agile during this phase. Your center of gravity has shifted, and your balance might not be what it used to be. The key here is to be patient with yourself. Remember, you're growing a life, and that's a magnificent feat!

Fatigue is often a constant companion in the third trimester. You might find yourself longing for those energetic days of the first trimester, when you could conquer the world with a simple brisk walk. It's essential to listen to your body and rest when needed. While staying active is important for your overall well-being, it's equally vital to recognize that fatigue is your body's way of saying, "Hey, I need some extra rest right now." Embrace naps and moments of relaxation without guilt.

Remember, the goal isn't to push your body to its limits but to maintain a level of activity that keeps you feeling good and promotes overall health. Always consult with your healthcare provider before starting any new exercise routine to ensure it's safe for you and your baby.

While the third trimester comes with its own unique challenges, it's also a time of anticipation and excitement as you prepare to welcome your baby into the world. Embrace your body's changes, listen to its signals, and prioritize self-care. Staying active in this phase may look different from earlier in your pregnancy, but it's still an essential part of nurturing your physical and emotional well-being.

Safe Exercises

1.Water Aerobics

Water aerobics is a fantastic exercise option during the third trimester. The buoyancy of the water supports your body, relieving the strain on your joints and muscles. It's an excellent way to stay active while reducing the risk of falls or overexertion. In the water, you can perform a range of gentle movements that will help you maintain cardiovascular fitness, tone your muscles, and relieve swelling and discomfort. Look for prenatal water aerobics classes at your local pool, where instructors are trained to accommodate pregnant participants.

2. Stationary Cycling

Stationary cycling, also known as spinning, can be a safe and effective exercise for the third trimester. It's a low-impact activity that doesn't put too much stress on your joints. Make sure to adjust the bike seat and handlebars to a comfortable position, and take it easy. You don't need to push yourself too hard; the goal is to maintain your cardiovascular fitness and leg strength while minimizing strain on your back and pelvis.

3. Pregnancy-Safe Stretches

Stretching is a vital component of any prenatal fitness routine, especially during the third trimester. Gentle stretches can help alleviate back pain, reduce muscle tension, and improve flexibility. Here are some pregnancy-specific stretches to consider:

- Pelvic Tilts: Stand with your back against a wall and your feet hip-width apart. Slowly tuck your pelvis in, pressing your lower back into the wall. Hold for a few seconds, then release. This exercise can help strengthen your core muscles and alleviate lower back pain.
- Cat-Cow Stretch: Get down on your hands and knees, and gently arch your back up like a cat, then lower your belly towards the floor while lifting your head and tailbone like a cow. This stretch can relieve tension in your back and promote flexibility.
- Leg and Ankle Circles: While sitting in a chair or on an exercise ball, make circles with your feet and rotate your ankles. This can help improve circulation, reduce swelling, and prevent leg cramps.

Remember to perform these stretches slowly and mindfully, never forcing your body into uncomfortable positions. As your pregnancy progresses, you may need to modify exercises further to accommodate your growing belly and changing center of gravity.

What to Avoid

Advanced pregnancy is a time for careful consideration and prioritizing safety above all else. While you might have to bid adieu to a few of your favorite exercises for now, it's all in the service of a healthy, happy pregnancy and a safe delivery. Stay active, but stay cautious, and keep nurturing that wonderful little life inside you. You're doing an amazing job!

Remember, the key is to listen to your body. If an exercise feels uncomfortable, painful, or just doesn't sit right, don't push through it. It's perfectly okay to modify or skip an exercise if it doesn't feel safe or comfortable.

While some of these may sound familiar from the first or second trimester, it is worth noting to ensure you and your baby are safe until he or she is ready for the big debut into the world!

1. High-Impact Aerobics
Let's start with the big one – those high-intensity, heart-pounding aerobics classes. While they might have been your go-to pre-pregnancy, during the advanced stages, it's time to swap them out for something gentler. The jarring impact on your joints can be uncomfortable and risky. Consider low-impact alternatives like prenatal yoga or swimming to keep moving without the jolts.

2. Heavy Weightlifting
We all love a little strength training, but it's time to put those heavyweight dumbbells on the shelf. Lifting extremely heavy weights can increase your risk of injury, strain, or even early labor. Instead, opt for lighter weights or resistance bands and focus on maintaining your muscle tone rather than bulking up.

3. Exercises Lying Flat on Your Back

Once you've reached the second trimester, it's essential to avoid exercises that involve lying flat on your back for extended periods. This position can put pressure on a major blood vessel, reducing blood flow to both you and your baby. Swap out those crunches and opt for exercises in a reclined or upright position.

4. Deep Twists
Twists can be incredibly beneficial for stretching and relieving tension, but deep twists that constrict your abdomen should be avoided in advanced pregnancy. These can put undue pressure on your uterus and may lead to complications.

5. Contact Sports
At this stage, it's time to hang up your soccer cleats and basketball shoes temporarily. Contact sports carry an increased risk of falls, collisions, and injury to the abdominal area. Safety is your top priority now, so consider non-contact sports like swimming or walking instead.

6. Hot Yoga and Hot Pilates
While yoga and Pilates are generally excellent choices for prenatal exercise, practicing them in a hot or overheated environment can lead to dehydration and overheating. Elevated body temperature can be harmful to your developing baby, so opt for regular temperature classes or gentle, prenatal-specific versions.

7. High-Intensity Interval Training (HIIT)
HIIT workouts can be intense and physically demanding, which might not be suitable as your pregnancy progresses. The rapid, high-intensity movements can put excess stress on your joints, ligaments, and pelvic floor. Consider lower-intensity forms of cardio like walking or stationary cycling.

8. Heavy Abdominal Exercises
Traditional abdominal exercises like sit-ups and leg raises can strain your abdominal muscles and increase the risk of diastasis recti, a condition where the abdominal muscles separate. Focus on gentle core-strengthening exercises like pelvic tilts and Kegels to maintain core strength without the risk.

9. High-impact Activities and Sports
In addition to contact sports, it's wise to avoid high-impact activities like running or jumping during the advanced stages of pregnancy. These activities can cause discomfort and increase the risk of injury or falls. Switch to lower-impact alternatives like brisk walking, swimming, or stationary cycling.

PREGNANCY~RELATED CONDITIONS

Now that you've learned the ins and outs of exercising during pregnancy, but there are a few curveballs that life can throw at you. Two of the most common are gestational diabetes and preeclampsia. While these conditions can be concerning, they don't necessarily mean the end of your exercise routine. Let's dive into how they might affect your fitness journey and what you can do to stay on track.

First, let's talk about gestational diabetes. This condition occurs when your blood sugar levels become elevated during pregnancy. It can throw a wrench into your exercise plans because it affects your body's ability to process glucose efficiently. But don't worry; it's manageable.

If you have gestational diabetes, you might find that your energy levels fluctuate. Some days you'll feel full of vim and vigor, while others you may feel a bit sluggish. On high-energy days, you can engage in your usual workouts, but be mindful on the low-energy days. Regular exercise can help stabilize your blood sugar levels, which is particularly important if you have gestational diabetes. However, you should monitor your blood sugar levels before, during, and after exercise. It's important to keep them within a safe range.

Additionally, consider the time of day when you exercise. Some women with gestational diabetes find that their blood sugar levels are more stable in the morning. If that's the case for you, consider scheduling your workouts accordingly.

When dealing with gestational diabetes, it's crucial to consult your healthcare provider before starting or continuing an exercise routine. They can provide tailored advice and ensure your safety. Staying hydrated and having a small, balanced snack before exercising can help stabilize blood sugar levels. If you experience discomfort or are unsure about the impact of a specific exercise, opt for low-impact activities like swimming, stationary cycling, or prenatal yoga. These are gentle on your joints and body. Keep an eye on your blood sugar levels and adjust your exercise routine accordingly. If

they spike or drop too much during exercise, it might be time to take a break or modify your activity.

Now, let's tackle preeclampsia, a condition characterized by high blood pressure and damage to organs, typically occurring after the 20th week of pregnancy. Preeclampsia can be a bit more complicated when it comes to exercise.

Preeclampsia can cause your blood pressure to spike, which can be risky during exercise. Elevated blood pressure can lead to complications like headaches, dizziness, or even fainting. Additionally, swelling in the legs and feet is common with preeclampsia. High-impact activities may exacerbate this, so it's essential to be cautious.

Consult your healthcare provider for guidance on exercise if you have preeclampsia. In some cases, they may advise bed rest or very light activity. If exercise is still allowed, focus on low-intensity activities like gentle walking or prenatal stretching. Avoid strenuous workouts or activities that could increase your blood pressure. Keep a close eye on your symptoms. If you experience severe headaches, vision changes, or sudden swelling, stop exercising immediately and seek medical attention.

In the grand scheme of things, gestational diabetes and preeclampsia can pose challenges to your exercise routine during pregnancy, but they don't have to halt your fitness journey altogether. The key is communication with your healthcare provider, listening to your body, and making modifications as needed. Remember, your health and the health of your baby are top priorities, so always err on the side of caution and make adjustments accordingly.

Conclusion

From understanding the nuances of prenatal nutrition to exploring a variety of recipes tailored for each stage of your pregnancy, this book has been a companion in your journey of nurturing a new life.

Remember, the choices you make today are not just for the well-being of your baby during these nine months, but they lay the foundation for a lifetime of health and happiness. The nutrition principles and recipes provided here are more than just guidelines; they are a testament to the power of mindful eating and the profound impact it has on both you and your baby.

As you move forward, remember that pregnancy is just the beginning of a lifelong journey of parenthood. The lessons in nutrition, the importance of self-care, and the joy of preparing and sharing wholesome food will continue to be invaluable as you nurture and watch your child grow.

Take pride in the knowledge you've gained and the steps you've taken to ensure the best for your baby. You've embraced the responsibility of motherhood with grace and commitment, and for that, you should feel empowered and proud.

In closing, I wish you joy, health, and a beautiful journey ahead as a parent. May the recipes and wisdom in this book not only nourish your body during pregnancy but also inspire a lifetime of healthy eating habits for you and your family. Thank you for allowing this book to be a part of your incredible journey.

**If this book has eased your journey into motherhood
then please leave a review on Amazon
so that others may profit from this incredible resource as well!**

Appendix A: Building the Perfect Prenatal-Friendly Pantry

For ease of use I have included here all the pantry items you will need to nourish your bay and yourself!

GRAINS

Grain Type	Nutritional Information (per 100g)	Health Benefits During Pregnancy	Pregnancy-Specific Nutrients	Recipe Tips
Whole Wheat	Calories: 340; Protein: 13g; Fiber: 10.7g; Iron: 3.5mg; Folate: 44µg	High in fiber; iron and folate for fetal development	Iron, Folate, B Vitamins	Use in bread, pasta, whole grain salads
Oats	Calories: 389; Protein: 16.9g; Fiber: 10.6g; Iron: 4.7mg; Magnesium: 177mg	Fiber and iron rich; magnesium for muscle function	Iron, Magnesium, Zinc	Breakfast porridge, baking, smoothies
Quinoa	Calories: 368; Protein: 14.1g; Fiber: 7g; Iron: 4.6mg; Calcium: 47mg	Complete protein; high in iron and calcium	Complete Protein, Iron, Calcium	Salads, rice substitute, stuffed vegetables
Brown Rice	Calories: 370; Protein: 7.5g; Fiber: 3.5g; Iron: 0.8mg; Manganese: 1.8mg	Slow-releasing energy; manganese for bone development	B Vitamins, Manganese, Selenium	Stir-fries, pilafs, side dishes
Barley	Calories: 354; Protein: 12.5g; Fiber: 17.3g; Iron: 3.6mg; Selenium: 37.7µg	High in fiber; selenium for immune function	Fiber, Selenium, Iron	Soups, stews, salad base
Buckwheat	Calories: 343; Protein: 13.3g; Fiber: 10g; Magnesium: 231mg; Iron: 2.2mg	Gluten-free; good for digestive health	Magnesium, Fiber, B Vitamins	Pancakes, noodles, porridge
Millet	Calories: 378; Protein: 11g; Fiber: 8.5g; Magnesium: 114mg; Phosphorus: 285mg	Gluten-free; phosphorus for bone health	Magnesium, Phosphorus, Fiber	Porridge, side dishes, gluten-free baking
Amaranth	Calories: 371; Protein: 14g; Fiber: 7g; Iron: 7.6mg; Calcium: 159mg	High in protein and calcium; good for bone health	Protein, Calcium, Iron	Salads, soups, as a rice substitute
Teff	Calories: 367; Protein: 13g; Fiber: 8g; Iron: 7.6mg; Calcium: 180mg	High in calcium and iron; gluten-free	Calcium, Iron, Protein	Gluten-free baking, porridge, stews

	Calories: 338; Protein: 14.6g; Fiber: 10.7g; Iron: 4.4mg; Magnesium: 136mg	High in B vitamins; good for energy	Iron, Magnesium, B Vitamins	Bread, pasta, salads
Spelt	Calories: 338; Protein: 14.6g; Fiber: 10.7g; Iron: 4.4mg; Magnesium: 136mg	High in B vitamins; good for energy	Iron, Magnesium, B Vitamins	Bread, pasta, salads
Rye	Calories: 335; Protein: 10.3g; Fiber: 15.1g; Iron: 2.7mg; Magnesium: 121mg	Fiber-rich; good for blood sugar control	Fiber, Magnesium, B Vitamins	Bread, crackers, porridge
Sorghum	Calories: 339; Protein: 11.3g; Fiber: 6.3g; Iron: 4.4mg; B6: 0.4mg	Gluten-free; antioxidant-rich	Iron, B Vitamins, Antioxidants	Gluten-free baking, pilafs, popped sorghum
Freekeh	Calories: 354; Protein: 14.9g; Fiber: 10.9g; Iron: 2.8mg; Zinc: 2.7mg	High in fiber and protein; zinc for immune health	Fiber, Protein, Zinc	Salads, soups, side dishes

LEGUMES

Legumes Type	Nutritional Information (per 100g)	Health Benefits During Pregnancy	Pregnancy-Specific Nutrients	Recipe Tips
Lentils	Calories: 116; Protein: 9g; Fiber: 8g; Iron: 3.3mg; Folate: 181μg	High in protein and folate; good for fetal development	Protein, Iron, Folate	Soups, stews, salads, lentil patties
Chickpeas	Calories: 164; Protein: 9g; Fiber: 8g; Iron: 2.9mg; Folate: 172μg	Rich in protein and fiber; supports digestive health	Protein, Fiber, Folate	Hummus, curries, salads, roasted as a snack
Black Beans	Calories: 132; Protein: 9g; Fiber: 8.7g; Iron: 2.1mg; Calcium: 27mg	Good source of protein and iron; calcium for bone health	Protein, Iron, Calcium	Burritos, soups, salads, black bean burgers
Kidney Beans	Calories: 127; Protein: 9g; Fiber: 6.4g; Iron: 2.9mg; Potassium: 403mg	High in protein and iron; potassium for heart health	Protein, Iron, Potassium	Chili, salads, stews, mixed bean dishes
Navy Beans	Calories: 140; Protein: 8g; Fiber: 10.5g; Iron: 2.4mg; Folate: 254μg	Rich in fiber and folate; supports fetal development	Fiber, Folate, Protein	Soups, baked beans, casseroles
Pinto Beans	Calories: 143; Protein: 9g; Fiber: 9g; Iron: 2.2mg; Folate: 229μg	Good for digestive health; folate for fetal health	Fiber, Folate, Iron	Mexican dishes, soups, bean salads
Green Peas	Calories: 81; Protein: 5g; Fiber: 5g; Vitamin C: 40mg; Iron: 1.5mg	Rich in vitamin C and iron; supports immune function	Vitamin C, Iron, Protein	Stir-fries, soups, salads, purees
Edamame	Calories: 121; Protein: 11g; Fiber: 5g; Iron: 2.3mg; Calcium: 63mg	High in protein and calcium; good for bone health	Protein, Calcium, Fiber	Snack, added to salads, in Asian dishes

| Soybeans | Calories: 147; Protein: 17g; Fiber: 6g; Iron: 8.6mg; Calcium: 197mg | Excellent protein source; high in iron and calcium | Protein, Iron, Calcium | Tofu, tempeh, soy milk, added to stews |

CANNED GOODS

Canned Goods	Health Benefits During Pregnancy	Pregnancy-Specific Nutrients	Culinary Uses
Canned Salmon	Rich in omega-3 fatty acids; good for fetal brain development	Omega-3 Fatty Acids, Protein, Vitamin D	Salads, sandwiches, pasta dishes
Canned Sardines	High in calcium and omega-3; supports bone health	Calcium, Omega-3 Fatty Acids, Iron	Pizzas, salads, on crackers
Canned Beans (e.g., black, kidney, garbanzo)	Good source of protein and fiber; aids in digestion	Protein, Fiber, Iron	Soups, salads, casseroles
Canned Lentils	Convenient source of protein and fiber; supports fetal development	Protein, Fiber, Folate	Stews, salads, side dishes
Canned Tomatoes	Rich in antioxidants; supports heart and skin health	Lycopene, Vitamin C, Fiber	Pasta sauces, soups, stews
Canned Pumpkin	High in vitamin A; supports vision and immune health	Vitamin A, Fiber, Vitamin C	Soups, baking, smoothies
Canned Peas	Easy to digest; good source of vitamins	Fiber, Protein, Vitamin C	Side dishes, in rice, pasta dishes
Canned Corn	Source of energy; high in fiber	Fiber, Vitamin B, Antioxidants	Salads, soups, as a side dish
Canned Beets	Good for iron levels; aids in blood health	Iron, Folate, Fiber	Salads, side dishes, smoothies
Canned Carrots	High in beta-carotene; supports eye health	Beta-carotene, Fiber, Vitamin A	Side dishes, stews, purees

HEALTHY FATS, OILS, AND NUT BUTTERS

Healthy Fats/Oils & Nut Butters	Nutritional Information (per 100g)	Health Benefits During Pregnancy	Pregnancy-Specific Nutrients	Recipe Tips
Olive Oil	Calories: 884; Total Fat: 100g; Vitamin E: 14mg; Vitamin K: 60µg	Supports heart health; rich in antioxidants	Healthy Monounsaturated Fats, Vitamin E	Salad dressings, drizzling over cooked dishes, dipping
Coconut Oil	Calories: 862; Total Fat: 100g; Saturated Fat: 87g; Lauric Acid: 49g	Supports immune function; high in lauric acid	Lauric Acid, Healthy Saturated Fats	Baking, sautéing, adding to smoothies
Flaxseed Oil	Calories: 884; Total Fat: 100g; Omega-3: 53g; Vitamin E: 0.47mg	High in omega-3 fatty acids; supports brain health	Omega-3 Fatty Acids, ALA (Alpha-linolenic acid)	Salad dressings, smoothies (not suitable for cooking)
Avocado Oil	Calories: 884; Total Fat: 100g; Monounsaturated Fat: 71g; Vitamin E: 10mg	High in monounsaturated fats; good for skin health	Monounsaturated Fats, Vitamin E	Cooking, salad dressings, drizzling on toast
Peanut Butter	Calories: 588; Protein: 25g; Total Fat: 50g; Fiber: 8g; Niacin: 13.1mg	Rich in protein and healthy fats; energy-dense	Healthy Fats, Protein, Niacin (Vitamin B3)	Spread on toast, in smoothies, baking
Almond Butter	Calories: 614; Protein: 21g; Total Fat: 56g; Fiber: 12g; Vitamin E: 26mg	High in Vitamin E and magnesium; good for heart health	Healthy Fats, Vitamin E, Magnesium	Spread on fruits, in oatmeal, baking
Sunflower Seed Butter	Calories: 617; Protein: 20g; Total Fat: 55g; Fiber: 9g; Vitamin E: 36mg	Rich in Vitamin E; good for skin and immune health	Healthy Fats, Vitamin E, Protein	Spread on toast, in sandwiches, as a dip
Tahini (Sesame Seed Paste)	Calories: 595; Protein: 17g; Total Fat: 53g; Fiber: 9g; Calcium: 426mg	High in calcium; supports bone health	Healthy Fats, Calcium, Iron	Salad dressings, hummus, sauces
Walnut Oil	Calories: 884; Total Fat: 100g; Omega-3: 10.4g; Vitamin E: 0.4mg	High in omega-3 fatty acids; supports brain development	Omega-3 Fatty Acids, Healthy Fats	Salad dressings, drizzling over cooked vegetables (not for cooking)

NUTS AND SEEDS

Nuts/Seeds Type	Nutritional Information (per 100g)	Health Benefits During Pregnancy	Pregnancy-Specific Nutrients	Recipe Tips
Almonds	Calories: 579; Protein: 21g; Fiber: 12.5g; Calcium: 269mg; Iron: 3.7mg	High in protein and calcium; good for bone health	Calcium, Iron, Vitamin E	Snack, salads, almond milk, almond butter
Walnuts	Calories: 654; Protein: 15g; Fiber: 7g; Omega-3: 9g; Magnesium: 158mg	High in omega-3 fatty acids; supports brain health	Omega-3 Fatty Acids, Magnesium	Snack, baking, salads, pesto
Chia Seeds	Calories: 486; Protein: 17g; Fiber: 34g; Omega-3: 17.8g; Calcium: 631mg	Rich in omega-3, calcium, and fiber; aids in digestion	Omega-3 Fatty Acids, Calcium, Fiber	Puddings, smoothies, yogurt toppings
Flaxseeds	Calories: 534; Protein: 18g; Fiber: 27g; Omega-3: 22.8g; Magnesium: 392mg	High in omega-3 and fiber; good for digestive health	Omega-3 Fatty Acids, Fiber, Magnesium	Smoothies, baking, as a yogurt topping
Pumpkin Seeds	Calories: 446; Protein: 19g; Fiber: 6g; Iron: 8.8mg; Magnesium: 592mg	Good source of iron and magnesium; supports energy levels	Iron, Magnesium, Zinc	Snack, salad toppings, granola
Sunflower Seeds	Calories: 584; Protein: 21g; Fiber: 9g; Vitamin E: 35.17mg; Magnesium: 325mg	High in Vitamin E and magnesium; supports skin health	Vitamin E, Magnesium, Folate	Snack, baking, sprinkled on salads
Sesame Seeds	Calories: 573; Protein: 18g; Fiber: 12g; Calcium: 975mg; Iron: 14.6mg	High in calcium and iron; good for bone and blood health	Calcium, Iron, Zinc	Toppings for bread, salads, tahini
Cashews	Calories: 553; Protein: 18g; Fiber: 3.3g; Magnesium: 292mg; Iron: 6.7mg	Good source of magnesium and iron; supports energy production	Magnesium, Iron, Zinc	Snack, cashew butter, stir-fries
Pecans	Calories: 691; Protein: 9g; Fiber: 10g; Magnesium: 121mg; Zinc: 4.5mg	High in healthy fats; good for heart health	Healthy Fats, Fiber, Zinc	Snack, baking, salads
Brazil Nuts	Calories: 656; Protein: 14g; Fiber: 8g; Selenium: 1917µg; Magnesium: 376mg	High in selenium; supports thyroid and immune function	Selenium, Magnesium, Healthy Fats	Snack, chopped in desserts, granola

DRIED FRUITS

Dried Fruits Type	Nutritional Information (per 100g)	Health Benefits During Pregnancy	Pregnancy-Specific Nutrients	Recipe Tips
Raisins	Calories: 299; Carbs: 79g; Fiber: 3.7g; Iron: 1.9mg; Potassium: 749mg	High in energy and iron; good for snacking	Iron, Potassium, Fiber	Snack, oatmeal, baking, yogurt topping
Dried Apricots	Calories: 241; Carbs: 63g; Fiber: 7.3g; Iron: 2.7mg; Vitamin A: 3604IU	Rich in iron and Vitamin A; supports vision and immune health	Iron, Potassium, Vitamin A	Snack, granola, baking, stews
Dates	Calories: 277; Carbs: 75g; Fiber: 6.7g; Potassium: 696mg; Magnesium: 54mg	High in natural sugars for energy; good source of fiber	Potassium, Magnesium, Fiber	Natural sweetener, energy bars, baking
Dried Figs	Calories: 249; Carbs: 64g; Fiber: 10g; Calcium: 162mg; Iron: 2mg	High in fiber and calcium; supports bone health	Calcium, Iron, Fiber	Snacks, baking, cheese pairings
Prunes	Calories: 240; Carbs: 64g; Fiber: 7g; Vitamin K: 59.5µg; Potassium: 732mg	Rich in fiber; supports digestive health	Fiber, Potassium, Vitamin K	Snack, baking, stewed as a dessert
Dried Mango	Calories: 319; Carbs: 78g; Fiber: 2.2g; Vitamin A: 2240IU; Vitamin C: 39.3mg	Good source of Vitamin A and C; supports immune health	Vitamin A, Vitamin C, Fiber	Snack, trail mix, cereal topping
Dried Cranberries	Calories: 325; Carbs: 82g; Fiber: 5.7g; Vitamin C: 0.2mg; Manganese: 0.36mg	Good for urinary tract health; high in antioxidants	Antioxidants, Fiber, Vitamin C	Baking, salads, yogurt topping
Dried Pineapple	Calories: 339; Carbs: 79g; Fiber: 2.3g; Vitamin C: 79.8mg; Manganese: 2.7mg	High in Vitamin C; supports immune system	Vitamin C, Manganese, Fiber	Snack, trail mix, granola bars
Dried Papaya	Calories: 296; Carbs: 76g; Fiber: 5g; Vitamin A: 95IU; Folate: 38µg	Contains enzymes aiding digestion; good source of folate	Vitamin A, Folate, Fiber	Snack, trail mix, cereal topping

SPICES AND HERBS

Herbs/Spices	Health Benefits During Pregnancy	Pregnancy-Specific Nutrients	Culinary Uses
Ginger	Aids in reducing nausea and morning sickness	Gingerol (active compound)	Tea, soups, stir-fries, baked goods
Turmeric	Anti-inflammatory properties; supports digestion	Curcumin, Iron	Curries, golden milk, soups, rice dishes
Cinnamon	Helps regulate blood sugar levels	Manganese, Antioxidants	Oatmeal, baking, smoothies, fruit salads
Fenugreek	Supports lactation; aids in digestion	Iron, Choline, Fiber	Curry powders, tea, spice blends
Fennel Seeds	Aids in digestion; may reduce pregnancy swelling	Fiber, Vitamin C, Calcium	Salads, breads, tea, seasoning blends
Mint	Soothes digestion; refreshing flavor	Vitamin A, Antioxidants	Teas, salads, water infusions, desserts
Dill	Good for digestion; adds fresh flavor	Vitamin C, Calcium	Fish dishes, salads, dips, pickles
Basil	High in antioxidants; supports immune health	Vitamin K, Iron	Pesto, sauces, salads, infused oils
Cumin	Aids in digestion; rich in iron	Iron, Magnesium	Curries, soups, spice rubs, beans
Oregano	Antioxidant-rich; supports immune health	Vitamin K, Antioxidants	Pizza, pasta sauces, salad dressings
Parsley	High in Vitamin C and iron; supports kidney health	Vitamin C, Iron, Folate	Garnish, salads, soups, sauces

Appendix B: Prenatal-Friendly Refrigerator Regulars

Now more than ever, you'll have to make sure to maintain good refrigerator hygiene, clean it weekly and preserve the food safely, rotating it often to avoid consuming foods that are past their prime.

VEGETABLES

Vegetables	Nutritional Information (per 100g)	Health Benefits During Pregnancy	Pregnancy-Specific Nutrients	Culinary Uses
Spinach	Calories: 23; Protein: 2.9g; Fiber: 2.2g; Iron: 2.7mg; Folate: 194µg	High in iron and folate; supports fetal development	Iron, Folate, Vitamin A	Salads, smoothies, sautéed dishes
Broccoli	Calories: 34; Protein: 2.8g; Fiber: 2.6g; Vitamin C: 89.2mg; Calcium: 47mg	Rich in fiber and antioxidants; supports immune health	Vitamin C, Fiber, Calcium	Steamed, stir-fries, soups
Kale	Calories: 49; Protein: 4.3g; Fiber: 4.1g; Vitamin C: 120mg; Calcium: 150mg	High in vitamins A, C, and K; supports eye and immune health	Vitamin A, Vitamin C, Calcium	Salads, smoothies, baked chips
Carrots	Calories: 41; Carbs: 10g; Fiber: 2.8g; Vitamin A: 835µg; Vitamin K: 13.2µg	High in beta-carotene; supports eye health	Beta-carotene, Fiber, Vitamin K	Snacks, salads, soups, roasting
Sweet Potatoes	Calories: 86; Carbs: 20g; Fiber: 3g; Vitamin A: 709µg; Vitamin C: 2.4mg	Rich in fiber and vitamin A; supports digestive health	Beta-carotene, Vitamin A, Fiber	Baked, mashed, roasted
Bell Peppers	Calories: 20; Protein: 1g; Fiber: 2.1g; Vitamin C: 128mg; Vitamin B6: 0.3mg	High in vitamin C; good for skin and immune health	Vitamin C, Fiber, Vitamin B6	Raw as snacks, stir-fries, stuffed
Tomatoes	Calories: 18; Carbs: 3.9g; Fiber: 1.2g; Vitamin C: 14mg; Lycopene: 2573µg	High in lycopene and vitamin C; supports heart health	Lycopene, Vitamin C, Fiber	Salads, sauces, roasted
Beets	Calories: 43; Carbs: 10g; Fiber: 2.8g; Iron: 0.8mg; Folate: 109µg	Good for iron levels; supports blood health	Iron, Folate, Fiber	Roasted, salads, juices
Zucchini	Calories: 17; Carbs: 3.1g; Fiber: 1g; Vitamin C: 17.9mg; Potassium: 261mg	Low in calories; high in vitamin C and fiber	Vitamin C, Fiber, Potassium	Grilled, stir-fries, zucchini noodles

Eggplant	Calories: 25; Carbs: 6g; Fiber: 3g; Vitamin B6: 0.1mg; Manganese: 0.2mg	High in fiber and antioxidants; supports heart health	Fiber, Antioxidants, Vitamin B6	Grilled, baked, in stews
Green Beans	Calories: 31; Protein: 1.8g; Fiber: 2.7g; Vitamin C: 12.2mg; Vitamin K: 14.4µg	Source of vitamins A, C, and K; supports bone health	Vitamin A, Vitamin C, Fiber	Steamed, stir-fries, salads
Cauliflower	Calories: 25; Carbs: 5g; Fiber: 2g; Vitamin C: 48.2mg; Vitamin K: 15.5µg	High in fiber and vitamin C; aids in digestion	Vitamin C, Fiber, Vitamin K	Roasted, steamed, in curries
Pumpkin	Calories: 26; Carbs: 6.5g; Fiber: 0.5g; Vitamin A: 426µg; Vitamin C: 9mg	Rich in vitamin A; supports vision and immune health	Vitamin A, Fiber, Potassium	Soups, baked, purees
Asparagus	Calories: 20; Protein: 2.2g; Fiber: 2.1g; Folate: 52µg; Vitamin K: 41.6µg	High in folate; supports fetal development	Folate, Fiber, Vitamin K	Grilled, roasted, steamed

FRUITS

Fruits	Nutritional Information (per 100g)	Health Benefits During Pregnancy	Pregnancy-Specific Nutrients	Culinary Uses
Apples	Calories: 52; Carbs: 14g; Fiber: 2.4g; Vitamin C: 4.6mg; Potassium: 107mg	High in fiber and vitamin C; good for digestion	Fiber, Vitamin C, Potassium	Raw, baked, in salads, applesauce
Bananas	Calories: 89; Carbs: 23g; Fiber: 2.6g; Vitamin B6: 0.4mg; Potassium: 358mg	Source of energy and potassium; aids muscle health	Potassium, Vitamin B6, Vitamin C	Raw, smoothies, baking, banana bread
Oranges	Calories: 47; Carbs: 12g; Fiber: 2.4g; Vitamin C: 53.2mg; Folate: 30µg	High in vitamin C and folate; supports immune health	Vitamin C, Folate, Fiber	Raw, juices, salads, zest in baking
Berries (e.g., strawberries, blueberries)	Calories: 32-57; Carbs: 8-14g; Fiber: 2-3g; Vitamin C: 35-97mg; Manganese: 0.3-0.6mg	Antioxidant-rich; supports skin and immune health	Antioxidants, Vitamin C, Fiber	Raw, in smoothies, desserts, yogurt topping
Watermelon	Calories: 30; Carbs: 8g; Fiber: 0.4g; Vitamin C: 8.1mg; Potassium: 112mg	Hydrating and rich in vitamins; good for hydration	Vitamin C, Potassium, Vitamin A	Raw, in salads, juices, fruit platters
Avocado	Calories: 160; Fat: 15g; Fiber: 7g; Vitamin C: 10mg; Folate: 81µg	High in healthy fats and folate; supports fetal development	Healthy Fats, Folate, Fiber	Salads, sandwiches, guacamole, toast
Grapes	Calories: 69; Carbs: 18g; Fiber: 0.9g; Vitamin C: 10.8mg; Vitamin K: 14.6µg	Source of antioxidants and vitamins; good for heart health	Antioxidants, Vitamin C, Vitamin K	Raw, in salads, frozen as a snack
Kiwi	Calories: 61; Carbs: 15g; Fiber: 3g; Vitamin C: 92.7mg; Vitamin K: 40.3µg	High in vitamin C and fiber; supports digestive health	Vitamin C, Fiber, Vitamin K	Raw, in fruit salads, smoothies
Mango	Calories: 60; Carbs: 15g; Fiber: 1.6g; Vitamin C: 36.4mg; Vitamin A: 54µg	Rich in vitamin A and C; supports eye and immune health	Vitamin A, Vitamin C, Fiber	Raw, in smoothies, salsas, desserts
Pears	Calories: 57; Carbs: 15g; Fiber: 3.1g; Vitamin C: 4.3mg; Potassium: 116mg	High in fiber; aids in digestion and heart health	Fiber, Vitamin C, Potassium	Raw, baked, in salads, poached

PROTEINS

Understood, I'll revise the table to focus exclusively on refrigerated protein sources excluding dairy, suitable for prenatal nutrition. This list will cover various meats, fish, eggs, and refrigerated meat alternatives.

Protein Sources	Nutritional Information (per 100g)	Health Benefits During Pregnancy	Pregnancy-Specific Nutrients	Culinary Uses
Chicken Breast	Calories: 165; Protein: 31g; Fat: 3.6g; Vitamin B6: 0.6mg; Niacin: 14.8mg	Lean protein; supports tissue growth	Protein, Niacin, Vitamin B6	Grilled, roasted, salads, soups
Lean Beef	Calories: 250; Protein: 26g; Fat: 15g; Iron: 2.7mg; Zinc: 5.3mg	High in protein and iron; supports blood health	Protein, Iron, Zinc	Grilled, stir-fries, stews, meatballs
Pork Loin	Calories: 143; Protein: 25g; Fat: 4g; Thiamin: 0.6mg; Selenium: 27µg	Good source of thiamin; supports energy levels	Protein, Thiamin, Selenium	Roasted, grilled, stir-fries
Eggs	Calories: 155; Protein: 13g; Fat: 11g; Choline: 251mg; Vitamin D: 2µg	High in choline; supports brain development	Protein, Choline, Vitamin D	Boiled, scrambled, omelets, baking
Salmon	Calories: 208; Protein: 20g; Fat: 13g; Omega-3 Fatty Acids: 2.3g; Vitamin D: 25µg	Rich in omega-3; supports fetal brain development	Omega-3 Fatty Acids, Vitamin D, Protein	Grilled, baked, salads, pasta
Tuna	Calories: 116; Protein: 25g; Fat: 1g; Omega-3 Fatty Acids: 0.3g; Vitamin D: 1.7µg	Lean protein; good source of omega-3	Protein, Omega-3 Fatty Acids, Selenium	Grilles, baked, salads
Liver (beef, chicken)	Calories: 135-167; Protein: 20-26g; Fat: 3.6-6g; Iron: 6.5-9mg; Vitamin A: 6,582-11,329µg	High in iron and Vitamin A; supports blood and eye health	Protein, Iron, Vitamin A	Pan-fried, pâtés, with onions
Turkey Breast	Calories: 135; Protein: 30g; Fat: 0.7g; Selenium: 28.8µg; Vitamin B6: 0.7mg	Low-fat protein source; supports muscle growth	Protein, Selenium, Vitamin B6	Roasted, sandwiches, salads
Ground Turkey	Calories: 203; Protein: 27g; Fat: 10g; Zinc: 2.5mg; Phosphorus: 203mg	Lean protein; good for overall health	Protein, Zinc, Phosphorus	Meatballs, burgers, pasta sauces
Tofu	Calories: 144; Protein: 17g; Fat: 9g; Calcium: 350mg; Iron: 5.4mg	Plant-based protein; high in iron and calcium	Protein, Calcium, Iron	Stir-fries, salads, soups, scrambles
Tempeh	Calories: 193; Protein: 20g; Fat: 11g; Fiber: 9g; Calcium: 111mg	High in protein and fiber; supports digestive health	Protein, Fiber, Calcium	Grilled, stir-fries, salads, sandwiches

DAIRY PRODUCTS

Dairy Products	Nutritional Information (per 100g)	Health Benefits During Pregnancy	Pregnancy-Specific Nutrients	Culinary Uses
Whole Milk	Calories: 61; Protein: 3.2g; Fat: 3.3g; Calcium: 113mg; Vitamin D: 1µg	Supports bone health; essential vitamins	Calcium, Protein, Vitamin D	Drinking, cereals, smoothies, cooking
Greek Yogurt (Full-Fat)	Calories: 97; Protein: 9g; Fat: 5g; Calcium: 110mg; Probiotics	High in protein and probiotics; digestive health	Protein, Calcium, Probiotics	Breakfast, dips, sauces, dressings
Cheddar Cheese	Calories: 402; Protein: 25g; Fat: 33g; Calcium: 721mg; Phosphorus: 455mg	Rich in calcium and protein; bone and muscle health	Calcium, Protein, Vitamin A	Snacking, sandwiches, gratins, baking
Cottage Cheese (Full-Fat)	Calories: 98; Protein: 11g; Fat: 4.3g; Calcium: 83mg; Phosphorus: 159mg	Source of calcium and protein; fetal development	Protein, Calcium, Phosphorus	Breakfast bowls, salads, dips, baking
Butter	Calories: 717; Fat: 81g; Vitamin A: 684µg; Vitamin E: 2.3mg	Essential fats and vitamins	Saturated Fat, Vitamin A, Vitamin E	Cooking, baking, spreads, sautéing
Cream	Calories: 431; Fat: 46g; Vitamin A: 882µg; Calcium: 101mg	High in fat and vitamin A; skin and eye health	Saturated Fat, Vitamin A, Calcium	Desserts, sauces, soups, coffee
Sour Cream	Calories: 198; Fat: 20g; Calcium: 98mg; Vitamin A: 431µg	Source of calcium and healthy fats	Saturated Fat, Calcium, Vitamin A	Toppings, dips, baking, sauces
Parmesan Cheese	Calories: 431; Protein: 38g; Fat: 29g; Calcium: 1385mg; Phosphorus: 760mg	High in calcium; bone health	Calcium, Protein, Phosphorus	Grating over dishes, salads, baking
Mozzarella Cheese (Full-Fat)	Calories: 280; Protein: 22g; Fat: 17g; Calcium: 505mg; Phosphorus: 354mg	Good for protein and calcium; muscle health	Protein, Calcium, Phosphorus	Pizzas, salads, sandwiches, melting
Ricotta Cheese (Full-Fat)	Calories: 174; Protein: 11g; Fat: 13g; Calcium: 207mg; Phosphorus: 158mg	Rich in protein and calcium; supports growth	Protein, Calcium, Phosphorus	Lasagna, spreads, desserts, baking

Index

A

apple, 14, 43, 49, 62, 65, 87, 92, 107
    apple & goat cheese bites, 49
asparagus, 11–13, 37, 41, 44, 53, 57, 64, 68, 73, 76–77, 91, 100, 106
avocado, 9–10, 12–14, 18, 22, 26–28, 43, 50–51, 56, 67–69, 71–72, 93, 96–97, 101–102, 109, 111, 126
    avocado and mango salsa, 97
    avocado toast, 22, 50–51, 93
    smashed avocado, 50

B

beef skewers, 66
beets, 31–32, 41, 44, 69, 90–91, 107, 125
bell peppers, 11–13, 30, 34, 39, 48, 53, 57, 66, 72–73, 79, 96, 98–100
berries, 12–13, 18, 23–29, 47–48, 56, 80, 90–93
beverages to avoid, 14
black bean, 8, 18, 27, 33–35, 59, 78–79, 98, 124
blueberry compote, 25–26
bone broth, 17, 38–39, 46–47, 77, 99
breakfast, 6, 21–22, 24, 26–29, 53, 56–62, 90, 92–93, 123
    breakfast burrito, 27, 59
    breakfast casserole, 57
broccoli, 9, 11–14, 36, 44–45, 53, 57, 64–65, 68, 90–91, 97, 102
brown rice, 65, 97, 103, 105, 123
butternut squash, 9, 12–13, 33–34, 76, 99
    spaghetti squash, 11, 35, 71

C

calamari, 75
canned goods, 125
cannelloni, 69–70
carrots, 11–14, 36, 38, 40, 46, 60, 65, 74, 77, 87, 94–95, 100, 104, 114, 125
cashew cream, 98
cauliflower, 11–12, 17, 21, 31, 39, 65, 74, 94
cheddar, 27, 39, 76, 79
chia seed, 8, 10, 21–22, 24–25, 27–29, 48–50, 56, 58, 62, 79–80, 87, 89–92, 115, 127
    chia seed pudding, 25, 91
chicken, 8, 10–12, 31–32, 34–35, 37–39, 42–45, 62, 65, 71, 74, 94–95, 100–102, 104–108

chicken and vegetable soup with bone broth, 38
    chicken breast, 8, 31–32, 38–39, 44, 62, 65, 95, 100–102, 107–108
    chicken livers, 42
    roast chicken, 94
chickpea, 8–9, 18, 31, 45, 47–48, 70, 74–75, 77, 96, 100, 107–108, 124
    chickpea stew, 96
chimichurri, 66
chocolate dipped strawberries, 51
cobalamin, 12
coconut milk porridge, 29
coconut rice, 67
coconut yogurt parfait, 80
cottage cheese, 12, 50
cravings, 20, 49, 55, 90–91, 108–109, 114
cucumber, 11, 26, 38, 47, 51, 63, 70, 76–77, 82, 93, 97, 102, 111, 114
curry, 67, 103, 124
    curried lentils, 103

D

dairy products, 17, 54, 85
dandelion root tea, 86
dates, 70, 78–79, 91, 109, 128
dill dip, 111–112
dinner, 6, 14, 31, 41, 94–95
dried fruits, 27, 49, 87, 94, 115, 128

E

egg boats, 28
eggplant, 11, 105
enchiladas, 98

F

falafel bowl, 70
farro salad, 90
feta cheese, 30–31, 34, 42, 45, 50, 53, 56–57, 64, 69, 71–72, 76–77, 83, 94, 101–102, 111
first trimester, 13–14, 18–19, 54, 117–119
fitness, 116–119, 121
flatbread, 75
fluid intake, 14, 20
food aversions, 20

G

ginger tea, 14, 20, 86
gluten-free, 8, 24–25, 28, 30–34, 36–42, 44, 48, 51–52, 59–61, 63–68, 73–

74, 80, 89, 93, 95–97, 100–102, 104–105, 107, 110, 112, 123–124
goat cheese, 44, 49, 90–91
grapes, 14, 47
grass-fed beef, 10, 12, 33
greek yogurt, 21, 23–25, 28–29, 47–48, 52, 58–59, 63, 72, 87, 101, 111–112
    greek yogurt parfait, 47
green beans, 9, 11–12, 32, 46–47, 76, 78, 97, 100, 104
    oven-baked green bean fries, 78
ground turkey, 39, 63–64

H

hemp hearts, 89
hot sauce, 101
hummus, 13, 26, 47–48, 51, 70, 78, 82, 124, 126

I

immunity boost smoothie, 21
iodine, 13, 15, 19, 82

J

jackfruit, 71–72

K

kabobs, 33
kalamata olives, 24, 75, 77, 81
kale, 9, 11–13, 17, 22, 31–32, 35, 38, 42, 47, 53, 57, 64, 79, 89, 104
kid friendly, 62, 76, 114
kiwi, 25, 48, 50, 58, 80, 90–91

L

lamb, 10, 12, 36, 63, 100
    lamb chops, 36
    lamb koftas, 63
    lamb shoulder, 100
    lamb tagine, 100
leafy greens, 11–12, 14, 17, 54, 69, 105
legumes, 8, 14, 18, 54, 85, 124
liver, 11–12, 16–17, 37, 42
lunch, 6, 31, 69, 94

M

mac'n'cheese, 76
mackerel salad, 38, 69
macronutrients, 8
mango and turkey jerky, 80

meal-prep friendly, 38, 46, 53, 57, 72, 75, 80, 87, 92, 94, 96, 98, 103–104, 107, 111, 113–114
micronutrients, 11, 30, 38
minestrone, 104
mint, 14, 24, 50, 63, 83, 102, 110
morning sickness, 7, 12, 14, 19, 21–22, 29, 89, 117
mozzarella, 39, 70, 105
muffins, 9, 53, 60
mushroom burger, 78
mushroom pilaf, 89

N
nuts and seeds, 8, 29, 49, 127
        nut & seed trail mix, 49

O
oatmeal, 8, 17, 21, 23, 61–62, 92–93, 126, 128
olive tapenade, 40, 75
omelette, 30
one-pot meal, 77, 82, 99
oranges, 12, 14, 44, 55, 93
overnight oats, 27, 56, 90, 92

P
parmesan cheese, 24, 35, 42, 69, 71, 76, 78, 88, 95, 104–107
pears, 14, 23, 43
pickled beets, 69
plate method, 14
poached eggs, 34, 43
pork loin, 64–65
pork tenderloin, 40–41
portobello mushrooms, 95
prenatal nutrition, 6–7, 16, 122
pumpkin, 9–10, 12–13, 22–23, 32, 47, 49, 61–62, 90, 94, 98, 115, 125, 127
pyridoxine, 12

Q
quinoa bowl, 87

R
red snapper, 68
rice cakes, 26
ricotta, 69–71, 80, 113–114
risotto, 99
roasted beet, 31–32, 41, 44, 90–91
roasted root vegetables, 40–41
roasted sweet potatoes, 32, 52, 66, 97

S
safe exercises, 117–119
salmon, 8, 10–12, 17, 32, 38, 42–45, 50, 61, 85, 100, 106, 125

smoked salmon, 50, 61
sardines, 10–12, 17, 40, 125
scrambled eggs, 24
sea bass, 96–97
second trimester, 7, 13, 54, 118–120
seitan and mushroom bourguignon, 74
senna tea, 86
shrimp, 10, 12–13, 17, 37–38, 42–45, 51, 67, 71, 73, 101
smoked mackerel, 38, 69
smoothie, 14, 21–22, 59–60, 79, 89, 123, 125–127
snacks, 6, 8, 11, 14, 47, 78, 108, 128
snap pea, 36–37, 71
so fast, 26, 42, 45, 47, 49–50, 69, 82–84, 92, 109, 111
soup, 20, 38–39, 46, 78, 82, 87–88, 100, 104, 123–125
spices, 84, 87, 96, 100–101, 103
stew, 20, 31, 74, 78, 96, 123–125, 128
stir-fry, 36, 65, 97, 123–124, 127
stuffed bell peppers, 39, 98
superfoods, 16
supplements, 7, 12–14, 16, 86
surf and turf skewers, 73
sweet potato, 18, 27, 40, 52, 59, 76, 112

T
tacos, 71–72, 101
tahini, 45, 48, 79, 126–127
tempeh, 125
thai beef salad, 102
third trimester, 7, 13, 85–86, 119
toasted muesli, 29
tofu, 36–38, 42–45, 67, 82, 85, 94, 97, 125
trout, 41
tuna, 10–11, 17, 109–110
turkey breast, 80
tzatziki, 70

V
vegan, 12, 29, 31, 35–36, 49, 51, 58–59, 74, 78–81, 83, 89, 94, 97–98, 108, 113
vegetarian, 12–13, 21–22, 25, 27, 29, 33, 43, 56, 58, 64, 67, 69–71, 76, 78, 88, 90, 102, 106

W
watermelon, 83
whole grains, 8, 17–18, 50, 54–55, 58, 85–86, 90, 104
        whole grain couscous, 96
        whole grain toast, 50
        whole rye bread, 61

whole wheat pancakes, 25, 58
wild rice, 89, 98–99

Z
zucchini, 11, 17, 33, 38–39, 60, 66, 71–72, 77, 80, 100, 104–106

Made in the USA
Las Vegas, NV
14 October 2024

96769035R00077